The Spy Story

The Spy Story

John G. Cawelti
Bruce A. Rosenberg

The University of Chicago Press
Chicago and London

John G. Cawelti, professor of English at the University of Kentucky, is the author of *Adventure, Mystery, and Romance*, published by the University of Chicago Press.

Bruce A. Rosenberg, professor of English and American civilization at Brown University, is the author of a number of books, including *The Code of the West*.

The University of Chicago Press, Chicago 60637
The University of Chicago Press, Ltd., London
© 1987 by The University of Chicago
All rights reserved. Published 1987
Printed in the United States of America
96 95 94 93 92 91 90 89 88 87   54321

Library of Congress Cataloging-in-Publication Data

Cawelti, John G.
    The spy story.

    Bibliography: p.
    Includes index.
    1. Spy stories, English—History and criticism.
2. English fiction—20th century—History and
criticism. I. Rosenberg, Bruce A. II. Title.
PR888.S65C38 1987   823'.0872'09   86-30716
ISBN 0-226-09868-0

For Katie and Ann

Contents

vii

Acknowledgments

We first conceived of this book during the year we spent together at the National Humanities Institute at the University of Chicago. We are grateful to the National Endowment for the Humanities for funding the institute, to Neil Harris, its director, and to the other fellows with whom we shared a very stimulating experience.

The title was suggested by Mary Catherine Flannery.

Rosenberg would like to express his gratitude to the John Simon Guggenheim Memorial Foundation and the Huntington Library for released time to develop a major portion of the book, and offers special thanks to Professor Josie Campbell, Ms. Marcia Lieberman, Ms. Ann-Marie Thigpen, and Professor Barton Levi St. Armand. Much of what he has learned of narrative and style was the freely given gift of Ann Stewart.

Cawelti is grateful to his colleagues at the University of Kentucky and the University of Chicago and particularly wants to thank Professor J. A. Bryant, Jr., for his continuing encouragement and friendship and, for diverse advice, Robert Hemenway, Gregory Waller, Armando Prats, Art Wrobel,

x   Acknowledgments

Thomas Blues, Walt Foreman, Kevin Kiernan, John Shaw-
cross, Joan Blythe, Joseph Gardner, and Steven Weisenberger.
Elizabeth Domene typed much of Cawelti's part of the
manuscript.

An earlier version of chapter 4 appeared in Joseph Wald-
meir, ed., *Essays in Honor of Russel B. Nye* (East Lansing,
Michigan: Michigan State University Press, 1978). We are
grateful to that press for permission to use it here.

Leonard Rubenstein's list of major spy films appears in
The Great Spy Films (Secaucus, N.J.: Citadel Press, 1979). We
are grateful to the Citadel Press for permission to reprint it here.

Introduction

We live in a time that has become deeply obsessed with espionage, conspiracy, and other forms of clandestinity. What Edward Shils called "the torment of secrecy" has pervaded our national life, as the exposure of the Watergate cover-up revealed. But Watergate was only one in a series of developments in American culture that had their roots in the aftermath of World War II. That conflict thrust America into a new global position where our potential vulnerability to the economic and military strengths of other countries came to seem more threatening than ever before. With their anxieties intensified by the fear of atomic weapons, political leaders and ordinary citizens became deeply concerned about secret conspiracies, both at home and abroad. While such obsessions have often appeared in the aftermath of wars—both the Civil War and World War I left a disturbing legacy of suspicion and suspension of due process in the attempt to counter secret conspiracies—it was only after World War II that Americans institutionalized clandestinity on a large and permanent scale. Our generation has harvested the first fruits of that major cultural change.

1

One may hope that revelations about Watergate and CIA abuses of power will slow down an accelerating trend toward clandestine operations at all levels of our life, but it is unlikely that a few exposures and confessions will succeed in halting a political and cultural process with a powerful dynamic of its own. Those in power and a substantial segment of the public have come to believe that clandestine operations are indispensable to the security of a modern nation. This belief, and the institutions, attitudes, and actions to which it gives rise, have had a profound cultural impact. Though we desperately need to understand the processes of clandestinity more fully, this is difficult because much of the necessary evidence remains buried in secret archives. Even if historical data are available, to evaluate the actual impact of clandestine operations is very difficult and has become a subject of considerable controversy among historians. Some believe that such clandestine coups as British and American codebreaking during World War II made the difference between defeat and victory, while others assert that much information gleaned by espionage has been useless and largely ignored by commanders in the field. Manifold ambiguities cluster around the subject of historical espionage. What does one say about the terrible fate of those thousands who perished in agony during the destruction of Coventry because Churchill feared that to give advance warning of the bombing would reveal that the British had broken the German code? On the other hand, could the Allied invasion of Europe have succeeded without those clandestine operations designed to mislead German intelligence about the actual site of the landings?

Whatever the actual military, economic, and political importance of espionage, the twentieth century has become in many ways the Age of Clandestinity. One symptom of the pervasiveness of secret operations in our lives is the fact that the spy story has become one of the major popular genres of our time. The secret agent protagonist is now one of our favorite mythical heroes and to study his evolution is the purpose of this book. In studying the development of the spy story, we cannot cast more than an indirect light on the larger problem of the role of espionage and clandestinity in the contemporary world. We do hope, however, to analyze how patterns of clandestinity have become a part of our popular fantasies, and how writers, responding to the need for such fantasies, have tried to understand and exploit them to produce successful novels and films, and even, in some cases, major works of art.

It has often been remarked that spying is at least the world's second oldest profession. In book x of the *Iliad*, Odysseus conducts a night raid against the Trojans in order to spy out their dispositions. In the *Odyssey*, he disguises himself as an old beggar so that he can find out who his true friends and enemies are. Joshua sent spies into Canaan, and, in one of the most famous biblical stories, the great warrior Samson was brought down by a neat bit of counterespionage work carried out by history's first recorded female agent. However, in spite of the long and fascinating history of spying, it was not until the twentieth century that the secret agent became the heroic protagonist of a major form of popular narrative. As the century progressed into the 1980s, the spy hero became still more important, increasingly replacing earlier popular heroic figures like the cowboy and the hardboiled detective. In this book we will explore the twentieth-century spy story in relationship to the literary and cultural influences that have shaped its evolution. We hope, in the process, to articulate some of the reasons why the spy story has developed as it has and why the figure of the spy has seemed so fascinating to the American and British public in the twentieth century.

To begin with, we would like to differentiate our approach from other recent discussions of the spy story. Of these, Jerry Palmer's *Thrillers. Genesis and Structure of a Popular Genre* (1979) is the most tightly reasoned theoretical analysis. Palmer uses a structuralist methodology to define the thriller and to establish its place in cultural history. He argues that the thriller is determined by the interplay of two major elements: an individualistic competitive hero and a conspiracy that threatens the orderly fabric of society. The thriller, Palmer believes, reflects an ideological conflict between individuality and sociality that is characteristic of the last 150 years in England and America. It is also based on a somewhat reactionary fear of the unruly masses as conspirators against the established social order. By destroying the evil conspiracy, the hero both resolves the conflict between sociality and individualism and abates the fear of social upheaval symbolized by the evil conspiracy.

While there is much of interest in Palmer's work, especially his commentary on the nature of "thrills" and his ideas about "what makes a good thriller," his approach is, from our point of view, too broad and abstract. Quite purposely, he intends his definition to fit such genres as the classical and the hardboiled detective stories as well as the spy story. However, it appears to us that his paradigm is equally applicable to the American Western or the British colonial adventure as in Haggard and Kipling. One could even argue that Palmer's paradigm fits still earlier genres, such as the picaresque novels of Fielding and even the adventures of Odysseus—certainly a competitive individual facing a social conspiracy. In fact, this is precisely what Bruce Merry argues in *Anatomy of the Spy Thriller* (1977). Merry thinks that the popularity of the spy story can be accounted for on the grounds that it is a contemporary version of the ever-popular epic folktale:

> The fit between the standard pattern of the folktale and the modern spy thriller is a strikingly precise one. What it illustrates once again—and this has been the prime motive behind the present study—is the universality of popular literature and the atemporality of its appeal. The epic quest, the magic mission, the fairytale encounter and the espionage assignment, appeal to the larger-than-life fantasy needs of the plebian audience and the imagination of popular readership in every age. The spy thriller caters to the same need in urbanized, technology-conscious modern man. (P. 235)

Palmer and Merry approach the thriller on different levels. Where Merry sees it as a contemporary embodiment of a universal archetype, Palmer traces its structure to the specific ideological conflicts of a particular period: "Only in the second half of the nineteenth century, . . . is [there] a social base both for the sense of permanent conspiracy and for the taste for competitiveness" (*Thrillers*, p. 204). However, Palmer's own historical awareness will not let him accept a completely determinate relationship between popular formula and social ideology. He notes quite interestingly that:

> Although the two elements that are brought together to form [the thriller] are tied to particular, temporary circumstances . . . the genre which has sprung from them is not: the resolution of ideological contradiction that it permits is of wider significance. So much so, indeed, that the thriller formula itself becomes a starting point for interpreting the world, and the original material out of which it was constituted can be discarded and another analogous set substituted, provided that it offers the same possibilities of a fictitious resolution between individuality and sociality. (P. 204)

Unfortunately, Palmer does not develop this idea much further, which is one of the reasons why his treatment of the thriller seems to collapse a number of different formulas into a single oversimplified paradigm.

Our approach is, we think, more specific and flexible than Palmer's and less broadly archetypal than Merry's. While we agree that there is value in constructing generic archetypes, we also think that the exploration of popular formulas requires that some attention be given both to the most important individual creators and to the changing narrative and thematic patterns within the genre. We are therefore less interested in the idea of the "thriller" than in the more specific notion of the spy story, which we define as a story whose protagonist has some primary connection with espionage. Clearly, there are many stories of which this is true which one would hesitate to call spy stories, and usually for good reasons. One example is Conrad's *The Secret Agent*, which figures deservedly in almost any discussion of the spy story. However, other interests in *The Secret Agent* are as important as the protagonists' involvement with espionage. Verloc is a pathetically comic figure, for one thing, and the real protagonist of the novel is the more tragic figure of his wife, Winnie. Spy thrillers, however gloomy and cynical, are not usually tragedies, as we can see if we compare the most glum of John le Carré's stories of betrayal and corruption with a tragic novel involving espionage such as *The Secret Agent*. Though Alec Leamas, of *The Spy Who Came In from the Cold,* is shot along with the woman he has come to love, there is a kind of moral triumph at the end. Leamas now understands the corrupt and evil nature of the forces he is involved with; he has learned how to differentiate between good and evil and to have the moral courage to reject a life of further servitude to these evil principles. Thus, his death is both a positive moral action and a symbolic stand against the perverted means used in fighting the Cold War. Leamas begins in apparent moral decay but his death at the Berlin Wall is a heroic as well as despairing rejection of the corrupt world of power politics.

In Conrad's *Secret Agent,* however, there is no heroism and no meaningful conflict between good and evil. The true protagonist, Winnie Verloc, is not even involved in espionage, and her inexorable descent to murder and suicide is grimly unrelieved by any sort of spiritual triumph. The world of *The Secret Agent* is one in which no group of characters has a moral advantage over the others. With the sole exception of the mad anarchist professor, everyone is in pursuit of some kind of personal advantage. Even Winnie, the most selfless character in the novel, is in many ways a betrayer. By marrying Verloc with the sole intention of providing a comfortable home and security for her brother, Winnie is unintentionally transforming herself into a potential murderess and suicide by creating a relationship between herself and her husband so lacking in mutual understanding and feeling that it can turn to murderous hate in a moment.

Verloc, himself, is a spy and a killer, but largely through laziness and inertia. He has no evil motives or intentions. Both the police who pursue and the anarchists who threaten him are motivated by the quest for personal advancement or advantage. The world of *The Secret Agent* is a dark and murky London of hopelessly conflicting human purposes about which it becomes meaningless to talk in terms of good and evil. Cynical and full of betrayal as it may be, John le Carré's world is not, like Conrad's, a place of fathomless darkness. Though the good may be threatened by modern social and political trends, we can still know what is valuable and see it embodied, however feebly, in a sympathetic and effective figure. In one of le Carré's early novels the author sums up the hero's view of modern civilization and shows that the hero's values are clearly related to his struggles against the enemy:

> He hated the press as he hated advertising and television, he hated mass media, the relentless persuasion of the twentieth century. Everything he admired or loved had been the product of intense individualism. That was why he hated Dieter now, hated what he stood for more strongly than ever before: it was the fabulous impertinence of renouncing the individual in favor of the mass. When had mass philosophies ever brought benefit or wisdom? Dieter cared nothing for human life: dreamed only of armies of faceless men bound by their lowest common denominators; he wanted to shape the world as if it were a tree, cutting off what did not fit the regular image; for this he fashioned blank, soulless, automatons like Mundt. Mundt was faceless like Dieter's army, a trained killer born of the finest killer breed. (*Call for the Dead,* pp. 147–48)

In defeat, le Carré's protagonists try to strike out against the soulless bureaucracies of the modern world, if only by finally choosing death rather than continued complicity. By identifying his protagonists with the good and their ultimate fates with some kind of triumph over the forces of evil, le Carré, for all the complexity, subtlety, and sadness of his stories, is not writing tragedy. Where Conrad used the background of anarchist intrigue and counterespionage as a means of "telling Winnie Verloc's story to its anarchistic end of utter desolation, madness and despair" (Conrad, "Preface to The Secret Agent"), le Carré and other writers of spy stories place their greatest emphasis on the representation of the intrigue and its ultimate resolution.

Ralph Harper has the distinction of being the author of the first book-length analysis of the spy story. His *World of the Thriller* (1969) is primarily concerned with "the existential themes of the thriller and, more particularly, in the psychology of the reader's involvement" (p. viii). His analysis of the major patterns of the thriller and their relationship to the reader's psyche is highly suggestive. His basic idea is that the spy story enables the reader to vicariously bring to consciousness some of his secret desires and fears in order to relate these to conscious attitudes and values. "More than any other genre, the thriller invites us to spread the untidy contents of our subconsciousness on the same floor with our approved attitudes, and decide which we want to take seriously" (p. 128). The result, according to Harper, is a simulation of existential choice: "experience of the self as empty, nameless, rudderless is for some people precisely what impels them to read thrillers. In that reading they will be given one more, and a very special, chance to choose themselves" (p. 129).

At times, Harper's "existential" reading threatens to turn good spy stories into novels of the human condition in the mold of Dostoevski, Camus, and Sartre. In spite of this, many of his observations about the psychological appeals of the thriller seem valid. Our major problem with Harper's analysis is that, like Merry's archetypal analysis, Harper's approach relates the psychology of the spy story to universal human characteristics. While we agree that there are basic psychological dynamics involved in the spy story, this still does not account for the special place of the spy story in twentieth-century Western culture, something which we think depends on particular cultural patterns as well as on the creative accomplishments of three generations of writers and filmmakers.

Our brief catalog of books on the spy story would not be complete without reference to Donald McCormick's delightful *Who's Who in Spy Fiction* (1977), a dictionary of major writers of espionage fiction, and to LeRoy Panek's *Special Branch: The British Spy Novel, 1890–1980* (1981). While McCormick does not even pretend to present a complete or definitive listing of writers in the secret agent genre, his brief biographical and critical entries are an excellent corrective to the large generalizations offered in much of the existing literature. We hope in our book to provide significant generalizations about the form, the psychological dynamics, and the cultural significance of the spy story, but also to flesh out this skeleton by giving more intensive analyses of major contributions to the shaping of the generic tradition of secret agent fiction.

Panek's *Special Branch* is organized as a survey of seventeen of the "most important or representative British spy novelists," and is particularly strong in its discussion of those writers mainly responsible for the initial emergence of the espionage novel in the 1890s and 1900s: William LeQueux, E. Phillips Oppenheim, and Erskine Childers. Panek's combination of biographical detail and brief analysis of each writer's contributions to the tradition of the spy story is very useful and, while he does not cover as many writers as *Who's Who in Spy Fiction,* those he does discuss are treated more thoroughly and in a more sophisticated critical fashion. However, Panek's study is limited to the British spy story and lacks serious treatment of the cultural significance of his subject and of the relationship between the spy story and other developments in twentieth-century art and culture. Thus, though his book is not "simply an *aficianado's* handbook," it is primarily concerned with spy fiction as a restricted popular tradition, while we are attempting to see it as a major expressive phenomenon of modern culture. Thus, Panek is most disappointing in his treatment of those writers who have had the greatest artistic impact outside the secret agent tradition—for example, Graham Greene and John le Carré—and in his account of the evolving cultural themes and artistic structures which have characterized the history of the spy story.

Our book is structured as follows. The first chapter offers a general account of what we see as the spy story's cultural and psychological significance and is followed by a brief history of the development of the spy story as a popular genre. After that, we turn to an analysis of the narrative patterns most typical of the genre. The second part of the book consists of four chapters dealing with major figures in the history of the spy story: John Buchan, Eric Ambler and Graham Greene, Ian

Fleming, and John le Carré. The concluding chapter is a more general analysis of the many types of spy story that have proliferated in the last two decades.

We conceived of and designed this book together, but have each assumed primary responsibility for certain chapters, Cawelti for chapters 1, 2, 4, 6, and 7 and Rosenberg for chapters 3, 5, and 8.

1 The Appeal of Clandestinity

While the flourishing of the spy story as a popular genre is primarily a phenomenon of the twentieth century, fascination with clandestine operations goes back to the dawn of history and the earliest surviving narratives and folktales. That most famous of clandestine operations, the Trojan horse, comes immediately to mind, but folktales are full of magical paraphernalia which can make the possessor invisible, and almost all epics contain at least one character who betrays the heroic leader. While the impact of historical espionage is highly controversial, clandestinity has always been an important part of war, politics, and commerce. One is tempted to hazard the speculation that the very fascination of clandestine activity as much as its practical necessity makes it a significant part of our history.

This chapter offers a generalized analysis of the patterns of clandestine activity and their psychological fascination in order to clarify some of the underlying archetypes of espionage and their psychology. The analysis is based on the fictional literature of spying and on historical accounts of espionage.

11

After we have presented the general paradigm, we will describe two historical episodes, one individual and one cultural, which seem to exemplify what we have defined as the "cycle of clandestinity" in all its aspects. The model is highly speculative and general, and we do not claim that it will fit every particular case. Rather it shows the psychological relationship between different phases of clandestine activity, only some of which may be evident in the career of any individual spy or in any particular espionage episode. At most, we hope that the model will bring into relief some of the underlying psychodynamics that seem to be involved in the practice of clandestinity and reflected in its fictional embodiment in the spy story.

Clandestine operations usually begin with a purpose. Either the individual is so deeply committed to some goal that he is prepared to step beyond the usual boundaries of action, or the end he pursues is by its very nature illegal. Two such purposes are revolutionary activity and the service of a foreign country. Either commitment invariably entails some kind of clandestine operation since the open practice of revolution or subversion is outlawed. There are, however, many other purposes which can lead to clandestinity. For example, when those in power feel that public opinion will resist or reject a certain course of action deemed vital to national security, or to the success of an administration, there may be a great temptation to resort to secret actions against a foreign power or against an organization that is felt to be a domestic threat.

Clandestinity is not entirely political. The pursuit of business in a capitalistic society often leads its practitioners into secret operations. Industrial espionage and defenses against it have played a significant role in modern history both between and within countries (Eells and Nehemkis, *Corporate Intelligence and Espionage*). Crime is another mode of clandestine operation and so are many forms of love. While there are obviously significant differences between these various forms of clandestinity, the basic patterns of a secret love affair and an espionage operation have many features in common. Like the spy, the secret lover must keep his actual commitment secret from his wife and family to whom he owes a legal and moral loyalty. Carrying out a love affair often requires many of the same practices as an espionage mission: secret communications, hidden rendezvous, complicated alibis, and elaborate disguises. Such lovers often experience the special closeness of people who share a dangerous bond unknown to others. Not surprisingly, poets have often noted the analogy between love and espionage. Shakespeare and Donne both use spy metaphors to express secret love, for example.

Clandestinity thus begins with a purpose requiring actions that must be kept secret because they transgress conventional, moral, or legal boundaries. But there are also innate psychological attractions in clandestinity which can give the initial involvement an added impetus. In our imaginations, the role of spy partakes of the very powerful fantasy of invisibility, a motif whose recurrence in myth, legend, and literature indicates a compelling appeal for many people in many different cultures. The spy is invisible in a number of senses: he is the secret observer who, himself unseen, watches through a peephole or, in our modern technological age, through a telescope or some electronic device; he is invisible in the sense that his commission as a spy frees him from responsibility and gives him license to do things he could not ordinarily do without serious consequences. James Bond, for example, has the "license to kill." These aspects of invisibility—voyeurism, self-concealment, and license—clearly have a powerful attraction quite apart from the purpose they are intended to serve.

Closely related to invisibility is the fascination with disguises, another fantasy connected with clandestinity. Again, folktales, myths, and stories indicate the perennial human fascination with disguise, the power of which very likely resides in the thrill of trying on other identities—social, racial, sexual, or chronological. Men often fantasize themselves as women, whites as blacks, rich men as poor men, young people as the aged, and vice versa. Disguise is one of the ways that we have of narrating or dramatizing this fantasy. Disguise is a temporary escape from one's own identity; the role of a spy contains the possibility of a controlled but total escape from the constraints of self. This ties in with a third fantasy deeply connected with many forms of clandestinity, the secret exercise of power. The secret conspiracy—actual and fantasied—has been ever present in human history. To imagine becoming part of a secret organization is a compelling fantasy not only in terms of the exercise of power without its responsibilities and risks, but also as a particularly strong image of belonging. To belong to a clandestine organization seems to carry with it a profound involvement, a relationship to other members of the organization deeper than that characteristic of other kinds of organizations because it requires life-and-death loyalty. This particular fantasy of clandestinity is probably especially powerful in modern industrial cultures where people feel relatively alienated from most of the organizations to which they belong. Mario Puzo's *The Godfather,* with its central theme of the clandestine family, exploited this fantasy just as the contemporary spy thriller does.

Ironically, the cycle of clandestinity often moves from the profound loyalty of the initial commitment to extraordinary forms of betrayal. Though his participation in a secret relationship requires total loyalty on the part of the spy (or the lover) toward his partners in clandestinity, this relationship is also a betrayal of existing relationships and prior commitments. This theme of betrayal, possibly impelled by a deep-seated oedipal urge to throw off parental authority, constitutes, along with the fantasies of invisibility, disguise, and secret conspiracy, the repertoire of psychological attractions which, along with compelling moral or political goals, are reflected in the fantasy of espionage.

From the outset, clandestine involvements are complexly ambiguous, often combining high moral purpose with contradictory psychological needs. As the process of clandestinity develops, the psychological state of the spy tends to become even more ambiguous. After the initial commitment to secret activity, the clandestine operative becomes involved with one or more persons in pursuit of his initial purpose. This association quickly creates what might be called a clandestine world, based on the special view of things which the members of the secret group share. The second stage of the cycle of clandestinity is the full development of this clandestine world, which then exists side by side with the ordinary world in the mind of the spy. Participants in clandestinity believe that their secret world is more real than the ordinary world and that it is exempt from the rules that govern those who are not part of the clandestine world. As Marchetti and Marks put it:

> Deeply embedded within the clandestine mentality is the belief that human ethics and social laws have no bearing on covert actions and their practitioners. The intelligence profession, because of its lofty "national security" goals, is free from all moral restrictions. There is no need to wrestle with technical legalisms or judgments as to whether something is right or wrong. The determining factors in secret operations are purely pragmatic: Does the job need to be done? Can it be done? And can secrecy (or plausible denial) be maintained? (*The CIA and the Cult of Intelligence*, p. 240)

Jeb Magruder, in describing the atmosphere of the cover-up discussions between some of the major Watergate participants, corroborates Marchetti and Marks's account of the special morality of the clandestine world and indicates some of the psychological tensions and ambiguities that exist within this world.

> The meetings in Mitchell's office were calm, low-keyed, and businesslike. Sometimes we discussed the campaign as well as the cover-up. Sometimes there were long pauses in our deliberations, as we confronted questions that seemed to have no answers, but there was no sense of embarrassment or shame as we planned the cover-up. If anything, there was a certain self-righteousness to our deliberations. We had persuaded ourselves that what we had done, although technically illegal, was not wrong or even unusual, and that our enemies in the press and in the political world were trying to make a mountain out of a molehill, trying to use this minor incident as a means to destroy Richard Nixon. After the Democrats nominated Senator McGovern, we felt that we were protecting the honorable peace that the President was bringing to Vietnam and avoiding the

national disaster that would follow if McGovern became President. We were not covering up a burglary, we were safeguarding world peace. It was a rationalization we all found easy to accept. We did not discuss the Watergate affair in terms of perjury or burglary or conspiracy. We would refer, rather, to "handling the case" and "making sure things didn't get out of hand." Essentially, we used management terms to discuss a legal problem. Yet we were not dealing with a tidy managerial problem. There were many loose ends and much confusion to the Watergate cover-up. We often didn't know what was coming next, and for a while the Federal prosecutors seemed to be as confused as we were. It was a time, for me, and I think for all of us, of intense pressure and pervasive fatalism. Fred LaRue and I used to joke that as the cover-up continued, our drinking was increasing and our sex drives were diminishing. (Magruder, *An American Life,* pp. 271–72)

Clandestinity generates not only a special view of the world based on shared secrets, but a different language as well as a different morality. As the clandestine worldview and the special words that manifest it proliferate, it becomes difficult for participants to receive information or feedback from the ordinary world. In effect, the clandestine world becomes increasingly shut off from the ordinary world, and its devotees find it more and more difficult to take seriously and even to understand the ordinary view of things. The secret planning for the Bay of Pigs operation described by A. M. Schlesinger, Jr., in *A Thousand Days* is a frightening instance of this pattern. Late in the planning, Chester Bowles, who had not been in on the affair from the beginning and therefore did not fully share in the clandestine world the group had created, happened to preside over a session in the absence of Dean Rusk. He was horrified at what he heard and wrote a memorandum to Rusk strongly opposing the invasion. Schlesinger reports that "Rusk reassured Bowles, leaving him with the impression that the project was being whittled down into a guerilla infiltration, and filed the memorandum away" (pp. 250–51). The clandestine group thus closed ranks to reject any outsider who might shake their worldview and the operation went ahead.

In the aftermath of the Bay of Pigs fiasco, Kennedy became very concerned about the dangers of this kind of planning, but the successive tragedies of Vietnam with its proliferation of secret operations suggest that little was done to restrict the growth of clandestine groups within the American government.

Participants in a clandestine world live in a state of psychological tension which resembles, in some of its characteristics, the pathology of schizophrenia. This tension results from their dual views of the world. First, there is the "reality" constituted by the secrets shared with other members of the clandestine group. Since these secrets commonly refer to states of affairs or events that are not known to those outside the group, the clandestine worldview seems more real. Yet, since the preservation of the clandestine group requires that these secrets remain hidden from all other persons, a clandestine participant must also live as a member of the ordinary world, pretending to share its view of reality. This double vision is difficult enough. The clandestine participant must remember the attitudes, perceptions, and words characteristic of both the clandestine world and the world outside, and he must manipulate both consciousnesses effectively enough to shift back and forth between them with ease. This slipping in and out of the ordinary world is characteristic of schizophrenic illness. Though one can say that the spy exercises a conscious and rational control over his different roles while the psychotic appears to have lost this power, there is a boundary area in which the anxiety surrounding divergent worldviews can become so great that the secret agent passes beyond that stage of complete rational control over his divided self. The tension and excitement of participating in a clandestine world are among the central motifs of the fiction of espionage:

> He found the air of happy gaiety, the complete unknowingness of the crowds, almost unnerving—tragic. Life was going on just as usual, no one realizing anything except those in high authority and a handful of men who tended AFPU ONE under the Official Secrets Act's gat. As Shaw made his way along, diffidently stepping out of the way of dark, buxom Gibraltarian girls and

their escorts, he wondered what those crowds would think if they could see into his mind, see the picture which he was carrying within him of the utter annihilation of a community— but no one looked twice at the tall, thin figure in the now rumpled tropic-weight suit, the figure with the worried, lined face and graying hair. They were far too intent upon their present pleasure. (McCutchan, *Gibraltar Road*, p. 68)

As indicated in this passage, the clandestine participant's attitude toward the ordinary world is a mixture of superiority, loneliness, and resentment. He feels that he has a better understanding of reality and therefore is not deluded by the illusions and facile pleasure-seeking of the majority. On the other hand, he feels terribly isolated by his secret and resents the innocent happiness of those who cannot share his frightening knowledge. As his participation in the clandestine world continues, the spy finds the two roles he must play increasingly difficult to relate to each other:

"He's changed!" she said. "You must have noticed that yourself. I wouldn't be surprised what he was mixed up in. He has this sort of schizophrenia and an obsession with secrecy. I don't know if you get like that in the secret service, or whether the secret service chooses that sort of man. But it's hell to live with, I'll tell you that." (Deighton, *Yesterday's Spy*, p. 22)

So long as the clandestine participant can share with others a secret view of the world and thereby receive support and knowing sympathy, the condition of clandestinity is tolerable. Those who form parts of secret bureaucracies like the CIA receive this support from their organizations. The bureaucratization of clandestinity does not prevent the delusions of the clandestine world from growing, but it probably does counteract some of its more devastating psychological effects.

Even the most stable of organizations cannot entirely remove the sense of isolation inherent in the condition of clandestinity, however. To offset this isolation, clandestine participants are often impelled toward renewed conspiratorial efforts, as if the re-creation of the clandestine group around some new set of secrets or plots could assuage the feeling of separation from other human contacts. The need for renewed conspiracy can be seen over and over again in the lives of spies. Georges Cadoudal, an anti-Bonaparte agent, was once supposed to have observed: "Do you know what we ought to advise the King to do? We ought to tell him that he ought to have both of us shot, for we shall never be anything but conspirators. We have taken the imprint" (Rowan, *Secret Service*, p. 159). The intensity and complexity of the growing obsession with conspiracy is strikingly instanced in Richard Rowan's observations on the career of Daniel Defoe, who was among other things, an early secret agent:

> Not only were [Defoe's] most famous characters fictions, but he himself was partly a figment of his own teeming imagination. He published some books anonymously, but signed his name to the introductions in which he recommended them to the consideration of the reading public. He encouraged himself in letters to his papers and reviled himself in letters to rival sheets. He corrected himself, he quoted himself, he plagiarized his own writings in works which he attributed to foreign commentators. He boldly reminded himself in print of his alliance with political gentry who were secretly employing him to oppose some policy of the government to which they belonged. Defoe, more than any other man who has ever lived, permitted his aptitude for secret service to infect every other practice of his almost innumerable vocations. (Pp. 113–14)

When the participant in a clandestine group reaches the point where he is obsessed with conspiracy and overcome with anxiety about his own isolation and vulnerability, he is likely to pass into the next phase of the cycle of clandestinity: the role of double or triple agent.

The double agent is a role that heroic spies in the tradition of John Buchan and Ian Fleming never accept, however much they are tempted. In the more complex tradition of secret agent adventure, which began with Maugham, Greene, and

Ambler and continues in recent writers like John le Carré, Len Deighton, and Adam Hall, double agentry is a central theme. Several different motives can impel a spy to turn double agent. There is the hope for material gain. The double agent's unique position is that he can come to know some of the secrets of both sides. By selling to more than one buyer, he can greatly increase his personal profit. Another motive is the fear of being exposed. Many double agents pretend to work for both sides in order to insure their personal safety. If an agent cannot keep his activities completely concealed from the enemy, the next best thing is to pretend to be one of the enemy's own agents. In many instances, intelligence agencies have used "turned" agents to pass controlled information to an enemy. Apparently some agencies consider it almost a basic principle that an agent who has been in the field for a long period of time is very likely to be "doubled." Also, the agent's isolation—the anxiety of being "out in the cold" alone—may impel him to some kind of negotiation with the enemy simply for the sake of human contact. The psychological complexities of this ultimate state of clandestinity are reflected not only in the number of double agents one runs across in the history of espionage, but in those many cases where one cannot ever be sure where the double agent's real loyalty lay, if indeed it was to anyone but himself.

In the end, the double agent becomes the most isolated human being imaginable, for he must act as if every man's hand is against him. There is no person with whom he can share his secret view of the world. He must lie to everyone. In such a state, the individual easily comes to feel that everyone is in a conspiracy against him, that no person can be trusted. Thus, the double agent becomes the ultimate paranoid:

> "Paranoia—it's the occupational hazard of men who've worked the sort of territories that Champion has worked." Dawlish stared at me. I said, "Like anthrax for tannery workers, and silicosis for miners. You need somewhere . . . a place to go and hide forever . . . and you never shake it off." (Deighton, *Yesterday's Spy*, p. 29)

With entry into the paranoid world of double agentry, the cycle of clandestinity is complete. It is no longer possible for the individual to join with others in the pursuit of a clandestine purpose since all possibility of trust is closed to him. Having begun the cycle as an individual with a purpose that required collaborative secret actions, he becomes once again an individual but is now enmeshed in the net of multiple lies which he must tell to all other persons. The double agent enters a state of moral and personal isolation so complete that there is no way out but death, exposure, or total flight. The only purpose that remains to him is that of self-preservation through an increasingly complex improvisation of stories to hide his true position of multiple disloyalty.

There are then, three principal phases in the cycle of clandestinity:

1. An individual or group conceives of a purpose which appears to require actions beyond the bounds of law or morality accepted by other members of their society.

2. To pursue these purposes a secret group is formed. This group constitutes a clandestine world defined by the secrets they share. To preserve the clandestine world, members of the group must continue to live as members of ordinary society with the resultant psychological tension between conflicting worldviews.

3. Gradually the individual participant in a clandestine group begins to feel isolated not only from ordinary society, but from other members of the group. This isolation may result from the fear of exposure, a desire for profit, or from a growing sense that all men are engaged in conspiracies against him. He signals his complete isolation by becoming a double agent, that is, by engaging in secret activities against the clandestine group or by apparently or actually betraying the group's secrets to its enemies.

What we have just defined as the cycle of clandestinity is a pattern of experience outlined in broad, abstract strokes. Neither historical spies nor the secret agents of literature necessarily follow this pattern in every respect. In fact, most of the employees of the CIA, the British Secret Service, and,

presumably, the KGB are less involved in clandestine operations than in the gathering and sifting of information. As
information-gathering has become increasingly dominated by
electronics and computer technology, the vast majority of intelligence activities involve sitting in an office and routing the
flow of information from various machines into the appropriate
bureaucratic channels. Not surprisingly, intelligence operatives
are among the most dedicated fans of secret agent fiction, since
they, as much as anyone else, need to have their daily professional and bureaucratic routines enlivened by the fantasies of
adventure, mystery, and romance.

It is in the lives of the most legendary of historical spies
and in the adventures of the most popular secret agents of
fiction that the archetypal patterns of clandestinity are most
evident. While the main body of this book is concerned with
the evolution of the secret agent genre in fiction, a few historical examples of clandestinity, first on the individual and
then on the collective level, will illustrate the pervasiveness
of the cycle of clandestinity and the way in which, in the world
of espionage, life can be as strange as fiction.

The life of a man who could be called the spy's spy, the ultimate
clandestine operator, began in 1869 in the town of Lyskovo
in Russia, when a poor Jewish tailor's wife gave birth to a son
who was named Ievno Aseff. Though a failure in business,
Aseff's father did manage to give his children an education at
the gymnasium, where young Aseff became involved, like
many students of his time, in revolutionary movements. After
leaving the gymnasium, Aseff worked at a variety of jobs—
tutor, reporter, clerk, salesman—while carrying on various
undercover revolutionary activities, such as printing and distributing pamphlets. This period was evidently his introduction into clandestine activities, and it led directly to the first
crisis of his life. In 1892, he was, or felt himself to be,
threatened with arrest for distributing a revolutionary manifesto. To escape this fate, Aseff absconded with the proceeds
of a consignment of butter and fled to Germany. There, in
Karlsruhe, he joined forces with a group of Russian émigrés

in the Social Democratic party and entered the polytechnic, where he studied electrostatics.

During his first year in Germany, Aseff became more deeply involved in revolutionary activities, but he also evidently started to worry about the possibility of being betrayed to the police. The upshot was that

> On April 4, 1893, he wrote his first letter to the Police Department. This letter was something in the nature of a feeler. "I have the honor to inform Your Highness," he wrote, "that two months ago a circle of revolutionaries was formed here whose aim is . . ." and so forth. There followed a list of names, and certain facts were cited to show that the writer of the letter was in a position to give information not only about the revolutionary temper of Russian students abroad, but also about the propaganda that was going on in Rostov. The letter contained no concrete suggestions about the future. The writer only begged that a registered letter should be sent to him at a given address if the police thought his information of any use to them. He did not mention his real name. (Nikolajewsky, *Aseff the Spy,* p. 25)

After various negotiations in the course of which the secret police quickly discovered the identity of their anonymous correspondent, Aseff was placed on the department payroll and received his first salary in June 1893.

Just what Aseff's motivations were at this early stage in his clandestine career are not fully clear. It is possible that he sought to use his police connections primarily as a means of supporting and covering up his authentic revolutionary activities. On the other hand, he may have been solely interested in the money, prepared, as it were, to sell his clandestine services to the highest bidder while retaining a foot in both camps. In any case, he returned to Russia in 1899 after receiving his engineering degree and quickly became even more fully involved in revolutionary activities with the full consent and collaboration of the secret police. By 1903, Aseff had worked himself into the heart of the Social Revolutionary party, becoming the head of its battle organization or terrorist section after the arrest of its previous leader, Gershuni. Interestingly enough, Aseff used his position with this terrorist group and his cover within the police to engineer the assassination of the anti-Semitic interior minister, V. K. Plehve. One reason it is very difficult to ascertain Aseff's motives at this time is that his own personal hatred of Plehve was well-known, not only in revolutionary circles, but to the police. As a Jew himself, Aseff clearly had his heart in the assassination of the man who was responsible for some of the bloodiest pogroms in Russian history. His personal commitment to this particular terrorist act was great enough that he did not hesitate to become involved in it, even though he had spoken of his feelings about Plehve to the police.

But if it was the act of a man with certain overriding moral commitments, Plehve's assassination was the last such act on the part of Aseff. Its success solidified Aseff's position in the Social Revolutionary party to such a degree that mounting evidence of his treachery failed to shake the party's faith in him until the middle of 1909. At the same time, this terrorist success naturally made the police highly suspicious of Aseff's trustworthiness as an informer, and they placed even more pressure on him to betray revolutionary plots. The more Aseff's information led to the arrest of revolutionaries under his leadership, the more the party insisted on further terrorist activities. For six years, Aseff walked the narrow, slippery tightrope of a double agent with remarkable skill. It is amazing to think of a man who can continue to function in a situation where he must play a slightly different role for everyone he meets and where the penalty for a slight discrepancy in action or story is imprisonment or death. Despite a mounting campaign of exposure, Aseff's credibility with the Social Revolutionary party's Central Committee remained unassailable until, ironically, one of his chief antagonists fell into conversation with a retired police officer and learned of Aseff's early police informing, something that even he had not suspected. When this testimony was presented to the members of the Central Committee, they were at last convinced and laid plans for Aseff's execution. But the ever resilient Aseff fled, took an assumed name, and with the proceeds of his clandestine ac-

tivities moved to Berlin, where he lived as an affluent stock-
broker under the name Alexander Neumayer. Unfortunately
for him, he had invested heavily in Russian bonds, which were
interdicted with the outbreak of war. Recouping what he could
from his losses, Aseff opened a fashionable corset shop in the
name of his mistress and was doing quite well with it when
he was interned by the Germans as a dangerous international
terrorist. Outraged at this, he bombarded the government with
petitions detailing his services to the Russian police, but was
ignored. He lived through the war but contracted various
debilitating conditions during his internment and died of a
kidney ailment on 24 April 1918.

Aseff's clandestine career was hardly typical in that he
passed through the different stages of the cycle of clandestinity
with remarkable rapidity and thoroughness. Nevertheless, those
historical spies who become legendary, as well as many fictional
spies, tend to exemplify most of the psychodynamics of the
cycle. Indeed, our examination of the spy novel in the twentieth century will show how the spy story itself gradually
developed from a variation of the nineteenth-century colonial
adventure story into an increasingly complex exploration of
the psychological, philosophical, and cultural significance of
clandestinity.

The cycle of clandestinity touches not only the lives of
individual spies, but also shapes the development of groups
and even nations in certain kinds of historical circumstances.
One such group consisted of those followers of former president
Richard Nixon who became involved in that complex of events
known as "Watergate."

Watergate apparently originated in a "moral" conviction
held by certain loyalists that Nixon's reelection was necessary
to the salvation of the United States and perhaps of the world.
The intensity of this conviction was such that those at the
center came to accept the idea that a number of activities could
be justified as essential to Nixon's reelection. Various clandestine groups were created within the administration and
entrusted with the running of secret operations against individuals and groups identified as particularly dangerous enemies

of the administration. Soon these groups, such as the notorious "plumbers" or the "dirty tricks" groups of Howard Hunt and Gordon Liddy, had developed clandestine worldviews of their own and the second phase of the cycle was underway. These clandestine worldviews very soon began to assume a life of their own and to exhibit the separation from ordinary logic and common sense that characterizes the insulated clandestine world. Residual adherence to the ordinary worldview by some powerful individuals like John Mitchell prevented some of the more bizarre fantasies of Gordon Liddy from being enacted, perhaps because Mitchell had not yet been fully initiated into the clandestine group. However, with the discovery of the Watergate burglary and the launching of the cover-up most of the inner circle of the Nixon administration became linked with these clandestine groups in a single secret worldview.

The fate of the cover-up exemplified the essential instability of the clandestine group and the tendency of individuals to pass over into the third phase of double agentry. In a sense, the attempt of administration higher-ups to maintain what was sometimes referred to as "deniability" was a form of double agentry since these leaders were quite prepared to betray other members of the clandestine group in order to maintain their own positions. Once the Watergate investigations were fully underway, double agentry became endemic within the administration as various former members of the clandestine groups scrambled to make deals with the investigating agencies.

In this case, the country ultimately benefited from the tendencies of the clandestine cycle, for without the increasing paranoia within the inner circle, the Nixon administration might have succeeded in its initial project of covering up the scandal.

It is possible not only for individuals and groups but also for whole societies to become involved in this pattern. One historical episode of this sort is the Dreyfus case in France (ca. 1894–1906). The Dreyfus case began as a result of the great national shock of defeat in the Franco-Prussian War. In the consequent search for a scapegoat to take responsibility for this defeat, Captain Alfred Dreyfus, the first Jewish officer to be assigned to the general staff, was accused of passing information to the Germans. A trumped up case against Dreyfus, patently manufactured by fanatic anti-Semites within the general staff, led to his conviction and sentencing to Devil's Island. For a decade French society was in turmoil as increasing numbers of French intellectuals and liberals became convinced of Dreyfus's innocence and launched a public campaign against imprisonment. Yet, Dreyfus had become a symbol of subversive elements within French society for much of the public, so that French society as a whole supported the honor of the army and thereby became involved in a cover-up of Dreyfus's innocence and the guilt of the army itself. The schizophrenic ambiguity of worldviews characteristic of the second phase of the clandestine cycle afflicted the whole structure of French society so much that many persons were no longer able to accept the plainest and most persuasive kind of evidence. For example, Félix Gribelin, archivist of the French Ministry of War, played an important part in exposing the forgeries that had been the only evidence against Dreyfus, yet he remained totally committed to the worldview that depended on Dreyfus's guilt:

> Gribelin readily traced the multitude of undisclosed forgeries as well as the disclosed ones. . . . He had all the perverted integrity that went into the make-up of the true Anti-Dreyfusard. To the last he preserved Henry's memory as a kind of cult. Nothing could have shaken his belief in Dreyfus' guilt. He knew that all the evidence was forged. He himself exposed such forgeries as not even the most convinced Dreyfusards suspected existed. But they made not one dent in that strange psyche bound in its private iron. (Halasz, *Captain Dreyfus*, p. 257)

This unshakable commitment to a belief is reminiscent of the fixed belief in the inevitability of the Bay of Pigs operation, which obsessed the secret planning group despite all evidence to the contrary.

But, as the Dreyfus cover-up persisted, becoming ever more hysterical, French society became increasingly paranoid,

more and more convinced of the existence of subversive conspiracies at every level. As Nicholas Halasz describes the
ultimate state of French society, prior to Dreyfus's final vin-
dication, we see the transition from a committed clandestinity
to the chaotic state of suspicion, distrust, and a concern with
pure survival that we have characterized as the final stage of
the cycle of clandestinity:

> Governments fell. Eventually no court, not even the highest,
> was trusted. The Chamber of Deputies passed a law to prevent
> France's highest criminal court from considering the matter
> further. With courts unable to rule in law, the nation came to
> the brink of anarchy. The fact that the truth was discovered very
> soon after the nation had accepted the lie made no difference.
> The lie had to continue to be accepted. To reject it was to reject
> the material force of the Army as a shield against Germany and
> embrace instead an abstract ideal as a refuge from brutal violence.
> The nation refused to do it. It sided with the lie and declared
> it the only truth. (P. 5)

The Cold War period of recent American history used
domestic radicals and suspected Communist sympathizers in
much the same way French society used Dreyfus and the Jews
as scapegoats for a frightening sense of national peril. Public
attitudes from the McCarthy crusade against Communists in
government in the early 1950s to the ultimate breakdown of
Cold War clandestinity in the chaotic conspiracies and double
agentry of Watergate show a number of significant points of
resemblance to the Dreyfus period in France and reveal the
psychodynamics of the cycle of clandestinity.

The history of spy fiction in the twentieth century also
reflects in certain ways the basic cycle of clandestinity, and
this evolution is the major subject of this book. The spy stories
of World War I and its aftermath, created by English writers
like John Buchan, Dornford Yates, and E. Phillips Oppenheim, were heroic stories of romantic gentlemen pursuing
moral purposes into successful, redemptive clandestine operations. These were fantasies of the early stages of the clandestine
cycle. The same kind of story was revived in popularity by Ian

Fleming, but in a later period, Fleming felt it necessary to cloak his romances of adventurous espionage in an aura of exaggeration and irony as if his readers could no longer take such heroics straight. In the 1930s a new kind of spy literature appeared in the novels of Eric Ambler and the "entertainments" of Graham Greene. Both Greene and Ambler specialized in stories of ordinary people suddenly caught up in the dangers and mysteries of international conspiracies. The interplay in their work between the ordinary world and their protagonists' new clandestine view of things clearly manifests the central themes of the second phase of the cycle of clandestinity, the "schizophrenic" ambiguity of clandestine and ordinary world-views. Finally, the most recent school of popular spy fiction—for example, John le Carré and Len Deighton—has become increasingly obsessed with the themes of loyalty, betrayal, and double agentry. Le Carré's *Tinker, Tailor, Soldier, Spy* told an amazingly involuted and paranoid story about the exposure of a Russian plot within the very heart of the British Secret Service, a plot carried on over a long period of years by a double agent who had an impeccably heroic and moral British background. It was as if John Buchan's Richard Hannay had been revealed as the kaiser's leading agent.

Clandestinity poses a particular problem for American culture because, in developing our version of democracy with its strong emphasis on publicity and openness, we have not created over the years a significant tradition of public clandestinity. If the interpretation of the cycle of clandestinity we have espoused here is at all correct, the lack of such a public tradition may be, in most respects, a saving grace. The short, incredible history of the CIA makes it quite clear, however, that when Americans settle down to the creation of clandestine establishments, they do so on the same monumental scale at which they generate other kinds of organizations. If the nature of international relations makes espionage and counterespionage vital necessities on certain occasions, the lack of a continuous tradition of public clandestinity means that we must face over and over again the same kind of irresponsible—indeed lunatic—proliferation of clandestine groups which developed throughout the

Cold War era. While the CIA is currently keeping as low a
profile as it can, and after Watergate the merest hint of political
clandestinity is likely to be exposed by the media, Americans
cannot afford to forget the profound psychological appeals of
clandestine power. If we are to avert the Watergates of the future, and even to bring the CIA of today under responsible
political control, we must develop a fuller understanding of
the psychological and cultural processes that are invoked by
the choice of clandestinity. It is our hope that this study of the
evolution of the fantasy of clandestinity in the popular genre
of the spy story will make an indirect contribution to this
understanding.

Though archetypal themes appear to play an important role
in the perennial fascination of clandestine activity, the question
of why the spy story has become a primary genre in the twentieth century still remains. In one sense, this question can
only be answered by acknowledging the contributions of many
individual writers and filmmakers to the creation, the broad-
ening, and the increasing sophistication of the spy story as a
literary and cinematic genre. In particular, the accomplishments of John Buchan, Eric Ambler, Graham Greene, Ian
Fleming, and John le Carré have shaped the evolution of the
spy story from romantic adventure to many-sided literary and
cinematic genre. Therefore, the analysis of these writers and
an interpretation of their significance in the tradition of the
spy story constitutes a major portion of this book.

The interests that impelled these writers to become part
of the espionage tradition and that motivated twentieth-century
readers and filmgoers to make the spy story one of their favorite
genres clearly go beyond the sum of individual accomplishments. For many reasons, the spy and clandestine activity have
come to be central symbols of the human condition in the twentieth century. Because this has been a century of total war and
totalitarian societies, espionage, both international and domestic, has become an increasing part of all of our lives. Even
in democratic societies, national intelligence organizations like
the CIA and the British Secret Service grew to unprecedented

size and influence in the aftermath of World War II. In addition, the protracted Cold War and the fear of imminent nuclear catastrophe have made espionage and counterespionage seem activities of the highest importance. Americans widely believed that "the enemy within," that is, Russian spies and their American agents, were responsible for giving vital scientific secrets to the Soviets, enabling them to become a nuclear power and a serious competitor for the conquest of space. During the McCarthy period, clandestinity became an obsession, for Americans were bombarded with claims that a large number of important government officials were Communist spies. Though these claims turned out to be largely groundless, cases like those of the Rosenbergs and Alger Hiss continued to feed fears of widespread subversion in America. These fears were intensified by the prolonged stalemate of the Korean War. The even greater tragedy of the Vietnam War led to an increasing concern with the role of clandestinity on the world scene. In this case, however, the concern was critical, stimulated by a growing fear of the uncontrolled power of the CIA on the international scene and the FBI within the country. Today, facing the bleak prospect of the annihilation of humanity, the public's attitude toward espionage can probably be characterized as profoundly ambiguous. On the one hand, there is a conviction that a strong intelligence community is necessary to prevent our national adversaries from gaining any political, military, or technological advantage that might threaten man's future. But there is also an increasing awareness of the way in which organizations like the CIA abuse their authority by fomenting problems that threaten the peace more than they work to preserve it. The development of the spy story during the Cold War period certainly reflects this ambiguity: one group of writers continues the heroic tradition of Ian Fleming and another presents stories of clandestine operators betrayed by their own organizations, as in many of the novels of Len Deighton and John le Carré.

Finally, though the increasing importance of espionage on the international scene has made the spy one of the central symbols of twentieth-century man, there is another important

reason why the clandestine protagonist has become an everyman figure. The situation of the spy "out in the cold" seems
to express the way many people feel about the basic patterns
of their lives. We first became aware of this phenomenon when
we were presenting earlier versions of our construct of the cycle
of clandestinity to meetings of various professional organizations for their suggestions and criticism. We were struck by
one quite unanticipated response: after each of our presenta-
tions and the ensuing discussion, members of the audience
would approach us privately to tell us how much our description of the patterns of clandestinity seemed to fit their perception of their own roles in contemporary society. People from
groups as diverse as psychiatrists, English professors, feminists,
and graduate students all reported feeling a sense of ambiguity
in their relationship to society and to their profession or organization which made them feel like either a participant in
a clandestine world, or a double agent, or both.

After reflecting on this surprising response, we have come
to think that there is a definite connection between the clandestine protagonist as a symbol of everyman in the twentieth
century and an aspect of modern culture which has often been
discussed in contemporary works of sociology, both popular and
academic: the alienation of the individual from the large organizations—corporations, bureaucracies, professions—which
dominate our lives. We think it is this sense of alienation and
the deep feeling of conflict between individual self and social
role which it engenders that makes the figure of the spy so
compelling as a contemporary everyman hero. Into the figure
of the spy trying to carry out his secret mission in a territory
dominated by the enemy or, even better, threatened by betrayal
from his own organization, the individual can project the frustrations he feels toward the limitations imposed on his actions
by his corporate employer, by bureaucratic regulations, or by
the conventions of his profession.

Thus, the spy story has become a primary twentieth-century genre by drawing on the archetypal power of the patterns
of clandestinity to express a compelling vision of contemporary
life into which readers can project their own fears and frus-

trations. This vision relates to the sense of anxiety the public feels about international conflict and to the possibility of nuclear catastrophe, as well as to the sense of alienation so many individuals feel. The present flourishing of the spy story is the accomplishment of three generations of writers and filmmakers who have contributed their creative skills and instincts about readers' needs and interests to the development of the genre. After a brief overview of this development and a closer look at some of the structures of secrecy which constitute the underlying patterns of the spy story, we will turn to a more intensive analysis of the writers who have done most to shape this tradition and to a fuller discussion of the spy story's continuing contemporary appeal.

2 The Spy Story's Story: A Brief History

The spy story gradually took shape in the nineteenth century and became a widely popular narrative formula around the time of World War I. The first novel to be entitled *The Spy* and to have a secret agent as one of its main characters was published by James Fenimore Cooper in 1821, shortly before Cooper began his major series, "The Leatherstocking Tales" with *The Pioneers* in 1823. Significantly, Cooper explored the possibilities of the spy in literature before he went on to develop the Western. He was apparently fascinated by characters caught in the middle between large opposing forces. His spy, Harvey Birch, was an American agent, but this was known only to the mysterious "Mr. Harper" (George Washington). To accomplish his mission, Birch had to pretend loyalty to the British. Caught between the Americans, who think he is a British spy, and the British against whom he is actually operating, Birch is perhaps the first figure in literature to be "out in the cold."

As early as the fourteenth century—possibly earlier—*no-mannesland* was an unoccupied wasteland, a place for hangings and the starting-off point for exiles. From the verge of societal order, the outcast was launched on his lonely way across desolation—topographical as well as cultural. Cooper made his Harvey Birch a denizen of liminal regions, of what in colonial days was a vast no-man's-land in New York State, seemingly neither royalist nor colonist rebel. He is thus profoundly mysterious, as his most sacred beliefs are known only to himself; only his control knows to which side, if any, he belongs. He is by ostensible profession a pedlar, carrying all of his inventory around on his back, perpetually transient, at home in no one place (he does have a home, but few even know of its existence). Birch has no fixed community to which he belongs, no society to which he appears to owe loyalty. Because the armies of both sides consider him harmless, Birch can roam the countryside freely, unhindered, unnoticed by prying eyes. He seems at home in the wilderness; it is his natural habitat, and so when he is in liminal lands he does not draw any notice. People expect to see him in no-man's-land. His modest hut is also in the wilderness; appropriately it is destroyed by some marauding cowboys. They too live just beyond the margins of established society, though they do so only to avoid the restrictions of law. Birch dresses and acts as though he is not a part of ordered, structured society; he is at home in the wilds, intimate with secret pathways and unknown hiding places. We would not recognize him in the genteel attire of contemporary Establishment merchants; and it would have been contrary to Cooper's vision to clothe him in anything besides shabby weeds.

The Spy seems to have been inspired by the debate over the capture and execution of Major André, who is mentioned several times in Cooper's novel. Many colonists and nearly all Englishmen and royalists (of course) felt that he was not "really" a spy and that in any case a gentleman should not be hanged, certainly not for such an infraction as André was accused of. Throughout *The Spy* the reader has difficulty deciding just who the spy of the title is: Washington himself appears in disguise behind enemy lines, Henry Wharton makes his way through enemy territory in disguise to see his beloved, and Birch is in a kind of disguise throughout. Cooper seems to be questioning the morality of clandestinity, implying that at one time or other a disguise can have honorable motives and purposes (the end does justify the means) and that just, honorable, the "right" causes can be correctly served by spies. He seems to question the nature of André's crime in this light.

Cooper is the first real spy novelist—that is, the writer of the first spy novel—because he saw what recent writers have had to rediscover, that the spy dwells in liminality, in no-man's-land; and he, Cooper, was able to imagine and to express what it was like to exist there and to describe the relation of liminal regions to those who dwell in the mainstream in or-dered, structured society. Most readers today find his novels unreadable; yet he was able to capture the essential sense of that characteristically "modern" phenomenon, life on the mar-gins, the borders, the limits of society, the interstices of its structure. *The Spy* is not Cooper's most honored novel; yet as the first literary exploration of liminality, it is underrated, a novel that should interest us much more today because it speaks so clearly to us.

Yet, interesting as he is, the spy Harvey Birch is not the major figure of *The Spy.* It is typical of Cooper's earlier novels that the protagonists are aristocratic lovers whose dynastic romance has been temporarily impeded by the divided loyalties of the American Revolution. Birch is from a lower class and is basically a comic figure whose central narrative function is to save the life of the gallant young Tory Henry Wharton so that Wharton's sister can eventually marry her aristocratic, loyalist lover, Peyton Dunwoodie. In many ways, Birch is similar to Cooper's initial version of Natty Bumppo, the first major western hero, in *The Pioneers.* Natty, like Birch, is a man in the middle, but the opposing forces are wilderness and civilization. As in *The Spy,* the Natty of *The Pioneers* is a loyal retainer who helps along the dynastic romance of Tory descen-dant Oliver Effingham and loyalist offspring Elizabeth Temple. Cooper later developed Natty Bumppo into the Leatherstock-ing, a much more heroic, mythical figure and thus invented the Western. But the many parallels between *The Spy* and *The Pioneers* suggest a basic kinship between the Western and the early spy story mainly because both are tales of adventure.

Cooper did not choose to develop the figure of the spy any further, perhaps because the Leatherstocking seemed a much more important symbolic hero of American culture. He may also have been influenced by the traditional animus against spies as traitors and mercenaries. Throughout most of the history of Western civilization, the most striking legends of espionage have developed around figures of treachery and evil. Two archetypal spies in the Judeo-Christian tradition were Delilah, who used her sexuality to bring down the mighty Samson, and Judas Iscariot, the betrayer of Christ. The legends of espionage are full of the progeny of Delilah and Judas. As Rosenberg indicates in *Custer and the Epic of Defeat,* most heroic defeats have their evil traitors who have gone over to the enemy. The sexy female betrayer is a perennial favorite from Delilah through Lucrezia Borgia to Mata Hari. The traditional image of the spy was one of treachery and greed—Judas's thirty pieces of silver—and this persisted for centuries. Even at the beginning of the nineteenth century, Napoleon is supposed to have said, when asked why he did not award the legion of honor to his great spymaster Schulmeister, "Gold is the only reward for a spy."

However the age of democratic revolutions and imperialism generated a new attitude toward the spy. The American Revolution produced its Judas-figure in Benedict Arnold, but it also gave rise to the legend of Nathan Hale, whose famous last words became a symbol of nobility and patriotism. The father of our country was himself a great spymaster as well as military strategist and created the first modern espionage organization with his extensive use of civilian sympathizers in British-occupied territory as double agents. Through such examples, the spy became a much more positive figure during the nineteenth century. While the traditional negative image of the secret agent continued to flourish in such stereotypes as the anarchist-terrorist and the radical agitator, Britain's colonial wars and the American Civil War generated a number of heroic legends about espionage. Such fascinating exploits as those of "Chinese" Gordon in China and Africa and of Sir William Sleeman against the thug cults in India created that compelling image of the Britisher disguised as a native to serve the empire, an image that not only served as a rich source of fictional characters but also had its impact on history by inspiring individuals such as Lawrence of Arabia.

In the American Civil War, spies on both sides of the Mason-Dixon line played a significant role. That this was a civil war made it difficult to portray these agents as vicious enemies. After the war, just as some of the Southern generals became heroes to the North as well, the memoirs of both Blue and Gray spies were widely read and their exploits admired. Most of these agents were amateurs, many of them women of unquestionable respectability. The war's most famous espionage professional, however, was Allan Pinkerton, who served as General McClellan's chief of secret service for the Army of the Potomac. Though he was probably one of the worst collectors of military intelligence in history, Pinkerton was a very effective self-promoter. His military adventures combined with his later counterespionage exploits against anarchists and labor agitators to enhance further the image of the heroic spy.

In later nineteenth-century America, counterespionage operations against the dreaded radicals and anarchists deemed responsible for political assassinations and terrorist plots like the Chicago Haymarket Riot further solidified the positive image of the spy as protector of the homeland against foreign threats. Even dime novel heroes like Nick Carter began to operate against anarchist villains in addition to their usual pursuit of garden-variety criminals. Thus, the spy and the cowboy were both heroes of the dime novel adventure continuing the related development of Western and espionage adventure stories Cooper had begun in the earlier nineteenth century.

In Britain, in addition to the growing fear of anarchism and labor violence, an increasing anxiety about foreign invasion paved the way for the growing popularity of the espionage adventure. In 1871, Sir George Chesney's "The Battle of Dorking" appeared in *Blackwood's Magazine* and became one of the first of many novels prophesying a German invasion of England. The popular genre of imaginary invasions became an international phenomenon in the last quarter of the nineteenth century, paving the way not only for a new kind of science fiction (e.g., Wells's *War of the Worlds*), but for a new kind of spy story. Erskine Childers's early spy story *The Riddle of the Sands* (1903) grew directly out of this tradition, as did the early adventure stories of William LeQueux, *The Great War in England in 1897* (1894) and *England's Peril* (1899), and the first spy novel of John Buchan, *The Thirty-Nine Steps* (1915).

By the end of the nineteenth century, the spy was not only attracting the attention of dime novelists and other writers of popular adventure, but of serious novelists as well. Dostoevski had used the theme of clandestinity in several of his novels, but it was Joseph Conrad who first created in *The Secret Agent* (1907) a modern tragedy with espionage as its central theme. Conrad had already dealt with the related theme of colonial adventure in *Heart of Darkness* (1902) and with revolution in *Nostromo* (1904). In 1911, he completed his portrayal of the world of clandestinity with *Under Western Eyes*. But Conrad's dark portrayals of intrigue and betrayal, of ceaseless but futile espionage between countries, were hardly models for a literature of entertainment and escape based on spying. For this, writers had to combine the theme of espionage with the form and mood of romantic adventure. To some extent, the great later nineteenth-century English romancers had already done this. Haggard and Kipling had spun out exciting tales of exotic adventure on the African and Indian fringes of the empire. Haggard's Allan Quartermain was one very important progenitor of the English gentleman as agent involved in heroic adventures against a lush and glamorous background. Kipling's *Kim* (1901), though obstensibly a story for children about the initiation of a young Anglo-Irish-Indian boy into the excitement of "the Great Game" of colonial espionage, remains one of the finest romantic spy novels, a dazzling embodiment of that mythical figure of the Englishman gone native. Stevenson not only explored the romantic possibilities of the Scottish countryside—an important example for John Buchan— he also transformed the fascination with anarchist terrorism into some of the first modern urban romances. Conan Doyle was also a dedicated writer of historical romance, but his most popular and successful creation, *The Adventures of Sherlock Holmes,* showed how the theme of espionage could be synthesized with the structures of mystery and detection. He, too, exploited clandestine operations on the colonial frontier (*The Sign of Four*), anarchist terrorism and labor agitation (*The Valley of Fear*), and specific acts of espionage ("The Bruce-Partington Plans") as backgrounds for Holmes stories. He also invented two figures who would later become stock characters in the spy story: Holmes's brother Mycroft, who appears as the shadowy head of the British Secret Service, and Professor Moriarty, the master criminal with an international network of agents.

The Boer War further stimulated public interest in stories of secret operations at the end of the nineteenth century. Winston Churchill's capture and adventurous escape as well as the daring raids of Boer commandos were headline news in Europe and America. Churchill, the epitome of the dashing gentleman-adventurer, launched a political career on the basis of his clandestine exploits. As international tensions mounted before the First World War, a new generation of English writers gradually turned from colonial adventures to tales of espionage. In 1903, Erskine Childers published *The Riddle of the Sands,* which narrated the discovery of a German invasion plot by two dauntless British gentlemen. Though Childers never published another spy story—he was executed in Ireland in 1922 for clandestine activity against the new Irish Free State—his novel was an important transition between the late nineteenth-century genre of imaginary invasions and the twentieth-century heroic spy adventure. Other writers, too, began to develop a new generic pattern in which the missions of a heroic agent or counterspy took place against the background of international rivalries and conspiracies aimed at destroying the British or American way of life. William LeQueux and E. Phillips Oppenheim turned from their early fantasies of imaginary invasions to sagas of the Secret Service, while Sax Rohmer built a highly popular series on his own variation of the conflict between Sherlock Holmes and that international master criminal, Professor Moriarty. Rohmer's Nayland Smith and Dr. Flinders Petrie were pale imitations of the original Holmes and Watson, but his supervillain, Dr. Fu Manchu, became almost as much a household word as the Great Detective himself.

But it was John Buchan who, more than any other writer of his time, synthesized these nineteenth-century traditions of adventure fiction with the theme of international espionage and created the first major version of the twentieth-century spy story. His *Thirty-Nine Steps* (1915) used both the natural settings popularized in the early nineteenth century by Scott and Cooper and the imperial backgrounds of Haggard and Kipling. His exploitation of such mysterious clues as "the Black Stone" and "the thirty-nine steps" showed much of Doyle's skill in using the unraveling of a complex mystery as a basic narrative structure. Finally, his creation of a plot based on a German scheme to steal British naval secrets in order to make the destruction of the fleet a prelude to the invasion of England capitalized not only on the coming of the First World War but on the late nineteenth-century tradition of imaginary invasions. Buchan added important elements of his own to this combination, as we will see in a later chapter, but it was, above all, his integration of these traditions of narrative adventure with current international espionage that made his work a basic model for writers of popular adventure through the twenties and early thirties.

The Buchan version of the spy adventure is a form of heroic romance which sends a hero of exceptional ability and virtue on a successful mission against a political, racial conspiracy against white Christian civilization as exemplified by Britain. This conspiracy is headed by a supervillain who is always of a different race and culture and a representative of malignant evil.

In Buchan's first novels, these villains were Germans. Later, just as Ian Fleming revamped his villainous organization from the Russian S.M.E.R.S.H. to the international criminal conspiracy S.P.E.C.T.R.E. when the Cold War became less heated, Buchan turned from the German enemy to a vaguer international quasi-Communist conspiracy and made his villains racial mixtures like the mysterious Irish-Spanish-Jew, Dominick Medina.

Buchan's villains, like Fleming's, are never primarily interested in monetary gain or military victory. Instead, they seek world domination and the power to make their own evil ideals prevail. Thus, they threaten not only the loss of money or sovereignty, but the wholesale corruption of the religious and moral values of the homeland. The theme which shapes the hero's mission and his confrontation with the enemy is the basic danger to a whole way of life threatened by another, malignant worldview. In other words, "they" are not simply another ambiguous political force different only in degree from "us"—a prevalent theme of the recent spy story—"they" are an alien civilization which threatens the very continuation of "our" way of life. In some ways, the role of the alien in works of science fiction like H. G. Wells's *The War of the Worlds* and even more recent fantasies like Jack Finney's *The Invasion of the Body Snatchers* is similar to that of the enemy conspiracy in the heroic spy story.

The hero of the Buchanesque spy story is, first of all, a gentleman who happens to be momentarily engaged in espionage activities, rather than a professional spy. His moral code is derived not from his allegiance to a secret service bureaucracy, but from his commitment to the preservation of the British way of life. He is, above all, a man of honor. Unlike his heroic successor, James Bond, he would not think of using his sexual prowess—which is, of course, hardly mentioned—or even of cheating at cards, to advance his mission. These are duplicities worthy only of the enemy, who is not above using glamorous women to tempt the hero from his righteous path. Though he may have a rough surface—Buchan's Richard Hannay is a colonial, Sapper's Bulldog Drummond is as tough as Sam Spade but impeccable in his moral attitudes—he is always recognized for what he is by other "true gentlemen." Though on the run through the wilderness, Richard Hannay is immediately able to persuade Sir Walter Bullivant of the Foreign Office of his bona fides. This tradition of the gentlemen spy may be one reason why Americans were so late in becoming successful writers of spy stories. Americans tended to find the English notion of gentility snobbish and effeminate and, at least in the first part of the twentieth century, preferred a similar combination of roughness and nobility in a less traditional form: the Western hero was always a "natural gentleman," a "gentle gunman," while Edgar Rice Burrough's Tarzan could outdo an ape in tree swinging, but was in reality the noble Lord Greystoke.

In this first phase of the spy story, the heroic spy's aristocratic character is related to the fact that the forces of good are usually an informal and temporary alliance of individual gentlemen rather than a permanent professional espionage organization. This informal alliance helps the hero carry out his mission and then disbands. Even Sax Rohmer's Nayland Smith, though he belongs to some vaguely described secret service, depends much more on his amateur fellow adventurer, Dr. Flinders Petrie, and other informal allies he picks up in the course of his mission than on the organization of which he is obstensibly a part. Retaining his amateur status is one way the early twentieth-century heroic spy overcame the traditional images of the spy as traitor and seducer.

Although the obvious formulaic pattern of the Buchanesque spy story is that of a highly moral amateur hero and his informal allies defending the English way of life against the threats posed by a deeply malignant conspiracy led by an alien supervillain, there is, as in most popular literature, a structure of less obvious meanings that at times run directly counter to the surface themes. In the case of the heroic spy story, this submerged pattern of meaning reflects a fascination with the enemy's power and way of life. Usually, the enemy's potency is symbolized by his complex organization and the way this has penetrated the homeland, by his superior command of technology, and by his relationship to the beautiful and exotic women he throws in the hero's path as temptresses. Though the heroic spy often has his own woman with qualities of chastity and maternity which will eventually make her an appropriate wife, he is also often momentarily attracted by the enemy seductress.

This set of contrary themes also appears in more subtle form in those characters like Sandy Arbuthnot who have both the ability and the need to temporarily "go native." But it is most obvious in the simpler and more stereotypical spy stories of Sax Rohmer. There is no doubt that Fu Manchu is a much more compelling character than his heroic adversary, Sir Dennis Nayland Smith. I have often asked groups of students whether they have ever heard of Fu Manchu. Though a small and diminishing number have actually read Sax Rohmer or even seen one of the many movies about Fu, they have almost all heard of him, while only one in a thousand can name his heroic pursuer. This is hardly surprising since, from the beginning of the series, Fu Manchu's exotic lairs, his stable of glamorous females, and his brilliant stratagems were the most interesting aspects of the Rohmer saga. In addition, Rohmer himself gave his archvillain an increasingly sympathetic character as the series progressed. In later stories, like *President Fu Manchu* (1936), Fu remains a putative villain—in this case he tries to control the American election in order to get his own puppet into the presidency—but more and more attention is paid to his benevolent side—in this case he uses his brilliant medical skills to save the life of a young boy. Throughout the heroic spy story, a fascination with alien cultures coexists with an overt fear and condemnation of these cultures. Similarly, in the colonial adventure, there is always the danger that one of the protagonists will be corrupted by the mysterious East.

This combination of fear and fascination is evidently a component of racism in many of its forms. Social psychologists have argued that the anxiety generated by the attractiveness of certain aspects of alien culture can intensify the fear and hatred felt toward it. Such a psychodynamic has been observed in phenomena like anti-Semitism, the English prejudice against the Irish and the Indians, and in American racism against blacks and Native Americans. Since racist ambivalence is apparently a pervasive social phenomenon, it is not surprising to find that it is an important component of the early twentieth-century heroic spy story.

The continuing appeal of the heroic spy adventure made Buchan and Rohmer, as well as writers like Dornford Yates, H. C. ("Sapper") McNeile, and E. Phillips Oppenheim, pop-

ular through the 1920s. This popularity probably reflected the
anxious optimism of that age. Though the white, Anglo-Saxon
gentleman hero always succeeded in defeating the plots of his
diabolical adversary, worldwide conspiracies of mysterious
Asiatics, dastardly Huns, or scheming Communists continued
to threaten the homeland. While heroic characters ostensibly
rejoiced at the return of peace and prosperity, their recurrent
need for more and more adventure and the increasing threat
of subversion and competition by the enemy suggested that
readers found "normalcy" more than a little boring and liked
to fantasize about the continuing danger of plots and conspiracies.

International Depression and the rise of fascism in the
1930s had an impact on adventure stories of all kinds, gen-
erating new kinds of heroes, villains, and adventures. In the
spy story, a change in mood was prefigured in the late 1920s
by the English novelist W. Somerset Maugham, who had himself been extensively involved in espionage during World War
I. Maugham's *Ashenden; or, The British Agent* (1928) has been
widely praised as the first "realistic" spy story, just as the
stories of Dashiell Hammett, which also first appeared in the
late twenties, have been characterized as the first "realistic"
detective stories. However, "realism" is a somewhat misleading
concept here. Although Maugham's stories were undoubtedly
based in part on his own experience and are probably more
accurate accounts of standard espionage practice than the melodramatic heroism of Buchan, Rohmer, and others, it is Maugham's antiheroic vision rather than the verisimilitude of his
stories that made his work a model for later writers. Maugham
says of his central character's espionage activities:

> Ashenden's official existence was as orderly and monotonous as
> a city clerk's. He saw his spies at stated intervals and paid them
> their wages; when he could get hold of a new one he engaged
> him, gave him his instructions and sent him off to Germany;
> he waited for the information that came through and dispatched
> it; he went into France once a week to confer with his colleague
> over the frontier and to receive his orders from London; he visited
> the marketplace on market-day to get any messages the old

butter-woman had brought him from the other side of the lake; he kept his eyes and ears open; and he wrote long reports which he was convinced no one read till having inadvertently slipped a jest into one of them he received a sharp rebuke for his levity. (P. 111)

This emphasis on the routine bureaucratic aspects of espionage had some impact on the spy story writers of the 1930s and has played an even more fundamental role in the genre since the 1960s. However, it was Maugham's mood of cynicism and his development of the antiheroic protagonist that was most strongly echoed in the work of his immediate successors, Eric Ambler and Graham Greene. Beginning with Greene's "entertainment" *Orient Express* in the early 1930s and continuing with such superb spy adventures as Greene's *This Gun for Hire* (1936), *The Ministry of Fear* (1943), and *The Confidential Agent* (1939), and Ambler's *Mask of Dimitrios* (1939), *Epitaph for a Spy* (1938), and *Journey into Fear* (1940), Ambler and Greene created a new version of the espionage genre that dominated the literature until the 1950s.

Ambler and Greene transformed the spy story from a heroic adventure into a more complex and ironic tale of corruption, betrayal, and conspiracy. Their typical protagonist was neither a gentleman amateur nor a professional agent. Instead, he was usually a quite ordinary person caught up against his will in a web of espionage. This hero's adventures took place not on a frontier or in enemy territory, but in the heart of what he had assumed was safe and friendly country. Having neither the strength nor the bravery of the heroic spy, the Ambler-Greene protagonist rarely brought a mission to a triumphant conclusion, saving the homeland from enemy threats. On the contrary, his greatest achievement was to narrowly escape with his life from the conspiracy into which he had been unwittingly and unwillingly implicated. More often than not, this escape was a result of blind luck or, in some cases, depended on the assistance of a more skillful and powerful person who sympathized with the hero's predicament. Sometimes, this rescuer is even an agent for what is supposedly an enemy power, as in the case of Soviet agent Zaleshoff in Ambler. In other cases, it is a friendly secret service that pulls the hero from the fire, and in Greene's two major spy novels of the 1930s a woman who falls in love with the hero is instrumental in his escape.

The Ambler-Greene antagonist is not an alien, but a respected member of homeland society, whose actions pose a dangerous threat to that society, usually because his economic interests lead him to favor war. The investigation and exposure of arms manufacturers who sold weapons to both sides in World War I had a great influence on the spy story in the 1930s, for those wealthy capitalists who profited from war were ideal villains for the Ambler-Greene story, partly because they were such dramatically appropriate antagonists for the innocent protagonist and partly because of the leftward leanings of Ambler, Greene, and much of their audience during the Depression decade. The situation in Greene's *This Gun for Hire* is a good example of this pattern. The assassin Raven is hired to kill a prominent European socialist leader in order to cause social unrest. His employer is a British arms manufacturer who hopes to profit from the consequences of the assassination. To cover up his involvement in the conspiracy, the manufacturer also tries to bring about Raven's death. The actual protagonist of the story is a young woman taken hostage by Raven as he tries to avenge himself against the manufacturer.

In the heroic spy story, the orderly and traditional patterns of homeland culture are threatened from without. In the Ambler-Greene story, the threat comes from within as well. The rise of European fascism is associated with the growth of fascist tendencies within the homeland itself. Though the protagonist initially has no interest in political and social developments, he finds that he cannot avoid their implications, even in his own personal life. Thus, the Ambler-Greene hero is, in effect, conscripted into the fight against fascism whether he wishes it or not. But his most dangerous adversary turns out not to be the external enemy, but betrayers in his own country.

Thus, the central theme of the spy story of the 1930s was the inescapability of the war against fascism. In these novels, even the least adventurous and apolitical of individuals are dragged into espionage activity and forced to take a stand, just as Ambler's mild-mannered detective story writer Latimer must finally shoot the international criminal Dimitrios, though his original interest in the character was only idle curiosity. So, too, Greene's protagonist in *The Ministry of Fear* must expose and help destroy a Nazi spy ring in England in order to save his own life. More of an everyman than a hero, the Ambler-Greene protagonist of the 1930s reflected the English and American public's anxiety about war. The late 1930s, when this version of the spy story was at its height, was the same time when Orson Welles's broadcast version of H. G. Wells's tale of Martian invasion (*The War of the Worlds* [1938]) generated mass hysteria in America, a phenomenon explained by social psychologists as largely a result of anxiety about the coming of war. However, there was also a countertheme in these stories which reflected disillusion with English and American society as a consequence of the international Depression of the 1930s. The figure of the corrupt tycoon and the arms merchant so prevalent in these stories raises some question as to whether the homeland is worth fighting for. Indeed, just as his unwilling involvement in espionage tests and transforms the Ambler-Greene protagonist from a selfish individualist to a politically committed hero, there is an implication that the challenge of the war may help purge the homeland of its corrupt materialism and end its domination by amoral business interests.

During World War II, the Ambler-Greene version of the spy story retained its popularity, and many of the two authors' books were made into movies, for example, *Background to Danger* (1943), *The Mask of Dimitrios* (1944), *This Gun for Hire* (1942), and *The Ministry of Fear* (1945). In general, these movies, most of them highly successful and involving some of Hollywood's best directors and stars, deemphasized the ironic countertheme of capitalist corruption and stressed the importance of commitment to the war. Perhaps the ultimate examples of this translation of Ambler and Greene's cynicism and irony into something more like the tradition of espionage as heroic romance were two of the most memorable films ever made: Michael Curtiz's *Casablanca* (1943), in which Humphrey Bogart, a disillusioned and cynical American nightclub owner in Casablanca, is moved to join the war against fascism by the patriotic dedication of Ingrid Bergman and Paul Henreid; and Howard Hawks's *To Have and Have Not* (1944), in which Hemingway's tragic social novel of the early 1930s was transformed into a vehicle for Bogart and Lauren Bacall by making Harry Morgan a cynical fishing boat captain who decides to join the fight.

After World War II, the spy story changed again, as the optimism of victory gave way to the disillusionment of the Cold War and the deep fears generated by the nuclear bomb. Ambler and Greene continued to be masters of the espionage theme, but their work changed considerably. In the decade or so after the war, Greene authored one spy story which was a darker version of his earlier studies of innocence encountering corruption, *The Third Man* (1949), and went on to produce the greatest burlesque of the spy story ever penned, *Our Man in Havana* (1958). After this Greene stopped writing the shorter narratives characteristic of his espionage "entertainments" and devoted himself to longer, more complex novels. In these works, the theme of espionage remains an important one, but usually as a source of tragedy, reminiscent of Conrad's use of spying in *The Secret Agent* and *Under Western Eyes*. In this vein, Greene's recent *Human Factor* (1978) is a compelling tragic novel and one of the most powerful artistic treatments of espionage in the history of the spy story.

Ambler also changed in this direction, though he continued to write shorter novels more concerned with intricacy of plot than the development of character, as in the case of Greene. His work, too, became more cynical, his protagonists less innocent, and his villains less evil. An example of his development is *The Intercom Conspiracy* (1970), in which two retired spies from both sides of the iron curtain successfully blackmail their former employers into giving them large sums of money by threatening to publish an international journal exposing the secrets they have learned during their careers. As McCormick points out in *Who's Who in Spy Fiction*, Ambler significantly begins *The Intercom Conspiracy* by announcing the disappearance of Charles Latimer, the decent but ordinary hero of his prewar book *The Mask of Dimitrios*.

A few writers like Helen MacInnes and Geoffrey Household continued after World War II to write spy stories which used something like the prewar Greene and Ambler formula with occasional elements of John Buchan thrown in, but the major change in the spy story in the 1950s was the emergence of a highly successful new version of the heroic spy story. Ian Fleming was the leading figure in this "renaissance." Beginning with *Casino Royale* (1953) and continuing long after Fleming's death in 1964, in novels and films created by various hands including Kingsley Amis and John Gardner, James Bond became the Cold War's favorite agent, the spy whom the public loved. Like Buchan's hero, Bond is a man of great courage and skill in violence with the manners and tastes of a gentleman. In the movies, he typically embarks on what will become some of his most violent escapades dressed in an impeccably tailored tuxedo. However, as we shall see in our chapter on Fleming, Bond is a very different kind of gentleman from the traditional clubland hero. For one thing, Bond is a professional spy and the secret service to which he belongs plays an important role in his adventures through such characters as M. (head of the service), Q. (specialist in technology who provides Bond with exotic weapons, communications, and transportation) and many agents in stations around the globe who provide the hero with support and information at crucial points. Fleming also drew on the heroic tradition for Bond's adversaries. His Goldfingers, Dr. Nos, Largos, and Blofelds are invariably nasty foreigners and frequently racial mixtures in the best Buchan-Rohmer fashion. Finally, the basic pattern of Bond's adventures drew on the formula elaborated by Buchan and Rohmer: the hero is given a mission; he enters enemy territory; he is captured, but escapes and finally defeats the enemy, thereby accomplishing his mission at the same time. Clearly, one source of Fleming's popularity was his ability to infuse a new variety and excitement in a pattern of action as ritualistic as that of the Lone Ranger and other superheroes.

Several aspects of Fleming's work were marked deviations from the Buchan tradition and were probably major factors in the Cold War success of the Bond saga. First of all, Bond is an organization man, but one with a difference: not only does he lead a life of high adventure and pleasure, he constantly disobeys his superiors and follows his own individual instincts. This aspect of Bond's character was delightfully portrayed in a scene at the end of a recent Bond film. After successfully completing his mission, the hero has a two-way television interview with Prime Minister Margaret Thatcher, while he is engaged in sexual dalliance with the heroine of the moment. Not surprisingly, Fleming's initial success came in a period when novels like *The Man in the Grey Flannel Suit* and works of popular sociology like Whyte's *Organization Man* became best-sellers by analyzing the growing role of corporate bureaucracy and its stress on conformity in American life.

Luxury and sex—along with technology—are two other central themes in Fleming's work. Bond has often, and rightly, been described as a hero in the image of *Playboy* magazine because of his many sexual adventures, his interest in expensive consumer products, and his involvement with fancy cars and other products of what we now call high tech. It is some testimony to the popularity of these themes with Bond followers that much of the fan literature that has grown up around Fleming's hero involves a cataloguing of Bond's tastes in women, clothes, liquor, food, and various brands of consumer products. However, there is also a significant countertheme in the Bond stories and films which portrays these objects as seductively dangerous and a cause of anxiety. Bond's women are never more than temporary conquests; the only time he supposedly falls in love, his wife is almost immediately killed by the enemy. Luxury is also the milieu of the villain who often uses it to try to deceive the hero and lull him into carelessness. Finally, technology is also an ambiguous element in the Bond adventures. Those fabulous weapons and communication devices which Q. provides for Bond are invariably used up or destroyed before the final confrontation with the enemy, and it is the villain's threatened use of military technology which poses the threat the hero must overcome. In recent Bond films, the hero's mission is most often generated by the villain's capture of nuclear weapons, which he threatens to use against the free world.

Fleming's most important contribution to the revival of the heroic spy story was probably the quality of humorous exaggeration or burlesque which he brought to his stories. Fleming's fanciful narratives of espionage became popular with a wide public not only because Bond's exploits resolved such value conflicts of the time as the fascination with and anxiety about technology, but because his adventures were presented with an omnipresent tongue in cheek. Fleming's narrative tone suggested that it was not, after all, necessary to take these things too seriously. By gently burlesquing the traditional elements of the heroic spy story, Fleming was able to revitalize such conventions of the tradition as the gentleman spy and the racial supervillain for an audience that would have found the moralistic seriousness of Buchan and his contemporaries hard going. These characteristics of exaggeration and self-parody were further intensified in the highly popular series of Bond movies produced by Albert R. ("Cubby") Broccoli and Harry Saltzman.

Fleming's great success generated a new phase in the development of the spy story. Many writers created their own versions of Fleming's fanciful epics of professional spies and archvillains. The American writer Donald Hamilton created a hard-boiled James Bond in his Matt Helm series, which became even closer to the Bond model in a series of films starring Dean Martin. Other writers, such as Alistair Maclean, Philip McCutchan, John Gardner, Gavin Lyall, and Trevanian, followed in Fleming's footsteps. Even E. Howard Hunt, ex-CIA agent and Watergate conspirator, included among his dubious accomplishments a series of spy stories that outdid even Fleming in their fantasies about heroes, sexy women, villains, and international conspiracies.

The heroic spy fantasy still delights large audiences. Between Fleming's appearance in the mid-1950s and the present,

many popular movies and such successful TV series as *I Spy,
The Man from U.N.C.L.E., Get Smart,* and *The Avengers* have
also made use of this formula, helping to complete the transformation of the spy story from a new type of heroic adventure
created in the early twentieth century into one of the most
important genres of our time. In general, there has been an
enormous proliferation of types of stories dealing with espionage and clandestinity. Out of the wave of political assassinations since World War II has come a subgenre of the spy
story, the assassination thriller, and some of its examples, like
Richard Condon's *Manchurian Candidate* (1959) and Frederick
Forsyth's *Day of the Jackal* (1971), have become best-selling
novels as well as highly popular films. The closely related
terrorist thriller centers around the development and thwarting
of terrorist plots such as airplane hijackings, the capture of
hostages, or attempts at mass murder, for example, Tom Harris's *Black Sunday* (1975), about a narrowly averted terrorist
plot to kill the entire audience of a Super Bowl game. Leon
Uris and Robert Ludlum, along with many others, have become international best-sellers by combining aspects of the
spy thriller with the large-scale social novel. Still other popular
creators who began in other genres have turned in recent years
to the spy story. Clint Eastwood, Sam Peckinpah, and Charles
Bronson became famous initially for their work in the Western
genre, but many of their recent movies have been forms of the
spy story, for example, *The Eiger Sanction* (Eastwood based on
Trevanian), *The Osterman Weekend* (Peckinpah based on Robert
Ludlum), and *Telefon* (Bronson based on Walter Wager). Works
that might once have been primarily police thrillers are given
a new twist by involving them with espionage and clandestinity
as in *Blue Thunder* and *The Belisarius Affair.* Thus, the spy
story is no longer a single generic pattern, but has become a
complex family of genres.

   Finally, just as Ian Fleming revitalized the heroic tradition
of the espionage adventure, recent writers like Len Deighton,
Brian Freemantle, Robert Duncan, Pierre Boulle, Noel Behn,
Adam Hall, and above all Graham Greene and John le Carré
have created a new kind of spy novel growing out of the earlier

tradition pioneered by Greene himself and Eric Ambler in the 1930s. In these stories, the heroes are usually professional spies, though they are not at all in the heroic mold of the Fleming vanguard. Instead, they are aging bureaucrats verging on despair like le Carré's George Smiley and Greene's Maurice Castle, or wisecracking antiheroes like Deighton's unnamed narrator, or innocent researchers like the protagonist of *Six Days of the Condor.* Most strikingly, the real antagonist in these stories is not an external enemy such as Soviet or Chinese espionage organizations, but secret conspiracies within the agent's own organization. The central theme of these novels is concern about the degree to which patterns of clandestinity have infiltrated and corrupted our intelligence organizations as well as the rest of society. At their best, as in Greene's *The Human Factor* and le Carré's *The Honourable Schoolboy* and *The Little Drummer Girl,* these novels are among our time's best works of fiction. In this respect, the spy story has come to fulfill the promise foreshadowed in the later novels of Joseph Conrad and in the romances of Rohmer and Buchan. It has become a source of much of our most popular entertainment and of some of our major literature.

3 The Forms of the Spy Novel

The setting of the secret agent adventure is quite different from the detective story or the Western. Whether the action all takes place in one country or the agent is sent on a secret mission from one country to another, the background is a conflict of international political interests. The spy story pretends to take us behind the scenes of world events as they are seen in newspapers or history books. It shows us secret conspiracies which apparently determine the fate of nations. A paranoiac aura typically tints the tale. Hidden secrets are everywhere. The innocent-looking office building is actually the headquarters of a secret society plotting to bring on another war; the respectable, seemingly harmless professor is really an enemy agent; the quaint teashop harbors a secret radio which gives instructions to a network of spies; the letter inviting Smith for a weekend in the country is a code message to assassinate the prime minister. Nothing is what it seems and everything is potentially dangerous. Only the agent knows something of the truth.

In addition to its background of international conspiracy, the secret agent formula usually centers around a particular military or technological secret. Alfred Hitchcock liked to refer to this element as the "MacGuffin."

> It's the device, the gimmick, if you will, or the papers the spies are after. I'll tell you about it. Most of Kipling's stories, as you know, were set in India and they dealt with the fighting between the natives and the British forces on the Afghanistan border. Many of them were spy stories, and they were concerned with the efforts to steal the secret plans out of a fortress. The theft of secret documents was the original MacGuffin. So the "MacGuffin" is the term we use to cover all that sort of thing: to steal plans or documents, or discover a secret, it doesn't matter what it is. And the logicians are wrong in trying to figure out the truth of a MacGuffin, since it's beside the point. The only thing that really matters is that in the picture the plans, documents, or the secrets must seem to be of vital importance to the characters. (Truffaut, *Hitchcock,* p. 98)

Hitchcock's insistence that the MacGuffin is an artistic device emphasizes one important point about the setting of the spy story. Although it is usually based on current historical situations, the background of the spy story is just as much a landscape of the mind as the country house of the classical detective story or the frontier town of the Western. Spying is an important activity of the modern state and contemporary espionage organizations like the Central Intelligence Agency operate in dangerously irresponsible secrecy, but espionage does not have the same world-shaking importance as the direct and open clash of national interests. The future of the world probably does not depend on real-life counterparts of Richard Hannay or James Bond. Indeed, the secret agent's fictional milieu with its omnipresent hidden secrets and conspiracies presents a picture of the world which is probably half reality and half extension to the international scene of the gothic castle with its hidden passages, secret panels, and lurking conspirators.

Two other common elements of the spy story reveal its original connection with gothic fantasy: the innocent hero and the supervillain. The gothic story commonly dealt with the trials of a heroine who whether by accident or design, was involved in the plots of some devious villain. Similarly, one of the perennially favorite spy heroes is the innocent amateur who stumbles by accident into the midst of an espionage conspiracy. This figure who, like the gothic heroine, enacts the nightmare of involvement, discovery, and realization that he is trapped and must play out the game to its end was a favorite character in the thrillers of John Buchan, Graham Greene, and Eric Ambler. Although the innocent amateur today seems to have become less characteristic of the genre than the professional agent, he still plays a role in many of the most successful and popular examples of the form, the works of Helen MacInnes, for instance. Later we will differentiate the amateur and professional spy heroes more carefully. For the present we need only note that they both play out the heroic role of accepting and accomplishing a secret mission. In the case of the amateur spy, the mission is forced upon him, whereas the professional accepts it voluntarily.

The tradition of the secret agent adventure has been particularly rich in colorful and exotic villains who, like their gothic grandfathers, are often more interesting than their heroic opponents and victims. Sax Rohmer's Fu Manchu has certainly become far more firmly implanted in the public imagination than his austere and colorless nemesis, Sir Dennis Nayland Smith; John Buchan's man with eyes "hooded like a hawk's" and Ian Fleming's wonderful gallery of spectacular rogues—Goldfinger, Dr. No, Le Chiffre, Sir Hugo Drax, Ernst Stavro Blofeld—contribute as much, perhaps more, to the reader's pleasure as Richard Hannay or James Bond. This particular emphasis on the villain seems to be a central feature of the spy thriller. In the classical detective story, the character of the villain is distinctly subordinated to his complex method of carrying out the crime. In the Western, the villain usually has a far less distinctive and colorful character than the hero. But in the secret agent story, even if the antagonist is not portrayed as an exotic master villain, the enemy organization plays a far more important role. In general, this strong treatment of the villain functions to give one the sense that the hero is isolated and alone in the midst of overpowering and seemingly omnipotent enemies.

This is as true of the simpler heroic spy story as of the more complex mid-twentieth-century clandestine novel. Le Carré's Karla is, if anything, more fascinating than Rohmer's Fu Manchu.

While it was once said of the mystery story that it was contingent upon the profession of the detective, the same cannot be said of the spy novel. We have always had spies—Moses sent two of them to reconnoiter the Sinai during the Exodus— but the spy novel is a genre of our time. Only in the twentieth century has its time come round at last. It is a kind of mystery/ suspense story that we are especially susceptible to, and it speaks to us today with particular cogency and effect. In this chapter we will discuss the effects the spy novel has on its reader and how the novelist achieves those effects. The methodology is essentially structuralist; we will examine the structures that are most likely to occur and the episodes within those structures that the novelist uses to achieve those effects. Our purpose will be, finally, to evaluate the messages that the structure of the spy novel sends to the reader.

The spy of fiction cannot operate without his own invisibility: it is the essence of his (fictional) being. Everything about him—his job, his leisure time, his genuine thoughts, his personal life, if he should be so fortunate as to have one— must be either clandestine or disguised. And, more than any other character or occupational type, the spy must have freedom of movement. Arrest, imprisonment, capture, or even revelation of his identity render his mission inoperative and his function in life useless. Thus, the spy of fiction should always be in danger of losing that mobility or in danger of exposure. Fear felt by the empathetic reader imparts the thrill to the thriller.

The nature of the work itself has expanded in recent years. Before the 1960s, it was thought by the public to be largely spying and catching spies, but recent covert activities extend well beyond those limits: arranging assassinations, financing revolutions and training the combatants, bribing foreign soldiers to defect with their aircraft or their tanks intact, salvaging vessels that have sunk while on classified missions. All of these activities and hundreds more are now properly the subject of those fictions called spy novels, though to date most writers have remained with traditional espionage themes—with good reason. The genre has been proven successful, the action of the surface suggests an excitement that is missing from most of our urban, well-regulated, bureaucratic lives, and the messages beneath the surface are compelling to our times.

The lives of real intelligence operatives, however, are frequently clerical and routine, at least as dull as our own. Some agents sit in an office from nine to five and clip out Russian-language articles about Nepal. Others monitor Rumanian radio broadcasts for clues about governmental attitudes which may, or may not, be interspersed among hours of Ionesco and popular music. An officer in naval intelligence during World War II has told us how painfully boring it was to be part of that department that once broke the Japanese code, especially since agency compartmentalization prevented his section from realizing what they had accomplished.

None of the tedium of a cryptographer's work was mimetically reproduced in Robert Littell's *Amateur,* and correctly so—that would have been an unforgivable commission of the imitative fallacy. One of *The Amateur's* minor characters is a "boxologist" with the CIA, probably not one of the agency's most interesting intelligence evaluation jobs, if it exists at all. Littell astutely makes of him a comic highlight of the novel, and of boxology (the determination of the contents of boxes and crates by an evaluation of their size, shape, and weight) a fascinating enterprise. Whether or not intelligence agencies train and employ such specialists as boxologists, some intelligence experts do this kind of analysis: in March 1985, U.S. Army Maj. Arthur Nicholson was shot in East Berlin because he had photographed the outside of a wooden shed of the kind used to conceal tanks. Presumably the picture was taken to assist intelligence boxologists to recognize such boxes when seen in aerial photographs. Boxologists in fiction may have to have their personalities and their jobs enlivened to make them interesting, but in this one instance, at least, the reality was more dangerous and dramatic than the fiction about it. Novels must not be permitted to replicate boredom, and the agent's death—heinous as it was in the real-life situation—must be given aesthetic form, drama, tension, and confrontation, just as in any competent fiction.

The most natural plot for the work of the spy should be determined by the kind of adventure we would most likely expect him to have—in enemy territory—a plot we call THE SPY GOES OVER. Adam Hall's best-selling *Quiller Memorandum* (1975) illustrates well many features in the narratives of this subgenre; understanding its success will help illuminate the others like it. In summary, the narrative follows British secret agent Quiller as he runs to ground an ex-Nazi war criminal who, since the end of the shooting, has risen patiently to become a high-ranking Bundesminister and, on the side, is Reichsführer of a neo-Nazi coven. In between the gambit and the end game, Hall deploys most of the formulas of the thriller to great effect, and his choice of them, as well as their con-figuration, makes them worth examining.

The first pages locate Quiller at a Berlin musical comedy, pleasantly anticipating his return to London, on this, his last night in Germany. The notion of a bored or aging agent looking forward to retirement is a common one. Bond suffers from ennui before being challenged by Goldfinger; le Carré's Leamas longs to come in from the cold; Anthony Burgess's protagonist-agent in *Tremor of Intent* has reluctantly agreed to give it one more try; even Greene's recent victim-hero Castle wants the information he gives his Russian friends (he is doubling for them) to be the last; such feelings are conventional human factors. But as with all of the retiring agents, Quiller will not be let go. His fellow agent, with the suggestive code name of Pol, contacts him and tells him that he must find the resur-rected Nazi organization Phönix not only because they are a world threat but because they have just slain his friend: duty is not incentive enough; Quiller finds the pull of personal retribution at least as compelling, and his own agency exploits these feelings.

John Buchan's enemy is the Germans—a few of them are redolent of an evil that is cosmic—but a lot had happened in the world between the era of Richard Hannay and that of Quiller to qualify our understanding of evil. Two cataclysms had been visited upon the peoples of Europe and Asia, and so, when Hall confronts us (and Quiller) with a conspiracy in which Phönix will retake the world, we are not so incredulous. Its operatives have gone underground and have risen out of the ashes of 1945 Germany in civilian attire to become the mercantile and political leaders of the new Deutschland. So they are in *The Wind Chill Factor* and *The Odessa File*. As in all of these novels, the probing agent (or civilian or reporter) does not know the scope of the enemy he is undertaking at first, but gradually his quest reveals more and more of the sinister and cosmic breadth of the evil he must vanquish.

Quiller's adventures are characteristic of the genre. Hardly anything befalls him that is not inflicted on or threatened to other (fictional) agents. Deciding that the best and quickest way to get a lead on Phönix is to induce their people to expose themselves, he manages to get into several news photographs with former Nazis he has helped capture. Phönix's first assassination attempt is with a crush car which slams against a wall inches from him as he walks back from a war crimes trial courtroom—a CLOSE CALL, though this first escape is due to no special ability on Quiller's part. He will get his chance to demonstrate his skills in evasion shortly.

CHASE and EVASION are the spy thriller's stock-in-trade. If the agent is caught (CAPTURE), then INTERROGATION will probably ensue, and most likely TORTURE (in recent years the agent is likely to be given a truth-revealing drug) and shortly the agent will be obliged to effect his NARROW ESCAPE. Then he will be ON THE RUN, though he may have been in that most characteristic of stances before apprehension. *The Quiller Memorandum* has all of these formulaic episodes.

Quiller's scheme to flush out the Phönix people by getting his picture in the newspapers as an aggressive Nazi-hunter pays off quickly. He soon senses their operatives TAGGING him, first on foot, then in a high-speed serpentine auto chase through Berlin's back streets. When he thinks that he has shaken his

TAGS, he looks in on an old acquaintance, Solly Rothstein, a bacteriologist, but that shortly gets Sol a bullet in the back. The *Polizei* want to immunize everyone who has been in Rothstein's lab during the past few days, but Quiller is given a knockout drug instead, and out on the streets again for only several minutes he falls into the clutches of Phönix: CAPTURE!

He revives in an apartment "encrusted with baroque marble, gilt, silk, and ormolu," where "Goering would have rolled . . . like a pig in clover," and is surrounded by five Phönix heavies (p. 80). Unarmed, Quiller estimates that the advantage will be his in a sudden bolt for freedom, because the Nazis, knowing he is weaponless, will be off guard. They are, but their recovery is quick and five against one is not fair. Quiller is again subdued, this time by muscle power, and injected with yet another kind of drug. He survives this INTERROGATION successfully: he tells them nothing. As in *Tremor of Intent,* the other party reasons at first that since the hero must reveal all the demanded secret information under narcosis, it would save them all trouble if the spy would talk now. It's no go, at least with Quiller. Injected, he uses various gimmicks— consuming nearly all of one chapter—to counter the effects of the drug, successfully overpowering its influence on him. Cleverness, knowledge of various drugs and their specific effects, and sheer will pull him through.

But his victory over the drugs has only infuriated his captors: he is injected with another serum, this one to knock him out, and the last words he hears are the leader's orders to his henchmen to "shoot him in the back of the neck, and drop him" over the Grünewald bridge (p. 98). When Quiller revives again, he is lying on the soggy bank of the Grünewald lake. Another NARROW ESCAPE. Reasoning that his assassins were frightened off before they could finish the job and that they dumped him assuming that he would drown before he could revive, Quiller goes to Inga's apartment. She is the woman he had met earlier on the way back from the courtroom when the crush car had narrowly missed both of them.

If the British agent has been playing a sly game of cat and mouse, Phönix can do him one better—at least. They have let him ESCAPE and survive his swim because they want him alive to try again to get him to talk. And from the little information they did extract during the first narcosis INTERROGATION, they reason correctly that, after crawling out of the lake, Quiller will head directly to Inga's place. They are there waiting for him; CAPTURE again.

This time the Phönix men do not experiment with drugs, but go directly to physical TORTURE, though with a diabolical twist: Inga, and not the hardened Quiller, is the victim. They know that he cannot be broken by anything they do to his body, but they gamble that he will soften when someone he loves is maimed. To heighten the effect, Inga is stripped in the adjoining room and the "treatment" begun with the door open. With the prospect of bestiality about to be visited upon a woman he cares for, whose cries of terror come shivering through the open doorway, Quiller reflects to himself that "we [secret agents] are not gentlemen," but to involve a "civilian" is a transgression, just as is the destruction of private property (p. 114). In Hartley Howard's *Assignment K* the other side abducts the agent's fiancée and threatens to debauch her forcibly unless the agent complies with their demands for secret information. In the event the agent discovers that the ABDUCTION has been planned only to entrap him and that his beloved is one of the enemy. Quiller will also later discover that Inga is a member of Phönix and that her TORTURE has been staged. Quiller ESCAPES again, this time by inducing a faint. The thugs from Phönix withdraw, and a physician is sent for to minister to Inga's "wounds."

TURNABOUT: the quarry turns hunter. John Buchan was one of the first spy writers to use this formula when he had Richard Hannay, who had been ON THE RUN for most of the book, reverse status and, in turn, hunt down the Germans. At first the English think him guilty of the murder of his companion and chase him over the countryside. But when Hannay's innocence is proven, he is able to join forces with them—actually to lead them—on the trail of the insidious enemy. Quiller pulls a TURNABOUT with no external assistance; when he leaves his hotel the next morning he quickly loses his TAG, doubles back on him, and follows him after he has received further orders. No avail; the TAG leads him back to his hotel where his erstwhile TAGGER has apparently been stationed until Quiller returns.

Being free is the only way an agent can function; it is his only acceptable condition. Quiller has chosen to violate that principle with Phönix in order to flush its agents, to know with whom he is dealing, but to the rest of his environment his cover is that of a traveling Red Cross representative searching for indigent refugees. The German police accept this ruse, and under this guise of innocence Quiller can move relatively freely. At this point in the novel, both sides of the "Spook War" are more or less known to each other; Quiller still does not know the identity of his ultimate objective, the war criminal Zossen, but he has met one of the Reichsführers, Oktober, and he has encountered several of his operatives. He moves freely in Berlin still because Phönix alternately allows him to (in hopes of following him to his control headquarters) or because while ON THE RUN he is able to evade their people. The game is something like an intricate chess match; winning involves capturing the enemy's headquarters, and yet his pawns cannot ever be completely eliminated because when threatened they can voluntarily be removed to a safe zone. And a final complication is that all the pieces are the same color.

Within these rules, Quiller remains free because largely invisible. Confrontations with the enemy are dangerous when he is known to them, but so is meeting other British agents, because their cover is still complete, and if they are seen communicating with Quiller their cover will also be blown. In principle, an encounter with the enemy—whether in disguise, as in *The Riddle of the Sands* or in *Greenmantle,* or in the clear—is extremely dangerous, and thus one of the sources of the thrills of the thriller. The situation is reversed in *The Thirty-Nine Steps* when Hannay, ON THE RUN to escape the local constabulary who still think him guilty of murder, stumbles into the country house of a congenial scientist. Safety! But Hannay's euphoria is as short-lived as it is cruelly destroyed: the amiable host who shelters him from the police suddenly reveals himself as the chief of the enemy's secret spy ring. Hannay is at once taken prisoner, but shortly after manages a NARROW ESCAPE. Danger lies also—already noted—in meeting with fellow agents. DROPS of any kind are dangerous, such as drops of information (on film or paper), money, or materiel. Equally perilous are EXCHANGES, whether of prisoners (as in *Funeral in Berlin* and *The Ninth Directive*), of goods, or of prisoners for goods (as in *The Ipcress File* movie version). The DROP in *The Quiller Memorandum* is between Quiller and Pol, alone in a silent park. Quiller needs a certain document; Pol is sure that he has not been followed; still, one can never be too certain. Pol leans through the window of Quiller's parked car "so that his body covered it" and then "dropped the envelope into the seat beside [him]" (p. 135).

A return to Inga's flat introduces another standard actor in espionage fiction, the DEFECTOR. This one calls himself Helmut Braun and claims to have stolen a top secret operations plan from Phönix headquarters, where he had until recently been an aide. It is Operation Sprungbrett, and it details the plan to recapture Europe by using the newly rearmed Wehrmacht in an assault on the troubled Mediterranean. Quiller asks Braun why he has DEFECTED: pathetically he replies that he is a Jew. Reason enough.

This situation bears several of the marks of the most recent spy novels. Although all the pawns are the same color, it is not the old straightforward game. Braun is not really a DEFECTOR from Phönix but one of their PLANTS. Operation Sprungbrett is phoney as well, thought up to induce Quiller to try to enter Phönix headquarters. As soon as the British agent gets the bogus file, he knows that it is a PLANT and that Braun must be DOUBLING, but he cannot let on that he realizes this. He decides to go to Phönix HQ, letting them think that he has been duped, thus giving him the advantage. Inga, who has been loyal to Phönix all along (because she had been in the Führer's bunker in Berlin during the last days and still worships his memory), has decided to DEFECT to the other—the right, the British—side. Quiller knows this implicitly because while she had always worn black, signifying death, at this meeting she wears red for life. Nevertheless, Quiller cannot afford to trust her completely, and though he knows that she has now DOUBLED back on her former allegiances, he pretends that he believes that both Inga and Helmut will support him. The early spy novels were not nearly so Byzantine. But Quiller can keep all of the entangling webs straight in his MI-6-trained head, and off they go to the Grünewaldbrück.

To the DEFECTORS, pretended DEFECTORS, DOUBLE AGENTS, and PLANTED MISINFORMATION, Hall adds the knowing agent who enters the enemy's den expecting them to be caught off guard because they will expect to surprise him. A CONFRON-TATION follows: Quiller is shown an elaborately staged Oper-ation Sprungbrett in the expectation that when he is released he will call his CONTROL, the call will be traced, and Phönix can then locate and raid their ultimate objective. A NARROW ESCAPE is unnecessary: Quiller is simply allowed to pass freely out into the night because, as the Reichsführer says, it will be too late to do anything about it. He knows that this is not true because there is no Operation Sprungbrett.

Quiller sees through him immediately, but he has to pre-tend to believe it. Once he is released, however, Phönix agents quickly realize that he is not going to contact CONTROL while they are TAGGING him. Quiller is forced once more ON THE RUN and, down to the last minutes before sunrise when he knows they must kill him, he plans his last NARROW ESCAPE. A bomb has been planted in his rented Mercedes 230 SL and when he finds it, he arranges to detonate it while at a safe distance. The Phönix men assume that he has been mashed in the blast, and while they admire their flaming handiwork, Quiller makes an inconspicuous exit. The rest is simple: back at CONTROL the destruction of Phönix's headquarters is planned, and in a final piece of personal diplomacy, Quiller visits the Bundesminister in his office, reveals that he knows that he is really Zossen, and with his suicide assured, returns to a cup of hot tea at CONTROL HQ.

The plot of *Quiller* shows how espionage fiction formulas work in context. The prime mover for the plot is the agent's mission, which must be accomplished in secret. From this premise the events and episodes which comprise the bulk of the agent's adventures are reasonably predictable. If secrecy and freedom of movement are the necessary conditions of his existence, then both must be continually threatened. Taking his clue from what he imagines espionage to be really like as well as from the genre's tradition, the spy novelist endangers his agent in several, commonly employed ways: the ASSASSINATION ATTEMPT, the CHASE, the DROP or EXCHANGE, and CAPTURE. While ON THE RUN the agent is continually threatened with exposure, with bodily harm, even with death, and his stance is always precarious, always uncertain, with disaster a constant possibility and the right path unknown. If he is CAPTURED, he may face TORTURE, either physical, as in *Marathon Man,* or mind-altering, as in *The Ipcress File* or *The Quiller Memorandum,* or exquisitely intricate, as in several of the 007 stories. The spy almost inevitably effects his NARROW ESCAPE from the clutches of the other party, whether it is simply a matter of blasting down a wall with happily found dynamite, as Hannay does in *The Thirty-Nine Steps,* or some intricately choreographed and electronically gimmicky affair, as is James Bond's good fortune. Or the NARROW ESCAPE can help the agent evade the enemy; it is one of the most flexible of formulas, not only in its positioning within the narrative and its function in the story, but in its multiform variety as surface structure.

In THE SPY GOES OVER stories the spy does not have to go overseas on his mission. Quiller is already in Berlin. For an English agent Germany is foreign territory, but before he agrees to go on the Phönix mission and thus change his network of secret involvements, he is on relatively safe ground. Once the mission has been accepted, however, his circumstances are altered radically: he is still ostensibly the Red Cross representative, but now his real purpose is entirely different, and it is this deep purpose that controls his relation to his environment. Now, though he has been in a foreign city all along, Quiller is in a new sense in an alien land. The new, deeper purpose, and not a change of location, marks his GOING OVER.

The Quiller Memorandum is only one of many fine books that employ this structure, the most popular instances of which include Buchan's *Greenmantle*, Burgess's *Tremor of Intent*, and le Carré's *Spy Who Came In from the Cold*, and (with a great many reversals and inversions of formulas) *The Looking Glass War*. One of the earlier, and most influential, books of the type, Graham Greene's *Confidential Agent*, exploits many of these conventional formulas yet still imparts considerable depth to its pivotal character. The novel's structure, though in its broadest parameters formulaic, exists largely to enable Greene to reveal the issues with which his characters deal. More recently Leon Uris has used this structure type, almost without characterization of any persuasiveness, for *Topaz*. The movie version does a more convincing job. More recently still, Jack Higgins has had German spies GO OVER in *The Eagle Has Landed*.

In a closely related structure, sympathetic characters strive throughout the narrative to achieve the BIG JOB, as in *A Kind of Anger*, where the JOB is selling secret papers to foreign agents, or *Topkapi*, not really a spy novel but one in which the JOB is a jewel theft from the Topkapi Palace in Istanbul, or *The Schirmer Inheritance* and *A Coffin for Dimitrios*, where the JOB is to find a particular individual. In all of these fictions a task motivates the pivotal characters, while the others act to aid or hinder him (or her or them). Often the pivotal character attempts to prevent a major and dramatic crime, as in *The Day of the Jackal*. Problems of reader empathy arise in such cases, and Forsythe does not handle them effectively: most of the book centers around the Jackal's assassination plans, and to be aesthetically successful, we must identify with him. But near the end of the book, and consequently near the culmination of the attempt, our sympathies must be twisted over to the side of the French detective who is on the Jackal's trail. We do not have such problems in Harris's *Black Sunday*, in which the BIG JOB is the explosion of a Goodyear-type blimp over the Superbowl, showering hundreds of thousands of fleshettes onto the thousands of fans. Nor, we think, would most readers find their loyalties tugged in more than one direction in Ambler's Middle Eastern story *The Levanter*.

A second type of plot posits the pivotal character or hero as victim, most commonly of an agency in a spook war, though recently the agency need not be on the other side. For a good part of the time in this plot type, the hero will be ON THE RUN, even within his own land. Again, the geographic location does not necessarily decide his deep condition; his own land may be even more sinister than foreign soil because while he is among those who are ostensibly friends or at least "on his side," they often enough turn out, in their deep purposes, to be the enemy. In one of the earliest uses of this formula, Buchan's Richard Hannay (in *The Thirty-Nine Steps*) has several NARROW ESCAPES at first when, as VICTIM-HERO, he is ON THE RUN not only from the bad guys but from his own police. As the story evolves, he gains confidence, is cleared of the domestic murder charge, develops his skills in the spy trade, and ends up in control of the situation. His early escapes are cleverly engineered—too cleverly, and they are not credible—and by the novel's end Hannay has doffed his rabbit's skin to become the hound of justice.

Background to Danger is, in its narrative outline, remarkably similar to Buchan's adventure, though Ambler's surface variations make a successful transformation. Kenton, a journalist, is over his head throughout with both the Russian agent Zaleshoff, whom he befriends, and the evil and avaricious Colonel Robinson (*née* Saridza). This is a much better novel than its .prototype, in characterization, in plausability, and in style, and the contrast between what each writer did with the same story is in itself the basis for an understanding of what good storytelling consists.

Len Deighton's Harry Palmer (the movie names him, but he is anonymous in the book) spends a short time ON THE RUN in *The Ipcress File*, though it, like *The Thirty-Nine Steps*, is in England. Again, it does not matter that the movie Harry Palmer thinks that his torture chamber is in Albania and that he is escaping (narrowly) from a prison in Tirana. After that, in the best Buchanian tradition, he too turns about, becomes the hunter, and though he is captured near the end of the

caper, he finally apprehends Housemartin. Geoffrey Household's *Rogue Male* victim is ON THE RUN throughout; Paul
Henissart's AVH man is also, from his own people as well as
from the CIA.

Published in the last few years have been several novels in
which the agent's own apparatus conspires against him, though
with slightly different outcomes: the VICTIM-HERO in James
Grady's *Six Days of the Condor* (only three days in the movie)
and Joseph Hone's *Sixth Directorate* happily escapes alive while
the real enemy, his own people—the CIA in the former book,
the KGB in the latter—are punished. In Robert Duncan's
Dragons at the Gate, the CIA man to be sacrificed is not only
able to extricate himself but to embarrass everyone in the
organization who has been responsible: he forces them to cancel
an operation he finds morally repugnant, gets his former boss
removed from his position of authority, and then "settles" for
a CIA pension to ensure his future silence and tranquility. In
The Winter Spy AVH Col. Paul Rappaport has been framed by
his superior and appears to be the killer of an American diplomat. (In characteristic baroque espionage fashion, the diplomat was a DOUBLE AGENT.) Rappaport is immediately ON
THE RUN, from the German and later the Australian police,
his own operatives, and the CIA. Near the novel's end he is
caught by the CIA and TURNED—willingly—against his former Hungarian masters. At the very end he meets a mercilessly
just finale: hated by his own, considered by the CIA to be
merely "one of theirs" and thus having been carelessly exploited
for its own ends, he is murdered by the daughter of one of
his victims.

One's own agency as the enemy is one of the most ominous
developments in recent espionage fiction. The spy novel derives
much of its appeal by striking a paranoid note: in earlier
espionage fiction, such as that written before the 1970s, the
secret agent had only to deal with the ostensible enemy and
an occasional seeming neutral. And nearly all of those were
identifiable because they were foreigners. In the past several
years the secret agent of fiction may find that his own people
are working against him, with lethal intent. His and their

surface motivations only seem consonant: their deep missions are on a collision course.

Of these novels, only *Six Days of the Condor* has had any great popular success, and so may seem to be an argument against taking this theme too seriously as an index of public perception of intelligence agencies. But most recently Graham Greene's superb narrative, *The Human Factor,* develops this formula as one of the book's subplots. Castle is actually leaking information to the Russians, but when his superiors in the agency trace the leak to his partner, Davis, they arrange to have him poisoned. (Coincidentally? Or perhaps not by accident; an Oklahoman named Davis was poisoned by British Intelligence during the early days of World War II when he refused to halt his oil shipments to the Germans [Stevenson, *A Man Called Intrepid,* pp. 325–26]). The fictional murder of British agent Davis, out of a mistaken understanding of culpability, sets in motion a series of formulaic episodes. The pivotal character, Castle, soon goes ON THE RUN, has a CLOSE ENCOUNTER with British authorities, makes his NARROW ESCAPE and ends up, "liberated," in Russia—without his wife and child whom the British are holding, without his country or countrymen, without the gratification that his morally motivated acts have gained him very much at all. BETRAYAL, by the Russian agent who had promised so much, is one of the lesser agonies he must live with. This briefest of summaries, and it is only part of the novel at that, does not begin to do justice to Greene's dramatic ironic power in a genuinely moving story; it only shows how the plot develops, in outline, formulaically.

The hero is also the intended victim in a variant plot type in which he must reach a destination at a certain time or with a particular cargo intact. Often that cargo is human, and the hero functions as bodyguard. We call this plot structure, and Greene's, after Ambler's novel, *The Journey into Fear.* In the book of that title the hero is on shipboard from Turkey to Europe and the cargo he must preserve is himself. He succeeds. Helen MacInnes's man on the run in her very successful *Snare of the Hunter* is trying to help the daughter of a Czech scientist escape to Switzerland, and the hunters are the murderous Czech secret police. The action is complicated, romantically and deliciously so, by the love of the American agent (who is an amateur, as is often the case) and his attractive Bohemian fugitive. *Midnight Plus One* of Gavin Lyall and the strikingly similar *Bearer Plot* of Owen Sela are both accounts of heroic attempts to be at the right place before a deadline; in both cases the trip to the destination is full of varied dangers threatening the hero ON THE RUN. The handsome salary he receives provides only a motivation for his undertaking the job at all and is not really central to the story. But once underway he cannot ESCAPE the gauntlet of circumstances that lie before him. Threading his way carefully, from danger to danger, from threat to threat, he is metaphorically as nimble as a halfback, and all the more skillful because he has valuable and brittle amateurs with him. Money may be all the reward the agent receives in payment, but satisfaction at having done it is important. In *The Bearer Plot* there is the added delectation that the rescued treasure is Nazi contraband.

A third structural type, also commonly used, parallels the detective novel in its manipulation of reader sympathies and employs many of the same strategies and formulas that detective fiction does because in it, too, a criminal is sought. But in the novel of counterespionage, TO CATCH A SPY (closest in form to the detective novel), the criminal is guilty of spying. *Tinker, Tailor, Soldier, Spy* is perhaps the best story of this kind yet written, a story in which the spy to be caught is a DOUBLE AGENT of the Kim Philby sort who has schemed his way into CONTROL's position. But the novel that we want to examine in more than a sentence is Greene's *The Human Factor:* if the reader's empathetic perspective were to be reversed, it would be a counterespionage plot. Much of the focus is on the upper ranks of British Intelligence and their efforts to determine which one of their operatives has been giving the Russians secret information. Logically and methodically they close in on their DOUBLE AGENT, and when they have identified him, they order his "accidental" murder. It is, to repeat, the wrong man.

But our sympathies are never with Greene's spy-hunters, and when Davis is in error eliminated, we are outraged because we empathize with the innocent and rather likable victim, and we are not merely remorseful at a piously intended and regrettable miscarriage of justice, which would have been our feelings had we identified with the Establishment. Castle must surely be the least personally attractive yet the most morally compelling spy in modern fiction. Married to a black South African whom he met while on duty there, he became indebted to Russian agents who smuggled his wife out of the country. They were not ones to let so valuable a source of information get away, and he became a pipeline of African-related intelligence to them in subsequent years. At the moment of the novel Castle has decided that he has given the Communists their last secrets. But the murder of Davis compels him, even though he realizes that it will probably mean his own destruction, to help the enemy one more time. He is right: it is his last. His moral sense, complicated and delicate in a simpleminded and brutal milieu, nearly destroys him. When he has his NARROW ESCAPE to Moscow, all that he has left is his corporeal being, and that is only minimally "life."

Other popular counterespionage stories include *The Ipcress File*, in which the spy is the agent's own section chief, as he is also in *Assignment K*, in which the agent's fiancée is in the enemy's employ. DOUBLE AGENTS prove particularly thorny and their innocence or guilt, or the side to which they ultimately owe their allegiance, has to be established by the pivotal agent in *Funeral in Berlin* and *Yesterday's Spy*. In *Spy Story* wealthy and politically influential English Brahmins are dealing privately with the Russians, and in MacInnes's *Neither Five nor Three* a wealthy young Madison Avenue type, and fiancé of the heroine, is recruited by the Communists to be their servile lackey in one of their wicked plots in the international conspiracy. TO CATCH A SPY novels develop through analysis and evaluation of events and character and implicitly argue that what is hidden can always be known, that the most cleverly concealed facets of life can be illuminated. In this respect it is consonant with the naively optimistic hopes for science in our century.

A certain kind of adventure is the spy novel's stock in trade. Its hero is like that of classical and medieval epic and romance; he must carry out his assigned mission, or capture an enemy agent, or merely save himself, despite formidable odds. Occasionally a knight of the Middle Ages conceals his identity behind his armored visor, and in book 4 of the *Odyssey* Helen tells Telemachos that she had once met his father while he roamed Troy in disguise on what we would today call an espionage mission. But for the most part the heroes of these eras, Achilles and Roland and Gawain, are actors of the surface. Their depths are psychological and philosophical, but they are seldom clandestine: they are not to be characterized that way. The contemporary spy must constantly conceal his identity, his loyalty, his mission, his beliefs. His enemy is usually also hidden or, to use the term now popular, covert. Enemy agents are likely to be skillful at deceit and treachery, the guilty are adept at EVASION and deception, and the innocent—if they are genuinely innocent—cannot be entrusted with the spy's secrets since they may unknowingly reveal him to the enemy or be made to betray him under TORTURE, or, as recently, under consciousness-altering drugs.

Given the limited range of effects most spy novels try to communicate (Greene and le Carré have been the most successful in expanding those limits) and the commensurately limited repertoire of plots, certain episodes are likely to occur frequently, so frequently that they have become characteristic of the species. The sphere of the fictional spy situates him alone in a potentially hostile environment in which most of the dangers are unknown to him and sometimes to the reader. His characteristic stance is ON THE RUN, the ideally expressive signifier of the man without roots, with no security, with no solace to be derived from his society because in reality he shares little with it: his occupation is a cover, he can ill afford to have friends on "the outside," and his fellow agents may well be conspiring against him. He may have no recourse to the law ("The Department will disown any knowledge of you"), and he is continually vulnerable to the hidden, silent enemy, within and without. Quiller muses on this subject: "We are alone. We are committed to the tenets of individual combat and there is no help for him who falls. Save a life and we save a man who will later watch us through the cross hairs and squeeze the trigger if he gets the orders or the chance" (p. 64).

The spy is trained to be suspicious of everyone: the reader, who must at least understand and hopefully share these feelings will have his own paranoid impulses foregrounded if he participates vicariously in the spy novel's action. Yet because those fears are not really and immediately his own, he can remove himself partially from the spy's predicament. The NARROW ESCAPE, the CLOSE CALL, the DROP, the DISGUISED ENCOUNTER with the enemy, the CHASE, even the CAPTURE—all of these events are exciting—they are thrilling. They are what the spy novel is all about, they are the feelings that this genre evokes most effectively. Nearly all of the episodes in these books are thus multiform variations of the same strategy intended to produce a limited range of responses in the reader. When the agent is ON THE RUN, what he fears is still only potential danger; during a NARROW ESCAPE it is actual; and when made to suffer TORTURE the phenomenon to be feared is more immediate still, though this is slightly more complicated since we and the agent may dread shame as well as physical pain, should secret information be revealed. But the effective emotional range of most spy novels, qua novels of espionage, does not transcend these parameters by much. Nevertheless, given their enormous popularity, especially during the past decade, they obviously reach deeply into us, if not broadly across our lives.

We are both participants and spectators in our experience with fiction, generally, and espionage fiction involves us in distinctive combinations of our stance vis-à-vis the text. That stance varies—in several modes, as reader-oriented criticism has highlighted in the past decade—but spy novels do have enough in common so that we can comment about their impact generically. Even Robert Ludlum shares affective features with Graham Greene. When everyone around him is a potential (or real) enemy, the secret agent must be detached, unemotional, dispassionately observant—in a word, cool. This is his legacy from the Raymond Chandler hard-boiled detective. This posture is necessary because his survival depends upon his constant, accurate evaluation of all around him, people and events. In that respect the spy is what many of us want to be; in that respect we participate in the action of the story. Puzzle-solving, code-deciphering, and character-analyzing are the modes of his survival. Quiller reports to his CONTROL (in writing) that "certain personal feelings toward [Inga] were now intruding," but that since he recognized this weakness he could control it: "but they did not of course interfere in any way with the pursuance of my mission" (p. 159).

Quiller is also able to break Solly Rothstein's coded message to his brother in Argentina, instructing him how to infect an entire community there with bacteria, ensuring that the German immigrants will be among the dead. The German *Polizei* cannot break the code by themselves, nor can CONTROL. But this ability is just one of many arrows in the agent's quiver. Richard Hannay has not even been trained, but he admits— why be modest in the face of facts?—that he has always been handy with codes.

The secret agent may be acting out our fantasies in his sexual adventures as well. This aspect has been thoroughly discussed and needs no supplement here: most spies have a compelling way with beautiful women, at least since the 1950s. Their occupations make our fantasies complete: the agency will not allow attachments or emotional involvements of any kind, and so the spy is not only free to love and leave, he is under national security orders to do so. Le Carré has reminded us, in his fiction, that even spies can have families, though for the most part his operatives are bound to their London offices. Greene's confidential agent was once married, but that was long ago and in another country; now, her haunting memory hinders his action. Bond tries marriage once and pays for it when the opposition murders his bride. It is much better, espionage fiction tells us, to remain detached. If you love a woman, you will get hurt.

If the fictional spy expresses (predominantly male) sexual impulses, he also is a medium for expressing our noblest aspirations. In his loneliness, his isolation, there is also the opportunity for heroism, manifested as self-possession, inner strength, the courage to do what he feels is right and to make such decisions while removed from societal pressures. There are no Joneses to emulate in his milieu. Thoreau would approve.

Matthew Arnold felt that he and his beloved "are here as on a darkling plain / Swept with confused alarms of struggle and flight / Where ignorant armies clash by night." Adam Hall picks up on that metaphor when he has Quiller's CONTROL tell him what it is like to be a spy in the field:

> There are two opposing armies drawn up on the field, each ready to launch the big attack. But there is heavy fog and they can't sight each other. You are in the gap between them. You can see us, but so far you can't see them. Your mission is to get near enough to see them, and signal their position to us, giving us the advantage. That is where you are Quiller, in the gap. (P. 136)

The spy alone, swirled in heavy fog, stands undaunted between poised armies. Therein lies his heroism, that quality with which the reader participates.

Spies occasionally get CAUGHT, are TORTURED, and threatened with death. The Geneva Convention sanctions much of it. But, "with a little bit of luck," one of the lyrics from *My Fair Lady* has it, "with a little luck I won't get caught." This is an apprehension that every person in the world experiences. In our world, in our lives, "getting caught" will not likely mean death or torture. We fudge on our taxes, jump red lights when no one is around, and overeat when we have resolved to cut down; in a thousand ways with nearly everyone we know, we do and say things that are not quite right, things that our ethical sense, if consulted, would proscribe. Our serious transgressions do not need elaboration: with a little luck we won't get caught at them, either (or especially). There is a part of all of us in the secret agent who "gets away with it."

Espionage fiction is not alone in allowing the reader to concretize repressed conflicts—in the case of spy novels, repressed anxiety—and once concretized as literary symbols, to deal with them safely. Objectified repressed matter can, without being acknowledged, be confronted and thus (as Simon

Lesser tells us in *Fiction and the Unconscious*) cathartically relieved. The spy novel also enables us, as spectators, to purge
and then obliterate the worst that is in us. Movie ads often
describe the spy's life as one of "cheating, lying, and stealing":
in what sphere of the psyche is that quite attractive? In what
sphere of our psyches do we want to be free to break any of
the rules we wish, as it is convenient, and never be held
accountable? The spy can do just that because he is invisible,
because he is an alien body in his host society. He moves
horizontally to intrude into the lives of others, but his own
life is structured vertically. We want to be a part of that life,
perhaps even to live that life, but in one sense only: we realize
that we cannot really lie, steal, and kill, that we are not really
like that. And so we observe—we are engaged spectators when
Szell drills Babe's tooth to the pulp, when Leamas is shot down
at the Wall, when Leiser is left to his fate among the rapidly
encircling Vopos.

We have always had spies, but only recently have we made
them our heroes. Their time has come round at last because
it is our times that see in their work a part of our own desires
and our fears. The spy novel, ostensibly so restricted in its
possibilities, allows us to pierce deeply into ourselves, where
the possibilities are infinite.

4 The Joys of Buchaneering: John Buchan and the Heroic Spy Story

oward the end of the nineteenth century, the secret agent adventure had begun to assume a definite shape in the work of writers like Kipling, Stevenson, and Conrad. A number of Doyle's Sherlock Holmes stories came close to being accounts of counterespionage activity, and on the eve of World War I, in "His Last Bow," Holmes came out of retirement in order to foil the plots of a German agent. But it was the generation which came of age in the early twentieth century that made the spy story a major literary archetype by producing masses of formulaic spy adventures (e.g., Rohmer's *Insidious Dr. Fu Manchu*, LeQueux's *Secret Service*, Wallace's *Four Just Men*) as well as a number of more complex fictions involving espionage as a theme (e.g., Childer's *Riddle of the Sands*, Kipling's *Kim*, and Conrad's *Secret Agent*). The Richard Hannay stories of John Buchan span the distance between the popular spy adventure and the novel of espionage. Like the popular stories, Buchan's tales are deeply romantic; his hero is a gentleman amateur, definitely one of that breed later labeled "clubland heroes." His enemies are supervillains who represent the threat of non-British races and cultures to the English hegemony. Their complex criminal organizations, like the international criminal syndicate of Doyle's Professor Moriarty, threaten the very heart of the homeland. With the help of a few other gentlemen friends, however, Buchan's dauntless hero is invariably able to uncover and defeat the supervillain's plots, saving the empire for the time being. Though his hero and antagonists sometimes lapse into the manichean simplicities of Sax Rohmer's Fu Manchu and Sir Dennis Nayland Smyth, Buchan's moral earnestness, his sense of humor, and his concern for literary values make his Hannay stories the very model of the early twentieth-century spy story.

If we are to take his own word for it, John Buchan would probably have written his stories whether they were successful or not. In his autobiography *Memory Hold the Door,* he tells us,

> It was huge fun playing with my puppets, and to me they soon became very real flesh and blood. I never consciously invented with a pen in my hand; I waited until the story had told itself and then wrote it down, and, since it was already a finished thing, I wrote it fast. The books had a wide sale, both in English and in translations, and I have always felt a little ashamed that profit should accrue from what had given me so much amusement. I had no purpose in writing except to please myself, and even if my books had not found a single reader I would have felt amply repaid. (P. 196)

There seems little reason to doubt that Buchan's account is essentially correct, that the stories were for him a pleasant and relaxing mode of fantasy, a refreshing escape from a life filled with problems, tensions, and achievements of a very wide range. The interesting thing is that Buchan's fantasies, coupled with his ability to put them into words, became the ground for a rich and varied series of collective fantasies. Buchan, more than any other writer, assembled the formula for the modern secret agent story.

In general, the comparison between Rohmer and Buchan is somewhat analogous to that between Mickey Spillane and Dashiell Hammett: Buchan, like Hammett, was the chief cre-

ator of a formulaic tradition which proved capable of complex
and various developments; Rohmer was, like Spillane, a prolific
popular exponent of the formula in its simplest and most
extreme form. Because of this, the study of Rohmer's writings
can sometimes reveal to us in an exaggerated way the themes
that lurk beneath the more balanced and controlled surface of
Buchan's work. The terror of racial degeneration, for example,
is clearly an aspect of Buchan's thinking, but never so obses-
sively as in Rohmer's portrayal of the threat of the "yellow
peril" in Fu Manchu and his minions.

Buchan's spy stories used highly colorful villains, plots,
and incidents, but he combined these with allegory, using
characters to represent general moral and social traits, thereby
suggesting that the whole fate of society was at stake. Generally, the most successful writers of spy thrillers have dealt
in this sort of combination, though for some, such as Graham
Greene, the sense of realism has been in tension with it. Few
spy writers have used the formula without feeling the temptation to transmute fantasy into allegory, and Buchan seems
to have had a remarkably clear perception of this aspect of his
psyche. We noted above his frank statement that his tales were
fantasy outlets strongly needed at certain periods of his life.
Early in his autobiography, he notes that the first and strongest
influences on his thought were the fairy tales his father loved
and collected and the strong Calvinistic discipline that was
also part of his parson father's way of life. These two influences
came together for Buchan when he discovered and read what
would become for him the basic literary work:

> The Pilgrim's Progress became my constant companion. Even to-
> day I think that, if the text were lost, I could restore most of
> it from memory. My delight in it came partly from the rhythms
> of its prose, which, save in King James's Bible, have not been
> equalled in our literature; there are passages, such as the death
> of Mr. Valiant-for-Truth, which all my life have made music in
> my ear. But its spell was largely due to its plain narrative, its
> picture of life as a pilgrimage over hill and dale, where surprising
> adventures lurked by the wayside, a hard road with now and
> then long views to cheer the traveller and a great brightness at
> the end of it. (Memory, pp. 17–18)

It is probably more revealing than exaggerated to suggest that
Buchan created the modern spy story out of his need to construct a contemporaneous fantasy that might have for him
something of the power of *The Pilgrim's Progress.* In any case,
his stories are full of Bunyanesque allusions and devices. This
is obvious in the case of *Mr. Standfast,* in which one of the
hero figures reads Bunyan throughout the novel and attempts
to pattern himself on a Bunyan character, finally going to his
death in emulation of Bunyan's Mr. Valiant-for-Truth. But,
in an even deeper sense than such explicit references to *The
Pilgrim's Progress,* the fantasy world of Buchan's spy stories
takes on the basic form of the pilgrim's quest. In each of the
novels, a hero sets out on a quest that takes him from the
comfort and security of the city into an increasingly jagged
and dangerous landscape. As he proceeds on his quest, he
becomes more and more isolated and alone. He confronts the
agents and the plots of a diabolical conspiracy that threatens
to overthrow the moral world. Finally, with the assistance of
a few courageous friends, he succeeds in uncovering the enemy's
conspiracy and overthrowing it.

Thus, Buchan was able to take the situations of modern
international intrigue and to cast them in the form of romantic
adventure, permeating them with the particular allegorical
intensity of a Bunyanesque sense of the world. At his best, he
was able to clothe this allegorical fantasy with enough verisimilitude to effectively disguise, at least from time to time,
the weaknesses inherent in his obsessive symbolic machinery
and his tendency toward a completely fantastic dependence on
providential coincidence. Perhaps the most important contrib-
utors to this surface verisimilitude are not such insights into
the workings of government which the novels offer us but the
moments of social comedy. Though basically a very serious
man, Buchan apparently had a larky delight in social eccen-
tricities and his best books are enlivened with incidents and
characters that add an earthy touch of reality to the fantastic
proceedings and remind us that the intense moral allegorizing
of the story is not to be taken too seriously. In fact, one of
the weaknesses of Buchan's spy stories was his tendency to let

the overinflated moral seriousness of his fantasy overpower these contrasting moments of eccentric humor.

Buchan usually achieved his most effective balance of fantasy, moral allegory, and humor in narrations of the pursuit across the landscape which always seemed to rouse him to his best efforts. His own insightful description of the peculiar narrative power of the chase reveals how compelled he was by it:

> I was especially fascinated by the notion of hurried journeys. In the great romances of literature they provide some of the chief dramatic moments, and since the theme is common to Homer and the penny reciter it must appeal to a very ancient instinct in human nature. We live our lives under the twin categories of time and space, and when the two come into conflict we get the great moment. Whether failure or success is the result, life is sharpened, intensified, idealized. A long journey, even with the most lofty purpose, may be a dull thing to read of if it is made at leisure; but a hundred yards may be a breathless business if only a few seconds are granted to complete it. For then it becomes a sporting event, a race; and the interest which makes millions read of the Derby is the same, in a grosser form, as when we follow an expedition straining to relieve a beleaguered fort or a man fleeing to sanctuary with the avenger behind him. (*Memory*, p. 184)

It was above all through his elaboration of the structure of the hurried journey or flight and pursuit that Buchan developed the basic rhythms of the spy story. One need only think of Latimer's journey from Istanbul to Paris in Ambler's *Mask of Dimitrios,* the train trips in Hitchcock's *The Lady Vanishes* and Greene's *Orient Express,* James Bond's stalking pursuit and desperate flights from his multifarious antagonists, and Alec Leamas's clandestine journey into East Germany in le Carré's *Spy Who Came In from the Cold* to realize how important Buchan's example was for this formulaic tradition.

Only one of Buchan's spy stories was completely organized around a single, sustained, hurried journey. This was the first and best of the Richard Hannay stories, *The Thirty-Nine Steps.*

By looking at this novel in greater detail we can see the reasons for the effectiveness of this kind of structure and the special and unique characteristics Buchan was able to give it.

The story begins on the eve of World War I in London and is narrated by the central figure, Richard Hannay, who introduces himself as a mature man who has made his fortune in South Africa. Now, returned to the comfort of London, he finds himself at loose ends:

> Here was I, thirty-seven years old, sound in wind and limb, with enough money to have a good time, yawning my head off all day. I had just about settled to clear out and get back to the veld, for I was the best-bored man in the United Kingdom. (*Thirty-Nine Steps*, p. 11)

Fortunately for his peace of mind, if not his physical comfort and safety, Hannay is soon plunged into an adventure as exciting as he might have wished. Returning to his lodging one evening, Hannay meets another tenant of the building on the stairs. Though they are not acquainted, this man, acting strangely and furtively, begs to be let into Hannay's apartment. Bolting the door, he announces suddenly; "Pardon . . . I'm a bit rattled tonight. You see, I happen at this moment to be dead" (p. 14). This curious gentleman reveals to Hannay that he is one Franklin P. Scudder, an American newspaper correspondent who has become a sort of amateur secret agent. He explains to Hannay that "behind all the governments and the armies there was a big subterranean movement going on, engineered by very dangerous people" (p. 16). In a typically Buchanesque passage he reveals how he has come upon their secret and how he has since scurried about Europe in disguise to avoid the enemy's agents:

> "I got the first hint in an inn on the Achensee in Tyrol. That set me inquiring, and I collected my other clues in a fur-shop in the Galician quarter of Buda, in a Strangers' Club in Vienna, and in a little book-shop off the Racknitzstrasse in Leipsic. I completed my evidence ten days ago in Paris. I can't tell you the details now, for it's something of a history. When I was

quite sure in my own mind I judged it my business to disappear, and I reached this city by a mighty queer circuit. I left Paris a dandified young French-American, and I sailed from Hamburg a Jew diamond merchant. In Norway I was an English student of Ibsen, collecting materials for lectures, but when I left Bergen I was a cinema man with special ski-films. And I came here from Leith with a lot of pulp-wood propositions in my pocket to put before the London newspapers. Till yesterday I thought I had muddied my trail some, and was feeling pretty happy. Then . . . " (Pp. 22–23)

The three motifs announced here, unravelling a mystery, the dangerous lone journey, and the series of disguises, become the basis of the development of *The Thirty-Nine Steps*. Scudder explains to Hannay that a plot is afoot to assassinate an important European statesman when he visits London and gives him tantalizing hints about the secret organization. He refers to a Black Stone, to a man who lisps, and to "an old man with a young voice who could hood his eyes like a hawk." But before he can get any further information, Hannay finds Scudder with a knife in his heart.

After this brisk opening, which Buchan accomplishes in a single chapter, Hannay's hurried journey begins. He realizes that if he waits for the police to arrive, he will certainly be arrested and probably convicted of Scudder's murder. Since he will not be able to do anything about the enemy plot if he is locked up in jail, he decides to elude the police by going to Scotland, where his Scots background will enable him to blend into the country and he can try to unravel the mystery of Scudder's death and the assassination plot. Disguised as a milkman, he leaves his apartment and boards a train for the North.

Hannay's arrival in Scotland marks the beginning of a series of narrow escapes from capture by both the police and the forces of the enemy conspiracy. The combination of these adventures is ineffably Buchanesque, a synthesis of moral allegory, fantastic scrapes, and social comedy which has never quite been duplicated by any other writer of spy adventures including, alas, Buchan himself. The chapter titles, with their reminiscent flavor of Sherlock Holmes's adventures, give a pretty good idea of the distinctive ambience of this major section of *The Thirty-Nine Steps:* "The Adventure of the Literary Innkeeper," "The Adventure of the Radical Candidate," "The Adventure of the Spectacled Roadman," "The Adventure of the Bald Archaeologist," and "The Dry-Fly Fisherman." Each "adventure" is a set of incidents that elaborate in a different way the same basic pattern: Hannay, isolated and alone, pursued by both police and enemy agents, must find someone he can trust in order to communicate his knowledge to the higher authorities. To find such a person and to elude his pursuers, he disguises himself in various ways, but his disguise is always given away by some unforeseen flaw. Moreover, many of the persons he meets turn out to be enemy agents. This patterning of the situation enables Buchan to generate a variety of suspense effects and sudden twists: Will Hannay's disguise be penetrated this time or will he get away? Will the friendly gentleman turn out to be a real friend or an enemy agent in disguise? Will the police capture Hannay before he locates the enemy? In addition, this complex of situation and setting leads Buchan to imagine a rather marvelous sequence of contrasting and paradoxical incidents which take on a special force because of their connection with the underlying moral allegory. Hannay passes through a striking series of disguises, from South African mining magnate in trouble with the diamond association, to a "trusted leader of Australian thought" addressing a local political rally on colonialism and free trade, to a dirty and drunken Scottish road mender. Despite their fantastic diversity, Buchan manages to make each of these impersonations a plausible thing for Hannay to do in the light of his background and ability. Each situation of disguise involves some humorous incongruity as well as danger, and Buchan is thereby able to take advantage of the emotional effectiveness of our uncertainty about whether a given moment will lead to fear or laughter. Alfred Hitchcock would later display an even greater mastery of this kind of suspense effect, but Buchan certainly showed the way to make this type of incident an important part of the spy thriller.

The overall structure of these adventures also embodies Buchan's flair for paradox and allegory. Each character Hannay meets has a Bunyanesque flavor and represents some moral or social characteristic. Hannay's own disguises and the perils he encounters are also the embodiment of temptations and obstacles to the accomplishment of the mission which, it becomes increasingly clear, is basic to the security of England. Even coincidence, which Buchan depends on to an inordinate extent, takes on something of a moral quality in the allegorical world of Buchan's fantasy. Throughout his adventures in Scotland, Hannay's flight leads him closer and closer to the heart of the enemy's power. Finally, with his pursuers close behind, Hannay comes to the isolated country house of a "benevolent old gentleman" and amateur historian and archeaologist of the local countryside. Certain that such a distinguished gentleman can be trusted, Hannay quickly blurts out his plight and the old gentleman turns away the pursuers with a misleading story. Then . . .

> I emerged into the sunlight to find the master of the house sitting in a deep armchair in the room he called his study, and regarding me with curious eyes.
> "Have they gone?" I asked.
> "They have gone. I convinced them that you had crossed the hill. I do not choose that the police should come between me and one whom I am delighted to honour. This is a lucky morning for you, Mr. Richard Hannay."
> As he spoke his eyelids seemed to tremble and to fall a little over his keen grey eyes. In a flash the phrase of Scudder's came back to me when he had described the man he most dreaded in the world. He had said that he "could hood his eyes like a hawk." Then I saw that I had walked straight into the enemy's headquarters. (P. 128)

The way in which Hannay's seemingly random flight leads him unerringly to a direct confrontation with the enemy is a sign of Hannay's instrumentality as the agent of some higher moral power. In Buchan's world, there is really no coincidence or accident. What appears to be chance is actually the mysterious and enigmatic working of providence. As Hannay puts it in *The Three Hostages*, "then suddenly there happened one of those trivial things which look like accidents but I believe are part of the rational government of the universe."

By his tenacity, his willingness to embark on a moral quest without assistance, his ability to disguise himself, his courage in facing the technology of airplanes and motor cars which his pursuers send after him, and the skills in wilderness living with which he escapes alone across the desolate moors of Scotland, Hannay demonstrates his worthiness to serve the cause of goodness. Thus, providential action leads him to the heart of the evil conspiracy and then puts him in touch with what might be called the good underground, the only political force capable of overcoming the threats of the evil conspiracy. Though captured by the enemy agents, Hannay manages to escape and find his way to the cottage of Sir Walter Bullivant of the Foreign Office. Bullivant has already received a letter from the late Mr. Scudder outlining the plot to assassinate the Balkan statesman Constantine Karolides. When the assassination occurs, Sir Walter knows that Hannay has stumbled onto a dangerous plot. By this time, Hannay has managed to solve the mystery of Scudder's mysterious hints about the Black Stone, and he realizes that the enemy agents have more important plans. As Hannay characteristically put it, "the fifteenth day of June was going to be a day of destiny, a bigger destiny than the killing of Dago" (p. 74). The final plot is to steal Britain's secret naval plans from the Admiralty and to use them in a surprise attack that would cripple the British navy. The remainder of *The Thirty-Nine Steps* deals with Hannay's tracking down the Black Stone, the secret group of German agents, capturing their leaders just as they are about to turn over the stolen plans to an enemy submarine waiting off the British coast. The thirty-nine steps are finally revealed as the number of steps down to the sea from the coastal villa where the group of enemy agents is captured. This last section of the story is marred by the kind of implausibilities that Buchan often could not resist; for example, the naval plans are stolen by an enemy agent disguised as the first sea lord, who takes them from a meeting with a group of military leaders who have been in intimate contact with the real first sea lord for years. But it is, on the whole, an effective continuation of the suspenseful chase initiated in the first chapter.

None of the later Hannay books is as completely successful as *The Thirty-Nine Steps*. Works like *Greenmantle, Mr. Standfast,* and *The Three Hostages* come alive when Buchan deals with the hurried journey motif, but are generally more rambling and digressive narrative structures with too many subplots and different phases of action. Though these later novels have many striking incidents and characters, they seem increasingly clotted by an attempt at seriousness and moralism, as if Buchan were increasingly seeing his fantasy creations as a vehicle for important social and political opinions. This trend reached a peak in later novels of international intrigue like *A Prince of the Captivity,* which is far too full of apocalyptic warnings about the vast conspiracies threatening Western civilization to be a very effective tale of secret adventure. Political ideologies inevitably play an important role in the spy story because the agent's mission must be related to larger political conflicts in order to increase our sense of its importance and to heighten our feeling of suspense about its outcome. However, the presence of political or moral attitudes that later audiences find outdated or noxious invariably leads to a fairly rapid decline in the appeal of the stories that contain them. We cannot respond emotionally to the story's suspense without taking its worldview with some degree of seriousness. Buchan's popularity has thus declined rather precipitously since the 1930s. In fact, his work seems most likely to continue to appeal to wider audiences mainly in the form of the superb film that Alfred Hitchcock based on the novel. In his film version, Hitchcock retained Buchan's excellent suspense structure, but eliminated most of his ideological moralizing. At the same time he strengthened the comic and satirical aspects of Buchan's original by inventing a witty and sophisticated romance which he made one of the main lines of the film's plot.

Yet Buchan's fantasy vision of the world retains a considerable historical interest because of the degree to which it was shared by other popular writers of the time, men like Dornford Yates, H. C. McNeile (pseud. Sapper), E. Phillips Oppenheim, and Sax Rohmer. Moreover, it is this vision that a later generation of writers, men like Eric Ambler and Graham Greene, inherited and had to struggle with. These writers faced the problem not only of maintaining the effective structures of suspense and action, which Buchan's generation had created, but of expressing these structures in terms of a very different vision of the world. Thus, Buchan's view of the world provides us with some clues about dominant moral fantasies in the first part of the twentieth century, and it gives us a point from which to measure the extent to which a later generation departed from these fantasies.

Richard Usborne, in a fascinating study of the heroes of Buchan, Sapper, and Yates, coined the rather nice term "clubland heroes" to describe Hannay and his compatriots Bulldog Drummond and Jonah Mansel. This characterization of the hero is an important aspect of Buchan's fantasy. Hannay is a clubman, which means that he is, above all, a gentleman and an amateur, a member of the upper classes with an independent income, and one who lives by a very strong moral and social code in which the ideals of honor, duty, and country play a primary role. He is not a professional agent, nor does he belong even temporarily to any formal secret service. Even during the height of the war, he does his spying while on brief leave from his main occupation, the traditional gentlemanly one of military officer. After the war, his great dream is to settle down in a lovely country house in the Cotswolds and serve happily as the local squire. In these respects, Hannay symbolizes the continuity of British social tradition, the vision of an ordered and hierarchical social world which has lasted from time immemorial. The search for reassurance that this tradition can go on is one basic impetus of Buchan's fantasy:

> Many of my pre-War interests revived, but, so to speak, on sufferance, for I felt that they had become terribly fragile. Would anything remain of the innocencies of old life? I was reassured by two short holidays. One was a tramp in the Cotswolds from

which I returned with the conviction that the essential England could not perish. This field had sent bowmen to Agincourt; down that hill Rupert's men, swaying in their saddles, had fled after Naseby; this village had given Wellington a general; and from another the parson's son had helped to turn the tide in the Indian Mutiny. To-day the land was as quiet as in the beginning, and mowers were busy in the hay. A second holiday took me to my Tweedside Hills. There, up in the glens, I found a shepherd's wife who had four sons serving. Jock, she told me cheerfully, was in France with the Royal Scots; Jamie was in "a bit ca'd Sammythrace", Tam was somewhere on the Artic shore and "sair troubled wi' his teeth"; and Davie was outside the walls of Jerusalem. Her kind old eyes were infinitely comforting. I felt that Jock and Jamie and Tam and David would return and would take up their shepherd's trade as dutifully as their father. Samothrace and Murmansk and Palestine would be absorbed, as Otterburn and Flodden had been, into the ageless world of pastoral. (*Memory*, p. 168)

Though this statement would sound right in Richard Hannay's mouth, it was actually made by Buchan, himself, in his autobiography.

But if the clubman's image of the world as a place of unchanging and stable social tradition is the ideal, Buchan was well aware of its fragility. It is significant that his hero is not only a club man, but a colonial and self-made man, accustomed to scenes of violence and at home in the wilderness, for only such a hero might be capable of coping with the manifold dangers which threaten "the innocencies of the old life." The traditional world is threatened both by external and by internal enemies. New forces of barbarism have arisen on the periphery of civilized society, that is, the British Empire. In addition, there are threats from within, for the average man's civilized restraints and his commitment to traditional social ethics are subverted by the increasing moral chaos of modern life:

The barriers between the conscious and the subconscious have always been pretty stiff in the average man. But now with the general loosening of screws they are growing shaky and the two worlds are getting mixed. . . . That is why I say you can't any longer take the clear psychology of most civilized human beings for granted. Something is welling up from primeval deeps to muddy it. . . . The civilized is far simpler than the primeval. All history has been an effort to make definitions, clear rules of thought, clear rules of conduct, social sanctions, by which we can conduct our life. These are the work of the conscious self. The subconscious is an elementary and lawless thing. If it intrudes on life, two results must follow. There will be a weakening of the power of reasoning, which after all is the thing that brings men nearest to the Almighty. And there will be a failure of nerve. (*Three Hostages*, p. 10)

External threats are most strikingly dramatized through the fantasy of a great racial drama which is being played out on the world stage. Buchan was by no means a virulent racist. As a man and a colonial administrator he appears to have been unshakably convinced of the superior virtues of the Anglo-Saxon, but there is little evidence that he was hostile to other races and cultures. Even in his stories he was no direct manipulator of the popular paranoia surrounding the "yellow peril," as Sax Rohmer was. Nevertheless, the adventures of Richard Hannay have an unmistakably racist tinge, as if in fantasy Buchan was able to give vent to feelings about racial good and evil which he would never have made the basis of calculated political action. Hannay's continual and automatic use of racial epithets like "dago," "nigger," and "wog," while doubtless a real enough characteristic of a colonial gentleman of his era, is one of those aspects of Buchan's work that most embarrassingly grates on the contemporary reader's ear, preventing us from accepting Hannay as a hero without serious reservations.

But, on a deeper level than that of racial epithet and the instinctive superiority of the Anglo-Saxon gentleman, Buchan's treatment of the drama of racial conflict reflects his sense that the English Christian social tradition is no longer able to cope with the larger social forces the twentieth century has unleashed in the world. Buchan presents these forces as spiritual and racial, rather than political and economic, and in a

number of ways he seems rather ambiguously attracted by the
enemy, though ostensibly his stories represent heroic victory
over the enemy's conspiracy. Indeed, the Buchan hero is often
strongly attracted by the racial or spiritual force represented
by the opposing supervillain.

> There would be no mercy from Stumm. That large man was
> beginning to fascinate me, even though I hated him. Gaudian
> [another German agent] was clearly a good fellow, a white man
> and a gentleman. I could have worked with him, for he belonged
> to my own totem. But the other was an incarnation of all that
> makes Germany detestable, and yet he wasn't altogether the
> ordinary German and I couldn't help admiring him. I noticed
> he neither smoke nor drank. His grossness was apparently not
> in the way of fleshly appetites. Cruelty . . . was his hobby, but
> there were other things in him, some of them good, and he had
> that kind of crazy patriotism which becomes a religion. (*Green-
> mantle*, p. 85)

In *The Three Hostages,* Hannay must use all his spiritual resources to overcome the psychological spell of supervillain
Dominick Medina, one of whose powers involves the almost
hypnotic control of others, the capacity to bring both followers
and opponents under his complete spiritual domination.

On the surface these supervillains and the forces they represent are evil because they pose a basic threat to the good
tradition of the clubland world. Yet, in Buchan's fantasy, the
new forces have a way of seeming far more compelling and
attractive than the ordered life for which the hero officially
yearns. After all, who would actually fritter away his life in
the routine pastoral joy when he might be dashing about the
world exposing secret conspiracies which are, fortunately,
everywhere? We recall that, at the very beginning of the Hannay saga, our hero had become so bored with civilized life in
London that he was about to return to the African veldt. The
murderous intervention of a German conspiracy saves him just
in time. Later, in pursuit of the Islamic prophet Greenmantle,
one of Hannay's friends regrets that the prophet's attractive
message of primitive fanaticism should have become perverted
to the evil ends of German imperialism:

"Well, Greenmantle is the prophet of this great simplicity. He speaks straight to the heart of Islam, and it's been twisted into part of this damned German propaganda. His unworldliness has been used for a cunning political move, and his creed of space and simplicity for the furtherance of the last word in human degeneracy. My God, Dick, it's like seeing St. Francis run by Messalina." (*Greenmantle*, p. 233)

A similar ambivalence reveals itself in Hannay's romantic life. In the course of his adventures he meets and falls in love with the beautiful Mary Lamington, who is the very epitome of English womanhood. Hannay dreams of retiring with his beloved Mary, but the real intensity of their romance results from the fact that Mary is also a secret agent, one of the most daring members of the informal espionage group Hannay himself works with. Not surprisingly, the supervillain Graf von Schwabing also falls in love with her and wrecks his own conspiracy by attempting to take Mary back to Germany with him. Even before his first encounter with Mary, Hannay's own feelings about the opposite sex had been most strongly aroused by the German agent Hilda von Einem:

> I see I have written that I know nothing about women. But every man has in his bones a consciousness of sex. I was shy and perturbed, but horribly fascinated. This slim woman, poised exquisitely like some statue between the pillared lights, with her fair cloud of hair, her long delicate face, and her pale bright eyes, had the glamor of a wild dream. I hated her instinctively, hated her intensely, but I longed to arouse her interest. (*Greenmantle*, pp. 218–19)

When Hannay finally marries his perfect English lady spy and settles down to the life of a country squire, it is not long before he is drawn back into the fascinating world of new racial and spiritual forces. The comforts of the traditional life quickly pale when a visitor brings news of new forces at work in the East:

> That took him to Central Asia, and he observed that if he ever left England again he would make for those parts, since they

were the refuge of all the superior rascality of creation. He had a notion that something very off might happen there in the long run. "Think of it!" he cried. "All the places with names like spells—Bokhara, Samarkand—run by seedy little gangs of Communist Jews. It won't go on forever. Some day a new Genghis Khan or a Timour will be thrown up out of the Maelstrom. Europe is confused enough, but Asia is ancient Chaos. (*Three Hostages,* p. 6)

The way in which the basic spy themes of conspiracy and disguise are treated in Buchan's works also illustrates a curious ambivalence. Though the British countryside is explicitly presented as an ideal world and the values of the British social tradition as the apogee of the civilized world, this way of life is also shown to be riddled with weakness and conspiracy. Significantly, the arch conspirators typically wear the garb of representatives of the tradition. The evil German agent with eyes hooded like a hawk is disguised as a Scottish country gentleman and amateur historian. The Graf von Schwabing has passed for many years as Morgan Ivery, liberal politician and philanthropist. And their agents seem to be average British citizens. English country life thus seems at once the epitome of human civilization and a base deception, riddled with enemy agents. Buchan's treatment of disguise is even more curious. His supervillains are, above all, men of many faces, and their skill at disguises is implicitly condemned by contrast with the honesty, openness, and integrity of the British character. Though Hannay's missions frequently force him to hide his identity, he usually feels extremely uncomfortable when he must pretend to act in a way contrary to his nature. Yet this moral contrast between honest pilgrim Hannay and the enemy agents who delight in their deceptions and disguises is undercut on numerous occasions by characters who reflect a fascination with the idea of the British identity swallowed up in some alien way of life. The most striking of these characters, Sandy Arbuthnot, was evidently based on the historical figure of T. E. Lawrence. The way in which Buchan develops this character suggests the profound ambivalence his generation felt toward the character and exploits of Lawrence. Sandy is as British as

they come, the offspring of an aristocratic Scottish family with
a long and brilliant tradition of political and social leadership.
Yet he has the capacity to become so totally identified with
an alien way of life that he ends up not merely as an effective
agent, but a leader of some bizarre tribe or sect:

> "Billy Arbuthnot's boy? His father was at Harrow with me. I
> know the fellow—Harry used to bring him down to fish—
> tallish, with a lean, high-boned face and a pair of brown eyes
> like a pretty girl's. I know his record, too. There's a good deal
> about him in this office. He rode through Yemen, which no
> white man ever did before. The Arabs let him pass, for they
> thought him stark mad and argued that the hand of Allah was
> heavy enough on him without their efforts. He's blood-brother
> to every kind of Albanian bandit. Also he used to take a hand
> in Turkish politics, and got a huge reputation." (*Greenmantle*,
> p. 23)

Sandy's extraordinary conduct seems to be the same kind of
dissembling for which the villains are condemned, and yet for
Buchan there is clearly an important difference. Here we encounter one of the prime virtues of the British race:

> Lean brown men from the ends of the earth may be seen on the
> London pavements now and then in creased clothes, walking
> with the light outland step, slinking into clubs as if they could
> not remember whether or not they belonged to them. From
> them you may get news of Sandy. Better still, you will hear of
> him at little forgotten fishing ports where the Albanian moun-
> tains dip to the Adriatic. If you struck a Mecca pilgrimage the
> odds are you would meet a dozen of Sandy's friends in it. In
> shepherds' huts in the Caucasus you will find bits of his cast-
> off clothing, for he has a knack of shedding garments as he goes.
> In the caravanserais of Bokhara and Samarkand he is known,
> and there are Shikaris in the Pamirs who still speak of him
> around their fires. If you were going to visit Petrograd or Rome
> or Cairo it would be no use asking him for introductions; if he
> gave them, they would lead you into strange haunts. But if Fate
> compelled you to go to Lhasa or Yarkand or Seistan he could
> map out the roads for you and pass the word to potent friends.

We call ourselves insular, but the truth is that we are the only race on earth that can produce men capable of getting inside the skin of remote peoples. Perhaps the Scotch are better than the English, but we're all a thousand per cent better than anybody else. Sandy was the wandering Scot carried to the pitch of genius. In old days he would have led a crusade or discovered a new road to the Indies. To-day he merely roamed as the spirit moved him, till the war swept him up and dumped him down in my battalion. (*Greenmantle*, pp. 31–32)

Richard Hannay, the muscular Christian squire who fights to protect the old stabilities of British social tradition from the dangerous forces which threaten it, represents one side of Buchan's fantasy. But there is an equally important side encapsulated in this description of Sandy: the lure of the exotic, the dream of casting off the burden of identity like a suit of old clothes and letting oneself be swallowed up in the mysterious spiritual worlds of alien peoples, the desire to escape from the dull routines of civilized life into a more primitive and daring world, the search for a crusade to deepen and intensify the sense of life, to get away from the orderly and civilized patterns of British life which seem so constrained and restrictive. In this area of his fantasy, Buchan reflected the same tensions that have been so characteristic of a stream of modern Western European literature. The quest for the exotic, the urge to cast aside the constraining roles of civilized man, the ambivalent fascination with colonial peoples—these are the same urges that were articulated more powerfully and tragically in the life of a *poète maudit* like Rimbaud or in later works of Joseph Conrad like *Heart of Darkness,* or in the life and paintings of Paul Gauguin. The social-psychological causes of these curious urges in modern European culture have been explored from many different perspectives. Freud argued in *Civilization and Its Discontents* that the development of civilized society inevitably brought with it a neurotic desire to escape and to destroy. His explanation seems compelling in many ways, though it does not completely account for one central feature of this cultural phenomenon, its relation to colonialism and imperialism. It would appear that at a certain point in the development of democratic imperialistic societies, there emerges a fascination with the idea of entering into the identity of the colonial peoples. One of the key features of this fascination is a lurking fear that these traditional cultures, which have been destroyed or transformed by imperialistic power, possessed some deeper insight into the meaning of life. While this feeling has been an important theme in the culture of Britain and France since the end of the nineteenth century, it has only recently become widespread in America, where it has particularly taken the form of a fascination with traditional American Indian cultures.

Important cultural themes or ambivalences like this are often explored on a conscious and articulate level in the work of philosophers, artists, and novelists. In twentieth-century English literature, for example, the theme of fascination with the traditional culture of colonial peoples was explored with great subtlety and insight in E. M. Forster's *Passage to India*. Popular literature, however, tends to work toward a resolution of value conflicts and a reaffirmation of convential beliefs or perspectives. With this in view, we are in a better position to see why Buchan's fantasy world was widely enough shared by his generation to make his stories highly successful, and also why more recent generations have found that they cannot become easily identified with the network of assumptions and attitudes that rules this landscape of the imagination. Buchan's work represents a world in which the Anglo-Saxon Christian social tradition is under attack but is still strong enough in the minds of men not only to be victorious over its enemies but to be revealed as an expression of the underlying truth of the universe. This latter characteristic is especially important in defining the spy stories of Buchan and most of his contemporaries in comparison with more recent works, like those of Ian Fleming. There are, as we will see, many fundamental similarities between the epics of James Bond and Richard Hannay, but one of the most striking differences is the almost complete absence in Bond's world of the sense of providential governance which played such an important part in Buchan's. We have seen how the sense of Bunyanesque moral allegory pervades the Hannay stories and how coincidence takes on the meaning of an illustration of higher powers taking a hand in human affairs. While there is certainly enough moral melodrama and coincidence in the works of Ian Fleming, there is never a hint that the confrontation between our hero and his enemies is being shaped by the decrees of providence or that Bond and his allies are being tested by transcendent forces. It is probably the association Buchan makes between Hannay's beliefs and actions and the symbols of religious tradition that makes it most difficult for contemporary readers to enter imaginatively into his stories. While Hannay's casual racist slurs might be accepted as no more than tics of character, or melodramatic artifices, the way they are in Fleming, when we are asked to associate Hannay's obvious ideological limitations with the views of heaven, the delicate tissue of plausibility and emotional identification breaks down and we become too conscious of dated moral attitudes to suspend temporarily our own commitments and attitudes.

If Richard Hannay were only a typical clubland hero defending British social tradition with the help of higher powers, Buchan's work would doubtless have faded into the oblivion that has swallowed up most of his contemporaries and followers like Dornford Yates and Sapper. However, Buchan also responded in his fantasies to a more contemporary sense of ambivalence about the social and religious tradition. While he worked to resolve this ambivalence through characters like Sandy Arbuthnot, who remains a cool British aristocrat despite his total involvement in Eastern ways of life, the fascination with the new forces unleashed in the world remains an important undercurrent of Buchan's fantasy. Though his works of adventure are optimistic on the surface and he imagines a revitalized Christian social tradition able to overcome the threats of the twentieth century, his stories also reflect on a deeper level a sense of the critical failure of modern civilization and a yearning for a more glorious, simpler, and more mystical way of life. On this level, he still speaks to some of the major currents in the fantasy life of men in the twentieth century. The modern spy story, even in the cynical and despairing intrigues of John le Carré and Len Deighton, has come to express this kind of feeling still more strongly. Thus Buchan was instrumental in giving both a model of form and an inner spirit to the story of espionage, giving it through his vision of the world a capacity to express in terms of contemporary international politics and intrigue the yearning for a lost world of fullness and heroism. In this respect it might be said of Buchan's fantasy vision what he himself said of one of his contemporaries:

> He was not quite of this world; or, rather he was of an earlier, fairer world that our civilization has overlaid. He lived close to the kindly earth, and then he discovered the kindlier air, and that pure exultant joy of living which he always sought. (*Memory*, p. 74)

5 At a Crossroads: Eric Ambler and Graham Greene

*E*ric Ambler and Graham Greene transformed the spy novel irretrieva-
bly. In tone, in characterization, in theme as well as in the
episodes and plots used to express all of these features, the
genre changed from the naive to the sinister, from a story of
adventure to one of treachery and betrayal. These important
novelists, whose writing careers span World War II, were
themselves altered by that cataclysm, but also helped bring
about those changes that now characterize the genre. Ambler's
early novels, those written before England's active entry into
World War II, are modeled on the plots and for the most part
the characters of his predecessors. This is especially true of
Background to Danger (1937), but is also the case with *Epitaph
for a Spy* (1939), *Cause for Alarm* (1939), and his most popular
early work, *Coffin for Dimitrios* (also 1939). *Journey into Fear,*
though published in 1940, is still prewar in spirit. Ambler
served in the British army until 1945 (being discharged a
lieutenant colonel) and then went to Hollywood, where he
wrote the screen plays for several movies, most notably the
script for *The Cruel Sea,* an Oscar nominee. His novel-writing

101

career resumed in 1951 with the publication of *Judgment on Delchev;* by that time, our understanding of the nature and commonality of espionage, of window-dressing political trials, and of Balkan intrigues had matured substantially.

The FBI had made us aware of sabotage, potential and actual, and the exploits of the OSS had been glamorized by such movies as *13 Rue Madeleine,* which starred James Cagney. But in the years following the end of World War II, America's and England's consciousness of the enemy within grew enormously. In 1951 fears of Communist subversion had been heightened by the activities of Senator Joseph McCarthy and then Representative Richard Nixon and their followers. The Rosenbergs were convicted of stealing atomic secrets and were executed for this crime. Alger Hiss, a former minor official in the State Department during the early years of the war, was accused of passing state secrets along to the Russians and was convicted of perjury in a second trial related to his putative treason. In Great Britain, meanwhile, atomic scientist Klaus Fuchs was found to have been informing the Russians about Western bomb technology, and Kim Philby and his friends Guy Burgess and Donald Maclean were discovered to be active Russian agents operating within the British intelligence apparatus. In 1952 a Russian cipher specialist stationed in Canada defected to the West, carrying an encyclopedia of espionage information with him. Igor Gouzenko was to provide Western intelligence operatives with an enormous amount of invaluable data, but he was also to heighten the West's popular apprehensions about the espionage activities of those on the other side of the "curtain."

Background to Danger owes much to Buchan's *Thirty-Nine Steps,* a short narrative which Ambler, in the "footnote" to *Epitaph for a Spy,* listed as one of those spy stories that demonstrate best the possibilities of the genre (1952, p. 263). (The others are Childers's *Riddle of the Sands,* Conrad's *Secret Agent,* and Maugham's *Ashenden.*) Buchan's hero—and this is an apt descriptive term in the case of *The Thirty-Nine Steps,* rather than merely main character or protagonist—is a visitor to London from South Africa. Richard Hannay is very much a fish out of water in the big city, away from the veldt. He describes himself, at thirty-seven, as "the best-bored man in the United Kingdom." But when Hannay returns to his flat one afternoon, he is approached by an American renting the room above, with a riveting story to tell. On a later night, when Hannay enters his flat, he finds the American flat on his back, a knife through his heart.

In *Background to Danger,* the person whose adventures we follow throughout the story is much less a hero than Hannay; nevertheless, these characters are related. Ambler's Kenton is also a bored neutral at the tale's beginning. Having lost all his money to another journalist in Nuremberg, he would have taken the Orient Express but settled for an affordable local train to Vienna to borrow money from friends when he is approached by a crumpled, grubby man who shares his compartment. Would Kenton do him a favor? Would he carry some documents across the German border near Linz for him, in return for 300 marks? Needing the money, Kenton agrees, and now the plot noticeably thickens. Herr Sachs is being followed, and to avoid the Gestapo—who, he says, are his pursuers—he begs Kenton to meet him in the Hotel Josef in Linz, for another 300 marks. Reluctantly, the reporter agrees. Later, at the hotel, he, too, like Hannay, is thrust violently into the midst of an international intrigue when he finds the mysterious Herr Sachs on the floor of his room, a knife in his side.

Both Kenton and Hannay are disinterested amateurs at the beginning of their adventures, but both become quickly involved, Hannay for the sake of adventure and to save the life of that honest man Karolides, Kenton because he quickly finds himself wanted for the murder of a German fugitive (Hannay is also wanted by the police for murder). And both men find themselves the victims of intrigues choreographed by professionals: the spy ring Hannay must expose is known melodramatically as the Black Stone, while Kenton's enemies are led by the deadly mercenary and confidential agent Stefan Saridza, alias Colonel Robinson. But more of him later. Almost from the start Hannay is able to cope with the dangers of his situation, first in effecting an escape from his flat disguised as the milkman, later while on the run from several enemy agents as well as from his own police, and finally in deciphering the clue that leads to the exposure and capture of the Black Stone. Kenton, on the contrary, is no match for Saridza's forces and is saved more than once by the good offices of the professional friendlies, in this case the Russian secret agent Andreas Zaleshoff.

Whatever stirs the hero from his lethargy at the beginning of the adventure, commitment to a cause, patriotism, or simply "the right," impels him once the action is underway. Hannay has been bored with his life in London, but after his adventurous spirit is roused by the murder of Scudder, he becomes a man driven to defeat the minions of the Black Stone. In the last chapters of *The Thirty-Nine Steps* Hannay has taken charge of the hunt, directing both Scotland Yard and the admiralty. Ambler's Kenton plays a more modest role, seldom being more than an interested bystander while the Zaleshoffs and their agents recapture their crucial documents: Kenton's role remains minor, though he gradually becomes deeply committed in the spook war around him. It is a scenario which tells us that though we readers are not professionals, such adventures are possible in the most routine of lives, and it enables us to see what events motivate men, from ennui to *engagement*. It is the pattern Ian Fleming will use again and again to show us how his jaded superagent psyches himself up for yet another mission. It is the condition of Childers's Carruthers, suffering through "the dismal but dignified routine of office, club, and chambers" (*The Riddle of the Sands,* p. 16), who will shortly risk his life to discover the riddle of the sands. By these means does an author signal the reader that the forthcoming adventure will be compelling. This movement, from boredom to involvement, is so prevalent and so natural a thrust for this genre, that we need not worry about direct attribution; it is simply one of the best ways to tell an adventure story. It prepares the reader for the exciting adventure to come, signaling that the author is about to exit the everyday-life world into the dark and dangerous universe of spy wars.

So, too, when Kenton helps to foil a plot that will permit the enemy to appropriate the Bessarabian oil fields, Ambler is following the spy novel's early tradition of presenting the threat in global terms. The enemy in the contemporary spy story has more limited, more realistic goals. Ambler's villain, Stefan Saridza, has the conventional mark of the evil man, a deformity: "on every occasion on which Saridza has been identified it has been through the fact that his left arm is incapable of full articulation at the elbow. This disability produces an unmistakable awkwardness in the use of the arm" (1973, p. 27). The chief of the Black Stone, also called by Buchan the "bald archaeologist," has quite another distinguishing trait: he "could hood his eyes like a hawk" (1915*b*, p. 77). In Hitchcock's movie version, two joints of his finger are missing.

Both Hannay and Kenton are captured by the enemy when they are the hunted; both effect narrow escapes, Buchan's hero through the luck of finding explosives in the barn in which he is locked, Ambler's with the aid of Andreas Zaleshoff, whose determination brings off the eleventh-hour rescue. In both novels the victim-hero of the first episodes becomes the hunter later on, but not until both have spent their time on the run, Kenton escaping across the Austrian border into Czechoslovakia, Hannay through the English countryside. *The Thirty-Nine Steps* and *Background to Danger* end, appropriately, near the moment of highest tension, at the apprehension of the Black Stone and the capture of Saridza.

None of this accumulation of similarities proves that Ambler based *Background to Danger* on *The Thirty-Nine Steps,* but we know that in 1937 Ambler could draw upon an extensive spy fiction tradition that had already been established, in large part by the influence of Buchan's work. Many novels depict the involved amateur caught up in a net of intrigue and espionage who soon comes to be a dedicated combatant; many novels had the hero thwart the other side's monstrous plot, but not until he had been captured, had effected a narrow escape, had been on the run, and had finally himself become the hunter. Buchan was not alone in the use of these formulas, but he was one of the first widely read writers to exploit them fully. Ambler had read *The Thirty-Nine Steps,* of course, but he had also read a number of its contemporaries, with their repeated use of narrative formulas, and his first several books reflect their imprint.

Spy novelists are often conservative in their politics, at the least patriotic in a narrow sense, if we are to accept the political stances of their heroes as being even vaguely their own. In his prewar novels, Ambler was more of an anti-Fascist than a British nationalist, and this placed him close to Russia in sympathies. But his leftist inclinations included a dislike of greedy capitalists, a strain that runs, though subdued, through *Background to Danger.* The plot of the enemy in this story involves the release of Soviet contingency plans for the invasion of Rumania to the Rumanian press. Though the plans are outdated, are merely contingency plans, and do not reflect Russia's real intentions toward her southern neighbor, the publicity that would result is intended by the plotters— Pan Eurasian Petroleum and their agent, Saridza—to throw the country into turmoil, enabling rightists sympathetic to Pan Eurasian's designs on Rumanian oil fields to take control of the country.

Significantly, the novel begins not in Rumania (or on the train to Linz) but in the corporate headquarters of Pan Eurasian in London. (Did Frederick Forsyth have this book in mind when he began *The Dogs of War* in a London corporate board-room?) Joseph Balterghen is "a very small man," "anything but pleasing to the eye," having once been described by an associate as looking like "a bunch of putty-coloured grapes with some of the crevices filled in" (*Background to Danger,* p. 1). His second secretary, Blundell, describes his employer's office to his wife as "a harlot's parlour," concluding that "even if you didn't know from experience what a complete wart the man is, that room would tell you" (p. 2). Ambler's portrait is not subtle, nor is the directors' meeting convincingly portrayed. Lord Welterfield, broadly drawn as a buffoon to contrast with Balterghen's cunning and efficient deceit, arrives forty-five minutes late, blustering, just in time for the chairman's evaluation of the company's Russian problems.

Pan Eurasian agents had been able to bribe enough highly placed officials to have existing oil concession leases revised—in their favor. But when denounced by a Bucharest newspaper, despite terrorists' attacks to prevent publication, motions for lease revision were tabled. Faced with this probable defeat of his schemes, Balterghen proposes hiring a propagandist, Colonel Robinson, to correct the situation. On learning that the newspaper in question was *The Work People,* Lord Welterfield denounces them as "Reds!" Balterghen corrects him: "actually . . . the United Socialists are not affiliated to the Communist International; but they are, I agree, very much to the Left" (p. 5). To Lord Welterfield, however, they are the "same thing." Colonel Robinson's credentials, his plans, and his methods are of no interest to Welterfield, "as long as the fellow isn't a Red, he can call himself anything he likes as far as I'm concerned" (p. 7).

Zaleshoff is more specific on the matter of Saridza and generally on businessmen, stating explicitly what we only felt strongly from the first pages:

> They say that persons like Al Capone and John Dillinger are products of America's corrupt administration and clumsy lawmaking. Saridza and his kind must be products of the world business system. The principal differences between Al Capone and Stefan Saridza is that while Capone worked for himself, Saridza works for other people. When Capone ordered his hoodlums to machine-gun a couple of men on the side-walk from an armour-plated coupe, it was to maintain or increase his own income. When Saridza ordered that Captain to beat you [Kenton] with a totschlager until you give him some photographs, it was to increase the income of what are called his principals in London. . . . You see, your business man desires the end, but dislikes the means. . . . That is why Saridza is necessary. . . . There is always dirty work to be done . . . but whatever it is, Saridza and his kind are there to do it, with large fees in their pockets and the most evasive instructions imaginable. (*Background to Danger,* pp. 11–12)

These are the words of Zaleshoff and not necessarily Ambler's own, but the Russian is the leader of the positive forces in the novel and carries, therefore, a heavy moral weight. He is again the champion of Good in *Cause for Alarm,* where he not only foils the Fascist enemy but aids their intended victim, the English protagonist Nicholas Marlow. Moreover, the "other side" is not allowed political statements of the kind Zaleshoff makes. We are led, then, by the action as well as by such explicit statements from the characters to infer which side, which politics, and which morality Ambler, and we, should admire.

After the war Ambler seems to have had a momentary period of disillusionment with the Russian empire, if we can judge his feelings at all from his first postwar fiction, *Judgment on Delchev* (1951). Actually the locale of the action is an unnamed Socialist nation in the Balkans; Yordan Delchev, leader of the former underground resistance to German occupation, president and secretary-general of the Provisional Government of National Unity at the war's end, and the most prominent member of the Agrarian Socialist party, is accused at the moment of the story of complicity with the reactionary Officer Corps Brotherhood, of "treason and the preparation of a terrorist plot to assassinate the head of the state" (1977, pp. 1–2).

Once again Ambler's protagonist is a journalist, again English (though the journalist is Dutch in *A Kind of Anger*), and the plots and counterplots unfold through his investigation of the background of the Delchev trial. We begin by feeling that Yordan is innocent, but eventually learn that his son, Philip, is part of an Officer Corps Brotherhood plot to assassinate the head of the People's party, Vukashin. The plotters have been infiltrated by a mysterious but very competent newcomer, Aleko, who almost at once improves on the murder plan. Philip and two accomplices are to wait on a roof for Vukashin to review a parade and kill him during the festivities. But when other members of the brotherhood discover that the gun given Philip for the murder does not have a firing pin, even more sinister aspects of the plot emerge. Pashik, the journalist Foster's guide through Balkan mazes and unwilling member of the brotherhood, correctly guesses that Aleko's real target is his temporary master Rankovich, minister of propaganda, and that this change in loyalty has come about because Aleko's cunning intuition has told him that he has a better chance of survival by serving Vukashin. Philip, only ostensibly a co-conspirator, is to be made the scapegoat of the murder and, according to the plan, is to die with his more famous father.

Little in this plot—which is actually more convoluted than this brief summary indicates—condemns Leftist politics specifically; and while it does take place in a Balkan Communist country (never named), Communists and communism per se are not explicitly criticized. Nevertheless, one feels that the lethal milieu Ambler describes could only happen in a postwar communist regime. Though only obliquely expressed, *Judgment on Delchev* marks Ambler's disenchantment with Russian political influences. The novels that follow usually steer clear of politics, though *The Levanter* is modestly sectarian. Placed in the Middle East—like many others, Ambler sets his tales in currently exotic and newsworthy locales—the Palestinian terrorists are depicted as irresponsible and murderous, but the Israelis are scarcely shown at all. Rather than being a political novel, *The Levanter* is, as much as anything, simply a good story of intrigue pitting a greedy, clever merchant against coercive terrorists who want to use him and his organization to further their own ends. In the end, the rapacious Michael Howell triumphs, but his victory is over those who get in his way, and the fact that they are Palestinians is not a political judgment. *The Levanter*'s theme—of the destructive power of aggressive capitalists—is a restatement of the political philosophy expressed in *Background to Danger*. Despite his disenchantment with Russia and her satellites, he remains something of a "lefrie."

The locales of other postwar novels have been influenced by news headlines. *Passage of Arms* (1960) follows the efforts of Girija Krishnan, who has stumbled upon a Communist weapons cache in Malaya, to sell his found treasure and set up his own bus company. *Doctor Frigo* (1974), one of Ambler's least successful efforts, is involved with a revolution in the French Antilles. We are taken to the Middle Eastern theater in *The Levanter* (1972), as we have just noted and as the title indicates. *State of Siege* (1956) returns to Asia in turmoil; *Dirty Story* (1967) follows through on the further adventures of Arthur Abdel Simpson, the victim-hero of *The Light of Day* (1963), also known in the American edition and movie as *Topkapi.*

The partisan politics of the real world are absent from all of these novels; Ambler has always placed his character in the borderlands of danger, the natural habitat of the spy and international intrigue. In these marginal areas the law is weak and order is shaky. Everything is in flux, and nearly anything is possible. This vision of liminal regions owes its debt, ultimately, to Cooper's *The Spy.* Before World War II the Balkans was the area of greatest intrigue, the Mediterranean in general a close second. After the war, the no-man's-land fraught with danger and the lawlessness that inspired intrigue and duplicity had shifted: for Ambler, as for so many other spy novelists, it was the Middle East, Africa, and Asia. *Judgment on Delchev* and *The Schirmer Inheritance* (1953) are the last times that the Balkans will hold any exoticism and adventure for him.

Eric Ambler's interest in the sense of place is remarkably superficial. He is seldom able—he seldom bothers?—to describe vividly even the exotic places where his characters operate. In *A Coffin for Dimitrios,* for instance, though the search takes us all through the Balkans with stops at Sofia and Bucharest, Ambler gives us no sense of what it is like to be there, not even any idea of what these exotic places are like. Not even Istanbul, where the action is at first set, is given any life. We are merely told that Latimer was in Sofia, or Bucharest, and finally Paris. Everything is left to the reader to imagine, except in the French capital which alone comes in for some descriptive attention. Istanbul, Sofia, and the rest—they are hermetic names without the scent or the sight or the sense of what it may be like to have been there; all the more disappointing, since Ambler has obviously chosen these cities because of their exotic associations. He must have felt that merely mentioning their names would suffice to evoke an exotic and mysterious presence.

If Ambler's descriptive powers are frequently flagging, he was unquestionably a master of the espionage novel's formulas. Ambler's prewar novels characteristically enmesh the pivotal figure in situations he cannot cope with, making him a victim rather than a quester. The relative helplessness of Kenton has already become standardized. *Epitaph for a Spy*'s central character is a most unlikely hero, a language teacher on vacation in southern France. He is, to further complicate his situation and to enhance the plot, a stateless person, from whose camera photographs of secret naval installations have been taken. *A Coffin for Dimitrios* features a writer, Charles Latimer, so intrigued by the personality of the title character that he tracks him down across the Mediterranean, through the Balkans into Switzerland and finally confronts him in Paris. But character, certainly the hero's character, is decidedly subordinated to adventure and to exotic locales—though these are barely described. So too with the English engineer, Nicky Marlow, in *Cause for Alarm;* so too the hale fellow Andreas Zaleshoff is rather conventionally and stereotypically portrayed. Stefan Saridza is almost wickedness personified, a villain without socially redeeming features, contrasting as the evil genius of the other side with his sadistic, coarse, brutal aide, Captain Mailer.

But by the time Ambler started writing again in the fifties he was paying even closer attention to his characters as individuals with some psychological complexities. Delchev is no hero of melodrama. His son is a fascist gunman; he is filled with self-doubts about his own nobility, and he hesitates, fatally, to fulfill his promise to his people for free elections: "Is it because," he asks himself, "you know that in your heart that you have become corrupt and that these reasons you invent for keeping power in your hands are mere devices to conceal the fact?" (p. 228). In *A Kind of Anger* (1964) a Dutch freelance reporter, Piet Maas, is assigned to cover a story about the wife of a recently murdered Iraqi official, alleged to have in her possession extremely valuable and saleable state secrets. Though Ambler tells us that Maas has a record of mental instability, which might add to our interest in him, he performs quite efficiently in the narrative. He finds Madame Arbil when no one else can, assists her in selling her secrets for a handsome profit, and becomes her lover: not like Ambler's usual main characters. The *Intercom Affair* has, possibly, Ambler's most distinctive plot: two NATO intelligence officers buy a Swiss technical newsletter and publish NATO secrets in it in the expectation of being bought out by the CIA. The editor of the previously innocuous journal *Intercom* is an irascible expatriate whom Ambler brings gradually, and often amusingly, to an awareness of what is happening to his journal and consequently to him. These people, Delchev, Maas, and *Intercom*'s editor, are given a dimension of personality and character missing from Ambler's early work. Arthur Abdel Simpson was such a successful victim-hero in *The Light of Day* (1963) that Ambler starred him again in *Dirty Story,* and despite the use of tried formulas (Simpson, like *Epitaph*'s protagonist, is a stateless person, a defensive wimp who makes a natural victim) and a newsworthy setting (a revolution in Africa) this sequel to Simpson's adventures seems to have fallen somewhat on its face. As a memorable character in the prewar stories, only Dimitrios is genuinely noteworthy, and he is offstage for nearly the entire novel; what we learn about him is as lethal as it is interesting, though nearly all of that is related by others. Aside from him, only Zaleshoff stands out from the stereotypes.

As must already be clear, Ambler had given a lot of thought to his plots as well between *Journey into Fear* and *Judgment on Delchev,* though the latter novel still employs the basic strategy of the innocent (writer or reporter) tracking down a character, plot, or story, as in *A Coffin for Dimitrios,* and revealing to the reader the many twists and convolutions, deceptions and surprises of his plots as his writer discovers them. It is with the less successful *State of Siege* (1956) that Ambler begins to vary the plot structures that his predecessors and he had found so successful. Here the setting is Asian, the situation a civil war, the characters Western and trapped as much by intrigue as by gunfire. *Passage of Arms* (1960) also departs from Ambler's previous plots, as we have seen, and *The Light of Day* (*Topkapi,*

1963)—one of his most successful—is not a spy story at all, but rather an account of the elaborate attempt to steal the Turkish national treasures from Istanbul's Topkapi museum. And though not always successful, Ambler has continued to produce plots that present their characters and their information in distinctive ways. Since *The Schirmer Inheritance* (1953), he has not used the formula of the writer trying to uncover a mystery: George Carey, the sleuth of this novel, is a variation on the pattern, a Philadelphia lawyer tracking down the heir to the Schirmer fortune. The first interesting woman in Ambler's fiction debuts in this novel, the earthily sensual interpreter, Miss Kolin, who has remained dispassionately aloof throughout until, on impulse, she gives herself with enthusiastic passion to the quarry, Sgt. Franz Schirmer.

Though Miss Kolin is the first of Ambler's characters to have anything of a sex life, it is quite briefly described; in this respect, as in many others, Ambler makes few concessions to the directions in which the contemporary spy novel will move. Sex is sparse, as his plots focus directly on the more important elements of intrigue and adventure. The obvious exception is Piet Maas, the sleuth-reporter of *A Kind of Anger,* who becomes the lover of the widow Arbil during the intricate process of selling her late husband's state secrets to the highest bidders, but with near impeccable discretion, Ambler has them conduct their private lives off the pages. As a formula writer, he will not let his characters' passion interfere with the suspense of the story. Actually, the close relationship between Piet and Lucia becomes a part of the plot, a convincing justification for several of their other actions. But this is one of the few exceptions, and in this respect, as in several others, though Ambler had changed somewhat with the times, he never carried his characters and their plots quite as far as a number of others who first began writing after the war. James Bond seduces nearly all of the women he desires; Ambler's spies are rarely given those desires.

Buchan's heroes were very much in control of their destinies, so it seemed, for despite the danger that continually threatened him, Hannay always extricated himself with relative ease: with a cunning disguise, the lucky discovery of an explosive carelessly stored in the barn in which he was imprisoned, that glib and oily art which enabled him to pass himself off as a political orator with almost no preparation. And his supreme confidence in himself is shared by those around him, even staff officers of the admiralty, who incredibly permit Hannay to take command of the operation to crush the Black Stone. Ambler's and Greene's early heroes are rather ordinary, far less than heroic amateurs, undistinguished people caught up in intrigues in which they need professional help either from the police or from friendly agents. And they are more believable for that. Exceptions are rare: *Passage of Arms* (1960) narrates the adventures of the very capable Girija Krishnan who, though also naive in the matters of international arms negotiations, nevertheless deals with the professionals on at least equal terms. In the end he gets his bus company, not bad for a rubber-estate clerk.

Those characters of formula fiction who seem most real to us, who seem to have lives quite independent of their fictional plots, have been invested with complexities and ambiguities that lift them out of the formulaic plots where we found them. Thus does the writer of formula fiction charge his characters with life. Graham Greene has always succeeded in infusing his people with a vital sense of reality—but that point has been made and illustrated throughout. It is one of the most salient features that raise him above the level of spy novelist to the writer of fiction of the highest merit whose characters happen to be spies.

Graham Greene's world vision altered less dramatically than did Ambler's during the war, if we are to take his writing as witness. Of his early "entertainments"—*Stamboul Train* (1932), *A Gun for Sale* (1936), *The Confidential Agent* (1939), and *The Ministry of Fear* (1943)—only the last two are really about spies, though the former pair use settings that can be vaguely called "international intrigue," and so marginally qualify for discussion here. Those earliest novels can also be classified as readily as crime/detective stories, one of the instances in which the two genres overlap. They are not heavily formulaic throughout, suggesting that Greene worked from conventional mainstream plot structures toward the spy novel formula only after he had considerable experience in writing.

The Confidential Agent anticipated much of the direction of the postwar spy novel and in several ways was to be a model for *The Human Factor* (1978). Ambler introduced to the spy story the hero enmeshed in intrigues too intricate and dangerous for him to deal with alone; Greene gave such a character (identified only as "D") a life that could be extended in the reader's imagination beyond his fictional habitat; he lived. How many of Ambler's characters (such as Arthur Simpson) do we remember two months after we have put down the novel? How many readers can forget about D or Maurice Castle? Greene's people have "the sense of life as it is lived" (his own standard, articulated in *Ways of Escape*, p. 209); they have vitality because they have human flaws—endearing, engaging flaws. We are drawn to them as compassion draws us to all vulnerable creatures.

Because Graham Greene was interested primarily in character in the early novels, and did not fully exploit the potentials of formulas, the outlines of the mature writer are visible in the skyline of the younger. *Stamboul Train,* written without actual experience with the real train (he couldn't afford to ride it, he says, but took his inspiration from listening to a recording of Honegger's *Pacific 231* [*Escape,* pp. 22–23]), tests the character of Jewish businessman Carlton Myatt and chorus line dancer Coral Musker on a liminal train ride into Yugoslavia. Political implications are represented in Dr. Czinner, an exiled Communist leader, on the express to return to his country. The train is stopped at the border, and Czinner and Musker are among the small group taken off. Coral is politically innocent, but Czinner has a political—and an ethical—manifesto to declare to his captors: how old-fashioned is your patriotism! (p. 165). To him, as to Greene, the world was "out of joint" (p. 169).

As happens in several of Greene's novels, two or three characters are brought together, physically, in a dramatic scene that tests them ultimately. The detainees are put into a convenient shed while the express rolls further down the track toward Belgrade. Czinner convinces the others with him that they should all try to escape. But the old Communist's feet are not as swift as his brain, and he is wounded and eventually recaptured. But while he lies dying Coral ministers to him, as best she can in the dark and the cold, expressing the compassion that has been in her from the beginning.

The railroad siding shed is the locale of the "key scene" in *Stamboul Train,* as is another shed in *A Gun for Sale* and the guerrilla's hut in *The Honorary Consul.* Yet *A Gun for Sale* has an even more important enclosure, the empty house where Raven (whose gun is for hire or sale) spirits Anne Crowder. He is on the run, having committed at the novel's opening moments a political murder; of vital importance to millions of others, it is indifferent to him. It was just another job, another paid commission. Greene made Raven, with his blatant harelip, out to revenge himself against what he reckoned as all of society's dirty tricks. He is, as Greene later realized, a "first sketch" of *Brighton Rock's* "Pinkie." Raven learns from Anne—who does care—that the man he has killed was a good, kind, compassionate leader, something of a populist. Raven is a frustrated, angry man, embittered by life in general, but now he wants revenge against those who hired him to assassinate his victim. And though on the run from the police, the hunted becomes hunter, and Raven sets out after his "employer," Sir Marcus. As Greene tells us in *Ways of Escape* (p. 55), the type of Sir Marcus is the villain for today.

Thus, in nearly all of these early books he questions capitalist society, though not acrimoniously nor at didactic length. He does not involve himself in that primary concern of serious spy novelists, an exploration of the implications of clandestinity in a free and open society. His responses were humanistic ones to the Depression and to fascism in Europe, and a rebellion against the smug savagery of the clubland Establishment at home. The corruption of his characters was of primary concern to him from the first, though in the later novels evil does not merely compete with innocence (and get to shoot it down, as Raven does Sir Marcus), evil destroys it. These early novels stop short of such catastrophes.

Greene did not pioneer the hero as victim in his fiction, but he is the first important writer whose hero's mission fails (well, almost fails; in the end it is a standoff with the mission of the agent of the other side). Heroics per se are slighted and even denigrated in these early books. Both sides are nearly equally culpable; the right is not at all easy to discern from the unjust. D reflects that "the people were certainly sold out by their leaders. . . . There was no trust anywhere. All over the world there were people like himself who didn't believe in being corrupted—simply because it made life impossible—as when a man or woman cannot tell the truth about anything" (*Confidential Agent,* p. 32). Greene examined loyalty and betrayal in D's thoughts just as he did four decades later in Castle's; their responses, their situations, more than any other features, mark Greene's fictional direction. When Rose questions the grounds of his loyalty to his country, D replies, "it's they, you know, who are always talking about something called our country" (p. 60). Rose keeps after him: "Then why don't you take their money?" To which Greene's hero declares his personal code of honor, the code that keeps him sane and committed: "you've got to choose some line of action and live by it. Otherwise nothing matters at all."

The Confidential Agent (1939) has remained one of its author's favorites. A formula spy story, it is nevertheless not like the models established by Buchan, Oppenheim, and the early Ambler. Greene would need the war to change him, but, to repeat, the change would not be great, since his interests were less with sectarian politics than with people's problems and their responses. *The Confidential Agent* already shows the direction of the mature Greene. Unlike Raven, D has matured, has accepted much of life, though his problems are more internal; unlike Raven, who hates the world and seeks revenge against it, D has to come to terms with interiorized problems of his own creation—with what life without the woman he has loved must hold for him and the realities of political life. Raven has been ignorant of politics and pretty much of the world around him, except as it relates directly and immediately to his safety and his comfort.

Czinner is D's prototype. When Greene chooses to kill him off near that book's conclusion, he does not in a major way alter the thrust of the story, since Czinner is secondary to Myatt and Musker, and the old radical's death functions primarily to illustrate the necessary responses in her. In *The Confidential Agent,* D's death would have changed the book radically. This novel is less about revenge and hatred than it is about coming to terms, compassionately, with violence and moral vacuum.

Still, D is one of the earliest examples of the spy who came in from the cold a failure, the humanized spy, one who learned that some things are more important than confidential missions, and who lived to tell about it. In contrast, Ambler's heroes were "humanized"—reduced in heroic stature—and always succeeded, with outside help, because their author was interested in the successful plot conclusion. Character being Greene's primary concern, and not formulaic endings so much, D is made to fail, but in the process gains an incentive to renew his life. This is the prewar-postwar contrast in Greene's writing, between *The Confidential Agent* and *The Human Factor.* In the early book D struggles to preserve the self through his political stance refined by his personal code; in the later novel Castle and Sarah are their own "countries" to which they are exclusively loyal. In the intervening four decades Greene had learned to value the power and the stabilizing sinews of love.

D has been debilitated by the memory of his deceased wife and the fulfilling life they led together. He does not have much energy either for the present or for the future until he is, first, driven to impassioned action when he learns of the death of the innocent Else (unlike the later Eduardo Plarr, he will be able to do something about it) and then when he is rescued, physically and spiritually, by Rose. She remarks of D's love for his former wife, "when you are dead, she can have you. I can't compete then. . . . you'll be dead very soon: you needn't tell me that but *now* . . ." (p. 206). Castle's love for Sarah has given his life a center and a structure. She has become his "country," deserving all of the loyalty and devotion that that entity traditionally evokes, but this love has also allowed the germ of corruption to enter.

In characterization, primarily, Graham Greene's abilities as a writer remove him from the class of formulaic novelists. And he would, no doubt, as much despise being called and thought of as a "spy novelist" as he resents the label "Catholic writer." D and Maurice Castle have rich dimensions as characters; they are so humanly multifaceted that plots coagulate around them; they do not exist merely to fill up slots in fictional structures. D is timid and ineffectual at first, a specialist in his former University Lecturer days on *The Song of Roland*. The relationship is not farfetched: both he and Roland are losers. The difference is equally patent: Roland dies heroically, choosing to stand with his people—among whom there is no questioning of loyalty—for a cause. Yet the comparison does not end there. D laments his solitary state, while Roland, at least, could die among friends, in fact chooses to die among his countrymen. But what did Roland die for? Country? Personal honor? D has rejected the former and his own highly evolved concept of personal honor is very different from that of the hero of the *Chanson*. The death of the innocent Else at the hands of the other side abruptly thrusts D from his spiritual torpor into vengeful activity; the hunted becomes the hunter. By the novel's end he is once again the hunted, but by then he has fought an active fight, and he has made contact with another human being—one of Roland's seeming failures—and that will sustain him.

The Human Factor does not end so gratifyingly for Maurice Castle. He had become involved with the Communists when he fell in love with one of their agents; they got her safely out of South Africa and in return Castle gave them secrets of state that passed over his desk. But secrets relating to Africa only— that is the limit of his defection. British counterintelligence and a visitor from its South African counterpart close in, though at first on the wrong man. To whom should Castle be loyal? The South African who despises his black wife, the English for whom he works but who kill, with terrible casualness, his friend who is mistakenly thought to be the "leak"? Or the Communists? In the end they turn out to be exploiting him more callously than his own agency. In *The Confidential Agent* Greene wanted to create the predicament of the agent with scruples who is not trusted by his own party and who realizes that his party is right not to trust him (*Escape*, pp. 70–71); Castle's confusion about the "right" party is even more convoluted. Unlike D, Castle's conflicting obligations force him to act duplicitously merely in order to survive. In the last moments of this superb novel Castle is spirited away to Moscow where, his usefulness as a source of information at an end, he is condescended to and for the most part forgotten. Castle had long before realized that "each side shares the same clichés" (p. 129), but he and Sarah were their own country (they had just as long ago decided) and to that country Castle owed his primary, overmastering allegiance.

Greene knew Kim Philby personally. They had served together in the Iberian section of SIS during the war. And when Philby's memoirs were published in England, Greene wrote the Introduction. Whether or not, as LeRoy Panek thinks (*The Special Branch*, p. 134), Philby is the model for Maurice Castle, in the making of this particular fiction it hardly matters. In any event Greene has explicitly denied the Philby-Castle connection. He says that he began writing *The Human Factor* before the Philby affair; the West's most notorious defector disappeared from Beirut in January 1963 after revelations in England convincingly identified him as an officer of the KGB. Because of the attendant sensation, Greene abandoned his novel, pointing out that Castle was not in the least like Philby and that he did not want it to be taken as a roman á clef (*Escape*, p. 228).

Two sentences of Joseph Conrad's are quoted in the epigraph: "I only know that he who forms a tie is lost. The germ of corruption has entered into his soul." That is the problem with the human factor; it cannot be predicted or controlled as precisely as some would like. As in his earlier work, allusions to medieval literary characters are important. Dr. Percival is Castle's bête noir, a high-ranking officer in the agency's bureaucracy. But unlike the Percival of medieval narrative, whose compassion finally enables him to attain the Holy Grail, this Percival arranges the death of agent Davis on his own intuition of his guilt. No conclusive proof is gathered (it does not exist), no trial is held, Davis is never allowed to confront his accuser. This Percival is a blundering, callous executioner; when his medieval namesake had to kill, it was in the name of God.

If "Percival" is meaningful, what of Maurice's surname? Castle reflects, "a man in love walks through the world like an anarchist carrying a time bomb" (p. 155). Did Greene have Conrad's bomb-toting anarchist in mind? But love is not the only human factor; Castle had once told his Russian case officer, Boris, "you'd do much better to employ a man who doesn't hate. . . . Hate's liable to make mistakes. It's as dangerous as love. I'm doubly dangerous, Boris, because I love too. Love's a fault in both our services" (p. 131).

Greene has confessed that as a young man he had been an admirer of the fiction of John Buchan (*Escape*, p. 54)—how often that name appears in the biographical writing of the important espionage novelists! But by the 1940s Buchan's mawkish sentiments and those of his pivotal character, Richard Hannay, had become dated. For Greene, as for the rest of us—but for him more sensitively than for us—the world had changed too much. Mussolini had risen to power in Italy, as had Franco in Spain, Stalin in Russia, and Hitler in Germany. Greene writes that one could no longer believe in the kind of simple, direct patriotism of Hannay and his creator, nor in many of Buchan's sentiments.

While Ambler once quipped about himself that he had always been "something of a leftie," Greene was for a few weeks a member of the Communist party. It was a lark, he now writes. Nevertheless, his association was thought to be sufficiently close by American authorities that he was classed according to the McCarran Act (in 1954) as a "prohibited immigrant." Almost nothing in Greene's writing, however, reveals any Communist doctrine. He has always been concerned most of all with human rather than with sectarian political problems—with guilt, evil, salvation, and suffering. His "entertainments" incisively explore the individual's loyalty and the issues of faith and betrayal. These themes, of course, are no more Communist than the concerns of any political (or economic) system. Since he has never appeared doctrinaire in his writings (D was presumably the confidential agent of the Royalist, anti-Fascist side in the Spanish Civil War, but was disillusioned with both sides) he did not noticeably turn away from any system or toward its opposite after the surrender of Germany and Japan in 1945. Neither side is the winner of *The Human Factor;* in the end, the Russians effect Castle's escape to Moscow, but after a widely broadcast propaganda press conference, they proceed to neglect him, into oblivion. A call is finally put through between Sarah in England and Maurice; he reaffirms his love and urges her not to give up hope. But the call is interrupted: "In the long unbroken silence which followed she realized that the line to Moscow was dead" (p. 302).

One of his stories about innocence betrayed is *The Honorary Consul* (1973). Innocent, innocuous Charley Fortnum is kidnapped and held for ransom by guerrillas in Latin America; in the end his friend (and the seducer of his wife), Eduardo Plarr, also politically innocent, is gunned down after having tried to save Charley. Terrorism, violence against the innocent, savage ideologues (often fighting for worthy causes) had by that time become part of the formula writer's repertoire. Greene, as he would so often, exploited narrative formulas to express profoundly human problems. Formulas are the vehicles of character and personality. Greene saw that no plots are "new" anymore and that human situations are as nearly repetitive. Character is individual, unique; that holds his interest, and that becomes the focus of his writing. In *The Honorary Consul* the reader is left with feelings appropriate to the terrible injustice of the slaughter of innocents (anticipating our reactions to recent victims of hijackings) and of individual personalities caught in an absurd and mortal situation; generic aspects of the novel are submerged in the face of these transcendent concerns.

Along with *The Confidential Agent, The Honorary Consul* remains one of Greene's favorites. He has stated, diffidently so it would seem, that while all of his early novels lacked life, *The Honorary Consul* has been worth his rereading. He has said that he prefers it to all of his others (*Escape,* p. 228). The world has changed since the days of John Buchan, even since the days of *Stamboul Train*. Success and failure as they are traditionally conceived are no longer serious issues. Charley Fortnum is a hapless alcoholic, only ceremonially a consulate officer. He is kidnapped by mistake; what careful political guerrillas would bother with him? A callous local administration will not do enough to rescue him. The murder of Fortnum is politically meaningless; it has value—human value—only in that it arouses his casual friend Eduardo Plarr to try to save him. Plarr fails, but in his dying attempt he redeems himself and thus gives value to Fortnum's life. This very basic narrative philosophy—giving meaning to a life and to one's principles through sacrifice—is one that will later inspire several of John le Carré's novels.

Plot and counterplot have always been a part of Ambler's arsenal; the surprise turn of events, the man or woman who is not at all what he or she seems, the reversal, the gradual unfolding of a conspiracy which turns our expectations around—all these Ambler has mastered from the first. But his world has never been as insidious as, say, that of the British agency in *The Looking Glass War* (or as riddled with insecurities and inefficiency). Despite the fact that Maas's employer has called him a psycho, that Michael Howell of *The Levanter* is a bloodless, amoral merchant egoist, that Dr. Frigo is, as his name implies, frozen meat—despite these explorations of Ambler's into more interesting characterization, he has not written about psychotics or such people as in *Black Sunday, The Wind Chill Factor, The Holcroft Covenant, The Chancellor Manuscript,* or *Marathon Man.* Man's darker side is ignored, while plot is foregrounded. Nor has Ambler been tempted by the more exquisite forms of torture his fellow writers seem to favor; very signif icantly, Stefan Saridza threatens Kenton with a dentist's drill when trying to intimidate him, to make him reveal the whereabouts of the papers, but it remains for William Goldman's Szell in *Marathon Man* (1974) to actually use it.

So, Ambler's postwar phase makes few concessions to the directions taken by other spy story writers. He lacks le Carré's deep questioning of clandestine agencies per se, Len Deighton's glibness and fast-moving action, Trevanian's sadistic cruelty, and Fleming's and Hall's fascination with technology. Ambler and Greene brought the spy novel a long way toward respectability. Ambler has disciplined himself in telling an engaging story of intrigue and suspense. And he has been getting better, now as he nears eighty. Greene has from the first seen the deeper implications raised by the existence of spies and their trade in an open society. He has explored the role of clandestinity in our world and has, perhaps deepest of all, scrutinized the values of loyalty and patriotism, obligation and commitment. More than any spy novelist (in his case especially, a writer who has written spy novels), Greene has returned the spy novel to the mainstream of contemporary fiction. It began as a story of adventure, moved to become a genre in its own right, and by the excellence of some of its most accomplished practitioners is moving back into the main currents of what is simply good fiction. Ambler may be, in the *San Francisco Chronicle*'s extravagant kudos, "the greatest spy novelist of all time." Greene, whose *Human Factor* revived talk of a Nobel prize (futilely), has surely given us, in the words of a UPI reviewer, "the best espionage novel ever written." In the full context of Greene's achievement, this is modest praise.

6 Bonded Excitement: Ian Fleming

Despite Ian Fleming's death in 1964, the James Bond saga marches on. As of this writing (May 1985), it has worked its way through several novelists and film directors, innumerable screenwriters, and two major stars. Only recently, longtime Bond film producer Albert R. ("Cubby") Broccoli announced that he planned to continue the series indefinitely, though Roger Moore, the second Bond star, has announced that he plans to retire from the role after his next production. It is not hard to conjure up a public relations man's dream of an international search for the new James Bond, somewhat along the lines of the quest for an actress to play Scarlett O'Hara. James Bond, then, seems to have become an institution. Each year new Bond films are traditionally released at Christmastime. Is it possible that in years to come James Bond will be annually resurrected along with Santa Claus, Ebenezer Scrooge, and the Nutcracker Suite?

Bond's metamorphosis from best-seller to "phenomenon" (i.e., repeated best-seller) to "institution" (i.e., part of the family's traditional Christmas plans) has been remarkably rapid. Few other figures or personae have done so with anything like this rapidity, Elvis Presley and the Beatles being two of the most notable examples. This cycle of transformed significance is one of the most important patterns of culture. In earlier times, passing through the cycle from person to hero to phenomenon to institution usually took many, many years. However, one of the characteristics of contemporary culture is that, because of the rapidity with which modern media relay images to very large audiences, cultural cycles have greatly accelerated. It remains to be seen whether the contemporary version of this pattern also implies an increasingly rapid disappearance of the images which enter the cycle. In any case, and for the time being, Bond lives.

The great popularity of James Bond has inspired a large critical literature offering explanations of the Bond phenomenon ranging from the theological to the sociological and the psychological. One frequent theme encountered in this maze of interpretation is the idea that Bond is successful because he is an effective reincarnation of some basic mythological or psychological pattern. Without denying the interest in these archetypal speculations, we prefer to explore something more limited as one basis of Bond's striking popularity: his position in the history of the spy story as reincarnation of the heroic spy created by John Buchan and his contemporaries. After the more cynical and realistic version of the clandestine adventure written by Ambler, Greene, and others in the thirties and forties, Fleming correctly sensed that the postwar public was ready for a return to the heroic adventures of a gentleman spy. But he also realized that this figure could not be successfully presented in its original straightforward and moralistic fashion. The public of the 1950s, tired of a devastating war and fearful of a nuclear future, clearly wanted escape, adventure, heroism, and romance but remained suspicious of the pieties, the ascetic moralism, and the high-toned patriotism of the Buchan tradition. Fleming gave this public exactly what it wanted: a heroic spy interested in sex and good living, presented with a strong dose of wit and a large tongue in the cheek. One could enjoy this hero's adventures and affairs without being burdened with a heavy load of political and moral seriousness. *Playboy* magazine, another phenomenon of the fifties, transformed the tradition of the monthly magazine in much the same way that Fleming changed the spy story from a set of images heavily loaded with moral content into stories suffused with an amoral hedonism. In this chapter we will explore how Fleming re-created the heroic spy story in a way more interesting and acceptable to his contemporary public.

The kinship between the adventures of Buchan's Richard Hannay and the missions of James Bond are readily apparent when we compare the two to the typical patterns of action, character, and theme developed by Ambler and Greene. While all of these writers usually employ the basic spy formula of a mission involving a journey into enemy territory, both Fleming and Buchan make their protagonists heroic initiators of action against an enemy conspiracy, while in Ambler and Greene, the protagonist is usually a more or less innocent bystander who is accidentally pulled into a web of intrigue. Once entrapped, the Ambler-Greene protagonist must journey into the enemy's stronghold in order to survive and prove his innocence, while the Fleming-Buchan hero's primary goal is the defeat and destruction of the enemy. To match the heroic actions they are called on to perform, Bond and Hannay are men of extraordinary courage, skill, and endurance. They are at their best when they confront the enemy face-to-face separated from their organization and its technology. Their sagas move toward a climactic scene which usually takes place in an extreme situation or locale, such as the wilderness or in the midst of a battle. Buchan loved to have this final confrontation take place in the mountains, while Fleming invented a variety of locales with a similar function, for example, Blofeld's mountain laboratory in *On Her Majesty's Secret Service,* the underwater battle that climaxes *Thunderball,* or the great attack on Fort Knox in *Goldfinger.* In Ambler and Greene, the protagonist commonly becomes more and more helpless as he is dragged away from his home base and when he confronts the enemy, is usually saved by a lucky accident or the fortunate appearance of the police.

Fleming's stories develop the same pattern of heroic action that Buchan employed, as well as a similar characterization of hero and villain. The conflict is melodramatic and manichaean. Bond and Hannay represent goodness without ambiguity, and they face a series of supremely sinister, evil, and grotesque villains, whose unbridled lusts and cruelty drive them toward world domination. The specific characterizations are also quite close. Bond and Hannay are both gentlemen of the upper-middle class and of relatively mature years. They have cultivated backgrounds and a private income in addition to whatever remuneration they receive for their professional services. Both are at home in the elite circles of their worlds and despite considerable differences in demeanor, particularly with respect to the opposite sex, the aura of the clubland world of the British upper classes clings to them. There is in Joan Rockwell's nice phrase a "ritual frivolity" about their style which establishes them as gentlemen-sportsmen and representatives of an ideal of elite superiority, "an expression" as Rockwell puts it, "of the prime myth of the British upperclass, the delusion that it is a genuine elite, distinguished by an 'effortless superiority.' It does everything better, with no trouble, than the lower orders do with great effort. This belief, which might be called the Pimpernel Syndrome, is persistently displayed in British thriller fiction" ("Normative Attitudes," p. 331).

While the gentleman-hero retains a kind of amateur status, the Fleming-Buchan villain is a professional entrepreneur of evil who falsely aspires to gentility. Despite his numerous scientific, cultural, and organizational accomplishments, it is obvious to the discerning eye that he can never be a gentleman. The villain's basic falsity is symbolized by his dubious racial heritage. Where the hero is pure Anglo-Saxon, the villain is invariably from an "inferior" race or some curious racial mixture. Buchan's supervillains are the Germans von Stumm and von Schwabing, and the sinisterly mixed Spanish-Irish Dominick Medina. Fleming's are such as dastardly Teuton Ernst Stavro Blofeld, Negro Mr. Big, or those curious mixtures, the German-Chinese Dr. No and the polyglot Auric Goldfinger. The blatant racist symbolism that Buchan and Fleming use to establish the fundamental opposition of hero and villain has been eloquently condemned by Mordecai Richler:

The minority man, as Norman Mailer has astutely pointed out, grows up with a double-image of himself, his own and society's. My boys are crazy about the James Bond movies, they identify with 007, as yet unaware that they have been cast as the villains of the dramas. As a boy, I was brought up to revere John Buchan, then Lord Tweedsmuir, Governor-General of Canada. Before he came to speak at Junior Red Cross Prize Day, we were told that he stood for the ultimate British virtues. Fair play, clean living, gentlemanly conduct. We were not forewarned that he was also an ignorant, nasty-minded anti-Semite. I discovered this for myself, reading *The Thirty-nine Steps*. As badly as I wanted to identify with Richard Hannay, two-fisted soldier of fortune, I couldn't without betraying myself. My grandfather, *pace* Buchan, went in fear of being flogged in some one-horse location on the Volga, which was why we were in Canada. However, I owe to Buchan the image of my grandfather as a little white-faced Jew with an eye like a rattlesnake. It is an image I briefly responded to, alas, if only because Hannay, so obviously on the side of the good, accepted it without question. This, possibly, is why I've grown up to loathe Buchan, Fleming, and their sort. ("James Bond Unmasked," p. 355)

While condemning such racial stereotypes in popular litera-ture, we should also recognize that racial characterizations derive from the dramatic imperatives of heroic adventures as much as they express actual racial antipathy. We have already noted that Buchan's stories show a powerful fascination with non-British races and cultures. Fleming often has the same passion for the exotic. His delectable heroines also often rep-resent other races or mixtures, for example. Whatever part British racism played in the thinking of Buchan and Fleming, their racial characterizations are an effective way of creating heroes and villains who are good and evil by nature and not simply through situation, thus giving the conflict of characters a metaphysical dimension. Umberto Eco analyzes this aspect of the Fleming saga:

Fleming intends . . . to build an effective narrative apparatus. To do so he decided to rely upon the most secure and universal principles, and puts into play archetypal elements which are

precisely those that have proved successful in traditional tales.
Let us recall for a moment the pairs of characters that we placed
in opposition: M is the King and Bond the Cavalier entrusted
with a mission; Bond is the Cavalier and the Villain is the
Dragon; the Lady and Villain stand for Beauty and the Beast;
Bond restores the Lady to the fullness of spirit and to her senses,
he is the Prince who rescues Sleeping Beauty; between the Free
World and the Soviet Union, England and the non–Anglo-Saxon
countries represent the primitive epic relationship between the
Chosen Race and the Lower Race, between Black and White,
Good and Bad. Fleming is a racialist in the sense that any artist
is one if, to represent the devil he depicts him with oblique
eyes; in the sense that a nurse is one, who, wishing to frighten
children with the Bogey-man, suggests that he is black. (Eco
and del Buone, *The Bond Affair,* pp. 59–60)

Fleming and Buchan make the spy story into mythic romance with their tales of epic confrontation between noble
heroes and diabolical villains, while the Ambler-Greene story
moves the thriller in the direction of the twentieth-century
naturalistic novel with antiheroes and an emphasis on the
deterministic power of environment. The Ambler-Greene hero
is more typically of the middle or lower-middle class, and he
is often a failure. Far from heroic victory over a devilish enemy,
this protagonist, if victorious at all, achieves a minor triumph
over his own weaknesses and the restrictive circumstances of
his life. Villains in the Ambler-Greene stories are almost never
grotesque and powerful representatives of an alien race seeking
world domination. Though they engage in sinister activities,
the Ambler-Greene villains are less evil figures than expressions
of the disorder and corruption of modern European society.
Eric Ambler's Dimitrios is sinister enough, but Ambler interprets him as the product of a social order made brutal and
anarchic by war and revolution. In Greene's *This Gun for Hire*
the cold-blooded murderer Raven is treated with increasing
sympathy. Though Raven appears to be a vicious killer without
any decent feelings, Greene reveals in the course of the novel
that he has been molded by a society in which the poor are
exploited and corrupted while the rich, whose greed for money

and power are the real source of evil, are highly respected. While Greene's social criticism in thrillers like *This Gun for Hire* and *The Confidential Agent* is appropriately more melodramatic than marxist, his socially oriented treatment of protagonist and antagonist is still a very different version of the spy story from the mythical confrontation of heroic good and diabolical evil represented by Buchan and Fleming.

Beyond these basic similarities in action and character, Fleming also shares a number of important qualities of tone and characteristic themes with Buchan and his contemporary romancers. In discussing Buchan, we noted his characteristic mixture of tones, the combination of moralistic allegory with fantasy and touches of verisimilitude and humor. This combination functioned fairly effectively to transform the basic elements of mythic romance into the more contemporaneous form of the spy story. Fleming further transformed this mixture of tones. The allegorical conflict of good and evil represented by James Bond and his repertory of villains is overshadowed by a large element of fantasy in such inventions as Dr. No's secret underground laboratory, by highly precise details about specific places and products which lard the Bond books, and, above all, by humor and self-irony, the feeling of not taking it all too seriously, which makes it easier for sophisticated modern readers to give themselves up to the fantastic world of heroic adventure. Thematically, Fleming also picks up a number of Buchan's most basic concerns: the defense of British tradition against the world; the ideal of the gentleman as the heart of that tradition; the fascination of the exotic; the paranoiac sense of international conspiracies extending even into the heart of the homeland; even the curious comradeship in adventure of Britain and America, represented in Buchan by the association of Blenkiron and Hannay and in Fleming by the partnership of Bond with Felix Leiter of the CIA.

These similarities indicate the extent to which Fleming's success at least partly resulted from his reincarnation of an established formulaic tradition of heroic secret agent adventure. It is also clear that he revitalized this tradition by transforming it in many ways. Most obviously, Fleming brought the Buchan formula up to date by translating the conflict of hero and villain, which Buchan had symbolized by the hot war between Germany and England, into the contemporaneous terms of the Cold War between England and Russia. Later, as relations between England, the U.S., and Russia became slightly less hostile, Fleming invented an international criminal conspiracy, S.P.E.C.T.R.E. to take the place of the Russians. This melodramatizing of the Cold War coincided nicely with the mood of the 1950s, a topicality which certainly did not impede the success of the Bond books. It is simple enough, however, for a writer to give his story a currently topical background. It is harder to seize upon some of the crucial symbols and attitudes that have a wide popular currency at a particular time and to make these central to the adventures. This Fleming was able to do with considerable skill, and because of it his novels, though cast in the mold of Buchanesque romance, are still popular in an era of cynical and antiheroic spy stories written by men like John le Carré, Len Deighton, and Adam Hall.

Fleming's world is totally secularized, and it is dominated by bureaucracies. In contrast, the moral universe of Buchan's stories was, as we have seen, still pervaded by the Christian idea of providence, the direct governance of events by some higher power. In Buchan's world, the only large espionage organizations were those of the enemy. Because their actions were aligned with the divine will, Buchan's heroes did not need complex organizations. Instead, they could count on providence to take care of any situations which an ad hoc group of gentlemen agents could not handle. This is one thing which makes Buchan's world hard for modern readers to accept. We are totally skeptical that a small temporary alliance of gentlemen could effectively cope with a complex international political situation. Moreover, the providential coincidences that help Hannay and his friends defeat the villains seem like contrived and implausible narrative devices. Fleming gets around this difficulty by replacing providence with the international bureaucracy of the secret service. Bond is part of a powerful and permanent government service. The resources of this organization include agents in every major country who help to carry out the narrative function which Buchan largely assigned to providence, the bringing of the hero face to face with his enemy. Fleming spends a good deal of time detailing the workings of this organization. He shows Bond in his relations with his superior, M., and the supporting branches, just as he describes at considerable length the inner structure of the enemy groups. However, where a writer like le Carré or Deighton would go on to suggest that the secret service to which the hero belongs is just as amoral and corrupt as the enemy organization, Fleming takes considerable pains to establish the goodness of the British Secret Service. It is interesting to note that he does this in very Buchanesque terms. Her Majesty's secret service is a group of patriotically dedicated individuals who perform their dangerous assignments out of a sense of duty and devotion to tradition. Their rewards are few and yet they are supremely brave and adventurous. The enemy organizations, on the other hand, are corrupt and totalitarian. Their agents are motivated by greed for money and power, lust for killing, or fear of the brutality of the higher-ups. The head of the Russian secret service, presumably an unimpeachable authority on these matters, describes for us the Fleming vision of the British espionage bureaucracy:

"Their security service is excellent. England, being an island, has great security advantages and their so-called M.I.5 employs men with good education and good brains. Their Secret Service is still better. They have notable successes. In certain types of operations, we are constantly finding that they have been there before us. Their agents are good. They pay them little money— only a thousand or two thousand roubles a month—but they serve with devotion. Yet these agents have no special privileges in England, no relief from taxation and no special shops such as we have, from which they can buy cheap goods. Their social standing abroad is not high, and their wives have to pass as the wives of secretaries. They are rarely awarded a decoration until they retire. And yet these men and women continue to do this dangerous work. It is perhaps the Public School and University tradition. The love of adventure. But still it is odd that they

play this game so well, for they are not natural conspirators."
General Vozdvishensky felt that his remarks might be taken as
too laudatory. He hastily qualified them. "Of course, most of
their strength lies in the myth—in the myth of of Scotland
Yard, of Sherlock Holmes, of the Secret Service." (*From Russia,
with Love,* p. 40)

As further validation of the relation of the modern espionage bureaucracy to the greater tradition, Fleming develops
the character of M., Bond's master, as an aging Hannay, retired
from the field and now bringing the same values to the organization. Like Hannay, M. is a former military officer and
an ascetic and totally dedicated man. He disapproves of Bond's
flippancy, his womanizing and drinking, and Bond himself
feels occasionally irritated by M.'s attempts to improve his
character. Yet, there is clearly a strong feeling of parental and
filial loyalty between the two. Thus, despite the presence of
a bureaucratic organization and the differences in character
between Bond and his earlier predecessors, Fleming clearly
relates his character to the tradition of Buchan.

Fleming's representation of the spy-hero as organization man
and his vision of the world as a totally secular complex of
competing organizations obviously reflect on the level of fantasy that sense of life as dominated by large corporations and
state bureaucracies which most members of the mid-
twentieth-century European and American middle-class share.
There are also other aspects of Fleming's treatment of the secret
service as bureaucracy that seem to strike a resonant chord, by
touching on some important interest or need of the public.
Perhaps the most striking of these is the idea of the organization
providing the hero with license or legitimation to commit acts
which are normally considered crimes for the average man. Of
all the symbols associated with James Bond, none has caught
the public fancy more than the idea of 007, the number that
gives an agent official sanction to kill. This peculiar emphasis
on the license to kill is a striking departure from the traditional
heroic tale where the hero's attacks on the villain were legitimated either by some kind of divine authority or through

some combination of his own individual virtue and the villain's evil. Richard Hannay was reluctant to destroy even the most vicious of his enemies and Buchan makes sure that his killings are sanctioned both by strong hints of divine approval and by the contrast between heroic virtue and villainous deviltry. Fleming, however, loves to skate on the thin edge of moral anarchy by making his hero a trained professional assassin and then skipping nimbly back from the gulf of amorality by interpreting Bond's aggression as part of the orderly bureaucracy of modern society. Perhaps we find some of the same interest involved in the recent public fascination with the organized assassins of large crime syndicates. The Mafia hit men of *The Godfather* and other contemporary gangster stories and films do not seem at first sight to have much in common with the elegant 007, but they share the same central characteristic of being loyal to an organization which gives their acts of murder the sanction of bureaucratic order and procedure. Fleming himself became, if anything, even more fascinated by the paradox of the bureaucratic assassin. In the last James Bond novel he actually wrote, *The Man with the Golden Gun*, Fleming based the plot on an enemy attempt to turn 007's licensed deathdealing back on M., the head of the organization which had created it in the first place.

While killing is the most important crime or sin legitimated by the organization, it is significant that Bond is called on to perform a number of traditionally disreputable acts as he pursues his profession: at various points he must become a gambler—even a cheater at cards—a seducer, a thief, a swindler. Richard Hannay would never have cheated at cards or seduced a woman, even to save the British Empire from destruction. Though he is certainly no prude, Bond himself occasionally feels a bit anxious about the moral, or amoral, demands of his profession:

> And now? Bond smiled wryly at his reflection in the Perspex as the plane swung out of the mountains and over the grosgrained terazza of Lombardy. If that young James Bond came up to him in the street and talked to him would he recognize the clean, eager youth that had been him at seventeen? And what would

that youth think of him, the secret agent, the older James Bond? Would he recognize himself beneath the surface of this man who was tarnished with years of treachery and ruthlessness and fear— this man with the cold arrogant eyes and the scar down his cheek and the flat bulge beneath his left armpit? What would he think of Bond's present assignment? What would he think of the dashing secret agent who was off across the world in a new and most romantic role—to pimp for England? (From Russia, with Love, pp. 85–86)

We suggested earlier that part of Buchan's success as a popular writer was due to his ability to reflect and resolve in fantasy the ambivalent hatred and fascination early twentieth-century Britons felt toward other cultures. The central analogue to these themes in the 007 saga would seem to be the role of organizations. The pressure and the inescapability of large private corporations and government bureaucracies constitute one of the most continually exasperating experiences of individuals in mid-twentieth-century Britain and America. At the same time it is difficult to imagine any longer how society could function without these vast corporate structures. We are therefore both inextricably bound to and basically alienated from the bureaucracies that order our lives. The Fleming version of the spy story generates comforting fantasies about organizations on two levels. First, there is the image of the devoted and selfless organization—the British Secret Service—dauntlessly protecting us from the anarchic and destructive schemes of powerful foreign or criminal syndicates: S.M.E.R.S.H. or S.P.E.C.T.R.E. On a deeper and more complex level, there is the fantasy of the good organization legitimating our individualistic impulses, providing the framework in which we can safely and officially indulge those secret anarchic urges toward violence and sex which would destroy us and society if they were not controlled. The Fleming image of the secret service with its 00 section enables us to identify with a hero who has the legal right to indulge in the kind of private action that modern organizations are at least partly designed to prevent. Thus, in fantasy, the tension between organizational control and individual impulse is resolved and the status quo is reaffirmed.

Two other aspects of modern corporate society play a central role in Fleming's fantasy of the spy as organization man: technology and Fleming's almost unique emphasis on brand names. Both are treated with the marked ambivalence which characterizes Fleming's representation of bureaucratic motifs. There is a typical pattern in the use of technology which recurs through many of the Bond stories. At the beginning, the hero is armed by the Quartermaster branch with a collection of new weapons and communications devices. These are usually rather quickly used up as the hero approaches the enemy's lair and, by the time a climactic confrontation takes place, the fancy new weapons have been exhausted, destroyed, or captured. At this point, there is no possible way for the hero to use the organization's elaborate technology to protect himself or even to call for help. When it comes to the crunch, Bond must be prepared to depend on his unaided physical and moral resources and not on the latest electronic gear. In the Bond films even more is made of technological motifs. Not only does the hero have his bag of mechanical tricks, but the villain's hideout typically resembles the laboratory of a mad scientist in a science-fiction film. Despite the cinematic delight in specially designed cars and individual flying machines, the end result is generally the same: technology runs out and the hero must finish his mission bare-handed. In *Goldfinger*, for instance, 007 starts after the villain in a fancy modern car equipped with such paraphernalia as radar, built-in machine guns, ejector seat, and bulletproof shields. But before his adventures are half over this ponderous machine has been destroyed. Bond is left with his bare hands and inner resources to overcome a huge and villainous organization. Without technological support he is far more successful than with it. Unaided, he not only defeats an almost invulnerable Korean karate expert in hand-to-hand combat, but he converts a lesbian to heterosexuality! With her help he then defeats Goldfinger's plan to irradiate all the gold in Fort Knox. Thus, technology is represented as a rather ambiguous factor in the Bond saga. It is preeminently the villain's weapon and so long as both hero and villain are dependent on technology, the villain is usually successful. However, once the hero has divested himself of mechanical and electronic encumbrances and is separated from his organizational support, he is victorious despite overwhelming odds. This outcome reaffirms the basic potency of the individual hero in an organized technological world.

Something of the same sort happens with respect to consumer products, another of the dominant motifs of Fleming's writing. One of Fleming's stylistic mannerisms is the constant parading of brand names to the extent that 007 fans have been able to construct entire books which compile catalogs of Bond's preferences in food, drink, clothing, cars, and toilet articles. The centrality of this theme to Fleming's work has made many critics see Bond as a popular symbol of the affluent society:

> James Bond, Ian Fleming's popular secret agent 007, is a brand dropper. Though Bond comes from a lowbrow background, he has acquired aristocratic tastes. He knows how to move in highbrow circles—to order the proper wine of the best vintage year of the most exclusive label all appropriate to a properly ordered meal. He has really arrived. His clothes, his cars, his handmade cigarettes all have snob appeal. Perhaps Bond is popular because all this appeals to our affluent society. (Starkey, *James Bond's World of Values*, p. 51)

No doubt this is one of the ways in which Fleming revitalized the romantic story. The continual reference to specific objects by name helps provide those touches of contemporary verisimilitude which fantasies of this sort need to maintain some connection with the reader's sense of reality. In addition, 007's implicit recommendations of certain brands of food, drink, clothing, or weaponry have for us something of the pleasure associated with reading Bloomingdale's catalog or looking at the advertisements in *The New Yorker* or *Playboy*. Social scientists have pointed out that both America and England underwent a considerable change in values as their economies shifted from an emphasis on production generated by a preindustrial scarcity of goods to a concern with consumption necessary to the ever increasing productivity of an industrial society. In such a society, consuming becomes a form of moral obligation and a primary measure of individual success and failure. In this climate of values, individuals enjoy fantasizing about more expensive and elegant objects than they are ever likely to possess and need to be reassured that the things they actually buy are highly virtuous forms of consumption. Many of the most successful contemporary magazines mix illustrations of the expensive and unobtainable with recommendations about products within the reach of the average reader. Fleming effectively builds the same combination into the Bond saga. The souped-up Aston-Martins, the elegant hotels, the $50 worth of Beluga caviar—it is pleasant to dream about the satisfactions of consumption on this level, even if it remains out of reach. But then there are also the down-to-earth recommendations of particular brands of cigarettes or cocktails which one can actually consume with the security of knowing that they are endorsed by a hero.

Though some of Fleming's success in reviving the Buchanesque spy romance came from his ability to reflect the values of a consumption-oriented society, a closer look at the way these themes are handled reveals important moments of ambiguity. We have already observed the way technology tends to fail the hero. We also find that at certain crucial points in his novels Fleming reflects a deep-seated uncertainty about consumption. For instance, the following passage is fairly typical of Fleming's product lyricism:

> There was everything in the bathroom—Floris Lime bath essence for men and Guerlain bathcubes for women. He crushed a cube into the water and at once the room smelled like an orchid house. The soap was Guerlain's Sapoceti, *Fleurs des Alpes.* In a medicine cupboard behind the mirror over the washbasin were toothbrushes and toothpaste, Steradent toothpicks, Rose mouthwash, dental floss, Aspirin and Milk of Magnesia. There was also an electric razor, Lentheric after-shave lotion, and two nylon hairbrushes and combs. Everything was brand new and untouched. (*Doctor No,* p. 119)

But alas, this elegant repertory of toiletries is a feature of Dr. No's "mink-lined prison"; the scented bath with rich soaps, the clean teeth, and the pleasant shave are all Dr. No's way of fattening the victim up for the kill. In this passage, as in many others in the saga, objects of consumption are potentially symbols of temptation, corruption, and betrayal. Just as the villain is a master of technology, so is he also a model of affluent consumership. His lair typically puts the most expensive hotels and restaurants to shame. He is surrounded with the finest luxuries, a walking Neiman-Marcus catalog.

Because he develops this intimate tie between the villain, technology, and affluence, Fleming is able to reflect both a fascination with the primary symbols of modern industrial society and a deep-seated fear that these works of man contain the seeds of corruption and destruction. The 007 stories carry a residue of the worldly asceticism which was still dominant in the moral universe of the earlier spy romances. Max Weber uses the term in his famous discussion of the Protestant ethic and the spirit of capitalism to describe the moralistic zeal with which the Protestant entrepreneurs of the seventeenth and eighteenth centuries dedicated themselves to production and accumulation. Weber argued that the business life of these men was shaped by a religious zeal to serve God by diligently pursuing their callings rather than by a personal desire for wealth and possessions. According to Weber, the prevailing ethos of the early capitalistic era was one of worldly asceticism—an involvement with the things of this world, but not for personal gain or satisfaction. We can see how important this ethos still is in Buchan's portrayal of Hannay. Though an adventurer, Hannay is a moral ascetic—a man of Christian purity and dedication—and his deeds, though they take place in the arena of international politics, have the implication of a Christian pilgrim's progress.

While the development of the mature industrial society has involved a shift from worldly asceticism to a pleasure-centered morality of consumption, the continued stream of critiques of this new morality indicate that many people still feel within themselves the voice of the older ethos, hinting that the new values are leading to corruption. Fleming expresses this residual ambiguity in such passages as the one just quoted and in a variety of other ways—Bond's relationship to

M., who embodies the traditional ethos; Bond's own basic
dedication; the sense that he possesses an inner moral core
which makes him give up his pleasures for the important
mission; and, perhaps most important of all, the sense which
Fleming often gives us that the sensuous, consuming Bond is
an imposture hiding deeper moral motives behind the mask
of pleasant hedonism. In fact, too much easy pleasure is ultimately just as distressing to 007 as it was to Richard Hannay:

> I returned from the city about three o'clock on that May after-
> noon pretty well disgusted with life. I had been three months
> in the old country and was fed up with it. If any one had told
> me a year ago that I would have been feeling like that, I should
> have laughed at him, but there was the fact. The weather made
> me liverish, the talk of the ordinary Englishman made me sick,
> I couldn't get enough exercise, and the amusements of London
> seemed as flat as soda-water that has been standing in the sun.
> (*The Thirty-Nine Steps*, p. 9)

This is Hannay at the beginning of *The Thirty-Nine Steps*. Here
is Bond at the opening of *From Russia, with Love*:

> The blubbery arms of the soft life had Bond around the neck
> and they were slowly strangling him. He was a man of war and
> when, for a long period, there was no war, his spirit went into
> a decline. (*From Russia, with Love*, p. 72)

In Bond's character this residual core of Hannay's asceticism is overlaid not only with the new morality of consumption, but with the image of the hero as sexually potent and
irresistible. Though sometimes fascinated by the glamorous
and exotic women he encountered in the course of his missions,
Hannay remained essentially monogamous and chaste. Bond,
on the other hand, is as striking for his gallery of exotic
feminine conquests as he is for his triumphs over supervillains.
As O. F. Snelling puts it:

> Offhand, I can think of no character in fiction so lucky in love
> as James Bond. Almost every personable female he meets seems

> more than ready to hop into bed with him at his merest nod. Waitresses brush against him provocatively, married women appear to be his for the asking, other men's mistresses forget their lovers when they see him and even expensive whores are willing to bestow their favours *pour amour*. Unmarried young bachelor girls, of course, are sitting ducks. (*007 James Bond*, p. 35)

Agent 007's extensive relations with the fair sex obviously reflect the impact of changing sexual values. For a contemporary reader, sexual chastity and restraint are no longer meaningful symbols of manliness and heroism. Therefore, in resurrecting the heroic secret agent, Fleming sensibly followed the example of the American hard-boiled detective writers by using his central character's unusual sexual attractiveness as a chief sign of his heroic prowess. Yet, Bond is not simply a casual philanderer who parades his prowess in a continual sequence of erotic episodes. Though Bond's sexual adventures are frequent and promiscuous enough, Fleming also develops a number of traditional romantic themes. The motifs of the woman as fatal temptress and of the love-death, the intensification of romantic feeling through the close association of love and death, are always implicit in Bond's affairs and sometimes come out on the surface, as in the killing of Bond's new wife at the end of *On Her Majesty's Secret Service*. The fatal temptress was also a dominant theme of the American hard-boiled detective story, but Fleming gives it a more romantic twist. Vesper Lynd and Tatiana Romanova are both femmes fatales under enemy orders to seduce and destroy the hero; Pussy Galore is a lesbian in the organization of Goldfinger; Domino Vitale is the villain's mistress in *Thunderball*; and Tracy di Vicenzo is the nymphomaniac daughter of an international gangster. This gallery of perverse, dangerous, and treacherous women is reminiscent of the Carmen Sternwoods, Brigid O'Shaugnessys, Little Velmas, and Charlotte Mannings of Hammett, Chandler, and Spillane. The big difference is that they all fall in love with 007 and become his allies, thus placing themselves in danger. Some of them are even killed because of their love for Bond. Those who are not literally destroyed are symbolically eliminated, for the romance invariably breaks up before the next adventure. Only the faithful secretary (e.g., Miss Moneypenney) whose relationship with the hero remains chaste but adoring, carries over from story to story in a way analogous to the secretaries of Sam Spade and Mike Hammer.

The motifs of the femme fatale and the love-death have been an important part of the legends of espionage from Samson and Delilah to Mata Hari. Fleming's rich elaboration of these themes and his way of restating them in terms of contemporary sexual mores is another important aspect of his revitalization of the secret agent romance. In fact, Fleming's curious synthesis of contemporary "liberated" sexual attitudes with traditional romantic symbolism makes an especially piquant combination. Overtly, 007 is an exponent of spontaneous and uninhibited heterosexual eroticism. There is absolutely nothing in his moral code that restricts erotic play between mutually consenting adults. A sexual relationship does not require romantic love or any other ideological or institutional sanction. Sex is its own reward. Still, there must be some tender feeling, some mutual link beyond the purely physical stimulus that brings the lovers together. Though he sometimes pretends to be one, 007 is not a satyr or a Don Juan—just a man who enjoys a good healthy screw between mutually attracted partners. Because this is his view, Bond does not enjoy the games of love and the elaborate rituals of courtship. He believes in going straight to the point in a natural and spontaneous fashion:

> With most women his manner was a mixture of taciturnity and passion. The lengthy approaches to a seduction bored him almost as much as the subsequent mess of disentanglement. He found something grisly in the inevitability of the pattern of each affair. The conventional parabola—sentiment, the touch of the hand, the kiss, the passionate kiss, the feel of the body, the climax in the bed, then more bed, then less bed, then the boredom, the tears and the final bitterness—was to him shameful and hypocritical. Even more he shunned the *mise-en-scène* for each of these acts in the play—the meeting at a party, the restaurant, the taxi, his flat, her flat, then the weekend by the sea, then the

flats again, then the furtive alibis and the angry farewell on some doorstep in the rain. (*Casino Royale,* p. 120).

Sexual pleasure without complicating and dulling sentiments, without conventional social rituals, without enervating feelings of guilt and shame—these are major aspects of the new sexual ideals which have become increasingly widespread in theory, if not in practice, among the American and English middle classes. But, at the same time that he makes his hero a direct exponent of these liberated views, Fleming tells us quite another story in image, characterization, and incident. James Bond's inner song of love is "your lips, they may say yes, yes, but there's no, no in your eyes."

Instead of being straightforward, uncomplicated, and full-blooded bed partners, the Bond heroines carry an aura of fatality, perversity, and helplessness. Kingsley Amis points out that "under a wide variety of covers—worldliness (Tiffany Case, Pussy Galore), outdoor-girl self-sufficiency (Honey), international-set glossiness (Tracy), belief in the organization (Tatiana)—Bond-girl is a defenseless child of nature, a wanderer in a hostile world, an orphan, a waif" (*The James Bond Dossier,* pp. 48–49). They are also typically characterized by lesbianism (Pussy Galore), by neurosis (Honeychile Rider is a nearly pathological man-hater, Tracy a nymphomaniac), or by treachery (Vesper and Tatiana are enemy agents). Finally, they are doomed. Poe pointed out long ago that nothing is quite as exciting as a beautiful dead woman. Certainly, the mortality rate of Bond heroines is strikingly high. The approach to the heroine typically involves a considerable degree of aggression on Bond's part: "As now he knew that she was profoundly, excitingly sensual, but that the conquest of her body, because of the central privacy in her, would each time have the tang of rape" (*Casino Royale,* p. 127). In addition, Bond himself must undergo great dangers and, frequently, a session of physical torture by the villain before he is permitted the brief pastoral idyll with the heroine that usually terminates his adventures. In *Casino Royale* Bond is actually beaten about the genitals by the villain and is, for a time, uncertain whether he has anything left for the heroine. Dr. No forces 007 to pass through a tortuous obstacle course before he is able to escape and rescue Honeychile Rider. In every story, the hero's relationship with the heroine is inextricably mixed with his peril at the hands of the villain. Only after destroying his enemy can he snatch a few brief moments of sexual pleasure.

Several themes seem to be mixed in Fleming's ambiguous treatment of the hero's sexual exploits. Most obviously, the symbols of perversion and aggression add feelings of guilt, shame, and danger to the representation of erotic episodes. They suggest that Fleming and his public may find the new ethos of natural, liberated sex insufficiently exciting for the purposes of fantasy. Instead, Fleming surrounds his hero's supposedly liberated sexuality with two traditional sexual attitudes: the importance of masculine aggressiveness in the sexual act and the feeling that sex is hedged about with danger and corruption. There is also another sexual theme in the Fleming stories, largely covert in its expression, though occasionally quite explicit: the play between polymorphous eroticism and heterosexuality. This is obvious in *Goldfinger,* where Bond confronts lesbian Pussy Galore and her gang. But it also plays a role in the erotic undertones in the relations between hero and villains. We have already mentioned Le Chiffre's assault on 007's genitals. In the film version of *Goldfinger,* the villain has the hero tied down on a table with his legs spread open and nearly "rapes" him with a laser beam. This was certainly an appropriate cinematic embellishment of the novel, where this particular incident does not take place, and suggests the extent to which the covert homoerotic character of the Bond-Goldfinger relationship was felt by the filmmakers. When Dr. No has captured and drugged Bond and Honeychile Rider, he comes in to look at them while they sleep and his voyeuristic attentions, as described by Fleming, can only be characterized as "loving":

> The man *spent longer* beside Bond's bed. He scrutinized every line, every shadow on the dark, rather cruel face that *lay drowned,* almost extinct, on the pillow. He watched the pulse in the neck

and counted it and, when he had *pulled down the sheet,* he did the same with the area round the *heart.* He gazed thoughtfully at the *hidden strength in the flat stomach.* He even bent down close over the outflung open right hand and examined its life and fate lines. Finally, *with infinite care,* the steel claw drew the sheet back up to Bond's neck. For another minute the tall figure stood over the sleeping man, then it *swished* softly away and out into the corridor and the door closed with a click. (*Doctor No,* pp. 122–23; italics mine)

In Fleming's world of fantasy even an ordinary heterosexual episode can become the object of more polymorphous fantasies. When Tatiana and Bond first make love in their elegant hotel room, Tatiana is dressed in the classic costume of sadomasochistic fantasy—"Nothing but the black ribbon around her neck and black silk stockings rolled above her knees"—and the whole scene is filmed from behind the walls by two Russian agents:

> And the view-finders gazed coldly down on the passionate arabesques the two bodies formed and broke and formed again, and the clockwork mechanism of the cine-cameras whirred softly on and on as the breath rasped out of the open mouths of the two men and the sweat of excitement trickled down their bulging faces into their cheap collars. (*From Russia, with Love,* p. 172)

This procession of lesbian, homoerotic, and voyeuristic episodes forms a continual counterpoint to the liberated heterosexual ethos which Bond officially practices. Indeed, these episodes are given greater emphasis except at the beginning and end of each story. It is as if Bond must leave the secure haven of spontaneous male-female relations to plow through the murky waters of polymorphous perversity before he can stagger limping and bedraggled into the loving arms of the heroine. This pattern distinctly resembles the shape of Bond's encounters with technology and consumerism as I noted them earlier. With regard to all three—sex, technology, and brand-name products—007 discovers the inherent dangers and corruptions which threaten him through their association with the villain's evil. Having encountered these dangers and survived them, Bond is able to enjoy his women, his products, and his machines. But apparently this satisfaction is only temporary. Soon the soft life becomes enervating. The hero must embark on another dangerous mission so he can recharge his capacity to find fulfillment in the sex, goods, and technology readily available to him.

The underlying theme of the Bond adventure is the recharging of sex and object consumption with the kind of power which comes from an association with danger and perversion. Bond's reward is that in exchange for his flirtation with evil—and the word "flirtation" is appropriate here in all its various senses—sex and consumption are recharged with heightened power for him. If this interpretation is correct, then Fleming is responding on the level of popular formula to a sense of modern life that many serious poets, novelists, and thinkers have expressed. This view is that in a secularized society oriented toward the achievement of material abundance through technology and bureaucracy everything becomes routinized and trivialized. The pleasures of sex and consumption, which once had the magical power of sin in a religion-centered economy of scarcity, became so easily accessible that they lost their magic and became ordinary aspects of the biological cycles of life. Wallace Steven's brilliant phrase "the death of Satan was a tragedy for the imagination" summed up his feeling that the secularization of culture had endangered the richness and intensity of human experience. Stevens tried to imagine a naturalistic ethos which would restore the fullness of life through a heightened awareness of the immediacy and transiency of sensual experience—"Death is the mother of beauty." Modern dystopian writers like Anthony Burgess in A Clockwork Orange have also pointed up the psychological dangers of the attempt to eliminate evil. In the totally abundant and controlled bureaucracy of Burgess's vision the mass of men have become sterile and empty husks; only those who retain the capacity for evil still carry the spark of imagination. On the popular level, it is possible to see in the contemporary spread of pornography a confused attempt to reinvest sex with an aura of evil, shame, and guilt in a world where the liberal sexual ideology would make sexuality as natural and routinized as breathing.

Like most highly successful popular writers, however, Fleming tends to conceal conflicting values and to reaffirm conventional attitudes in a new cultural situation. The adventures combine the values of sexual liberation and material abundance with the traditional magic of guilt and sin, just as they integrate the world of technology and bureaucracy with the tradition of the dedicated individual hero. This is quite an achievement since all but the most unsophisticated sections of the public are well aware of the basic conflicts between secularism and religion, bureaucracy and individualism, liberated sexuality and the tradition of eroticism as obscenity, and spiritual values and materialism. Indeed, these conflicts are among the staple topics of newspaper editorials, sermons, and think pieces in both popular and intellectual magazines. How then does Fleming make us swallow a formulaic fantasy in which these basic modern tensions are reconciled in a story of heroic adventure? How does a writer like Fleming make us suspend our basic awareness of reality in order to enjoy something we know is not only a fantasy but in many ways an obsolete one? Here, I think the answer lies in Fleming's special tone and style. Fleming always lets the reader know that his hero's fantastic adventures are not to be taken too seriously, at least not for long. For an ironic and skeptical age like the middle of the twentieth century, any writer who tried to create a heroic spy in the serious moralistic manner of John Buchan would probably be laughed out of court. But mid-twentieth-century audiences, even rather sophisticated intellectual ones, are evidently willing to enter a world of derring-do so long as they are protected from having to accept it without reservations. Fleming is no ironist or satirist, yet there is always an edge of irony and burlesque in his style and in his inventions. Stylistically one can never be quite sure whether or not we are being put on. Fleming constantly makes inappropriate juxtapositions which one cannot be certain are intended that way, for example, the opening of *Goldfinger*: "James Bond, with two double bourbons inside him, sat in the final departure lounge of Miami Airport and thought about life and death" (p. 7). To what extent is Bond being ironically undercut here for sharing the usual maudlin sentiments brought on by sizable potations? Is that pun on final departure intended or a slip? If intended, is it not rather inappropriately funny?

There are burlesques of the traditions of the pulp thriller, such as the opening of *Moonraker* (p. 7):

> The two thirty-eights roared simultaneously. The walls of the underground room took the crash of sound and batted it to and fro between them until there was silence. James Bond watched the smoke being sucked from each end of the room towards the central Ventaxia fan. The memory in his right hand of how he had drawn and fired with one sweep from the left made him confident. He broke the chamber sideways out of the Colt Detective Special and waited, his gun pointing at the floor, while the instructor walked the twenty yards towards him through the half-light of the gallery.

The first sentence is an outrageous pulp cliché, but as the paragraph proceeds one becomes less sure that Fleming intends it parodistically. But then the reversal of our expectations with the appearance of the instructor again makes us wonder just who is being kidded.

Another important dimension of the Bond books is the running travelogue which we can never be quite sure whether to call a burlesque of travel writers or another example of Fleming's general sloppiness and indiscriminate dependence on hackneyed language and feeling: "It was one of those beautiful, naive seaside panoramas for which the Brittany and Picardy beaches have provided the setting and inspired their recorders, Boudin, Tisso, Monet ever since the birth of plages and bains de mer more than a hundred years ago" (*On Her Majesty's Secret Service,* p. 9). Almost every page in the Fleming opus has at least one or two sentences which hint at some form of put-on or self-parody. Some of this is conscious, some doubtless unconscious, perhaps most of it. Fleming wrote rapidly and without any serious artistic commitments. Bond was largely a commercial enterprise for him, though he must, like Buchan, have enjoyed the fantasizing. He was not a great stylist and his writing has little of the controlled and complex expressiveness of Dashiell Hammett or Raymond Chandler. Yet Fleming's style with its approach to irony, wit, and sophistication is a very effective vehicle for the kind of fantastic story he has to tell. Whenever our belief in the plausibility of character and event is strained far beyond the point of incredulity—a not infrequent event in the 007 saga—the edge of irony in Fleming's style reassures us that it is all a delightful game that neither author nor reader must take with seriousness. Thus Fleming can carry off the most outrageous inventions—villains who would not be out of place in the pages of Sax Rohmer, schemes for world domination whose absurdity is exceeded only by the means which the hero employs to defeat them, and heroines whose character and predicament bear closer resemblance to the early nineteenth-century gothic romance than to contemporary situations—without causing even his most sophisticated readers to insist upon measuring these inventions against their sense of reality. Because of his unique combination of fantasy and irony, Fleming's formula and manner have been more widely imitated and burlesqued than any thriller writer since A. Conan Doyle. Yet it is perhaps the final measure of Fleming's special gift that he remains his own greatest parodist.

Fleming revitalized the heroic version of the spy story, creating a new formula that would be widely imitated in novels, on film, and in television. His work combined traditional narrative patterns with a tone of irony and cynicism which made the patterns of heroic adventure more acceptable to the public in an age of skepticism and doubt. In addition, Fleming found ways of building into his stories the elaboration and resolution of certain key conflicts of value which were of central concern to English and American publics in the mid-twentieth century: the tradition of individual action versus modern bureaucracy and technology, the tradition of worldly asceticism versus contemporary hedonism, affluence, and abundance, and the traditions of romantic love and monogamous relations versus contemporary sexual liberation. By making the spy story into a fantasy structure in which heroic action overcomes these conflicts, Fleming enables us to temporarily enter a fictional world in which we are freed from the ambiguous feelings that characterize our ordinary lives. For so long as the fantasy holds, we share the hero's triumph over the restrictions of organizations, the dangers of technology, the ambiguities of affluence, and the uncertainties of sexual liberation. Because real frustrations and tensions are eliminated by Fleming's rhetoric and fantasy, the reader can experience the fundamental satisfaction of simultaneously affirming and escaping from his sense of reality.

The Fleming formula has achieved massive public popularity not only through Fleming's own works, but through a tremendous number of imitations. Fleming's tongue-in-cheek manner and his treatment of organization and technology were taken over on a large scale by television, becoming the basis of such successful series as *The Man from U.N.C.L.E.*, *I Spy*, *The Secret Agent*, and *The Girl from U.N.C.L.E.* The same elements, coupled with a greater stress on the cool elegance and hints of sadism found in the 007 saga, were effectively deployed in a British counterpart, *The Avengers*. The American writer Donald Hamilton has also exploited Fleming's combination of organization, technology, sex, and exotic locales in his Matt Helm series. Though the tone and style of the Hamilton novels is more in the tradition of the American hardboiled writers, the Matt Helm films starring Dean Martin have been much more in the manner of Fleming. Numerous writers of spy adventure fiction have followed the Fleming formula, and there have even been at least three pornographic pulp series in this vein, *The Man from O.R.G.Y.*, *The Lady from L.U.S.T.*, and *The Girl from B.U.S.T.*

Thus, Ian Fleming invented a hero and his adventures which so powerfully echoed the interests and feelings of his era that it could serve as a basic pattern for innumerable popular novels, films, and television series. Though few of these followers achieved anything like Fleming's unique integration of elements, their efforts indicate the extent to which the public had developed an inexhaustible appetite for Bonded adventures, an appetite no single writer could satisfy. As they enjoyed the works of his followers, it seems likely that fans were really looking for more 007 exploits and were willing to accept lesser substitutes if they could not have more of the real thing. In fact, the character James Bond has had such a basic impact on the contemporary imagination that his saga has given rise to a subsidiary literature of the sort that rarely grows up around formulaic stories. Not only have several full-length parodies of Fleming been quite successful—two of the most amusing being *Alligator* and *Loxfinger,* the latter with a Jewish Bond— but there have been critical anthologies, such as *The Bond Affair,* semipopular critical analyses such as Kingsley Amis's *James Bond Dossier* and O. F. Snelling's *007 James Bond: A Report,* sermons such as L. M. Starkey's *James Bond's World of Values,* and even straightforward fan books, such as Tanner's *The Book of Bond,* which simply catalogs the characteristic clothes, weapons, foods, drinks, and the like favored by the hero. The only earlier figure in the history of the popular thriller to develop such a dedicated and articulate following is Sherlock Holmes. Indeed, these writings on Bond are quite reminiscent of many of the works of the Baker Street Irregulars and it will be interesting to see whether Fleming's stories will eventually occupy a position in the hearts of sophisticated readers like those of Conan Doyle.

In any case, Bond seems to be a creation who, like Holmes, has transcended the boundaries of the formulaic tradition to become an archetypal figure, another way of saying that he has become an institution. If we ask what qualities seem to be imperative to the creation of such characters, we can get some answers by looking at the immortal characters of that writer who is universally recognized as the master of striking and memorable characters who live beyond the boundaries of the specific work in which they were created. This is, of course, Shakespeare, whose major characters like Hamlet, Othello, Macbeth, Lear, Falstaff, and many others have come to have an existence of their own in the public imagination as symbols of basic human problems and qualities. Many readers of Shakespeare have observed that these great characters seem to have such a fascinating power because they are striking combinations

of qualities that we usually think of as contradictory or in-
congruous. For example, Sir Edward Elgar, speaking of his
symphonic study of Falstaff points out that Shakespeare's
creation

> is a conception hardly less complex, hardly less wonderful than
> that of Hamlet. This complexity has been summed up by Mor-
> gan as follows: He is a character made up by Shakespeare wholly
> of incongruities—a man at once young and old, enterprising
> and fat, a dupe and a wit, harmless and wicked, weak in principle
> and resolute by constitution, cowardly in appearance and brave
> in reality; a knave without malice; a liar without deceit; and a
> knight, a gentleman, and a soldier, without either dignity,
> decency, or honor. (Parsons, Chicago Symphony program notes
> [26 October 1972], p. 19).

Great popular character creations, like Sherlock Holmes,
or tremendously popular movie stars, like Valentino, Garbo,
or Chaplin, seem also to be derived from a striking synthesis
of contraries and incongruities. Holmes was at once the su-
perrationalistic scientific inquirer and the *poète maudit*. When
he was not keenly peering through a magnifying lens at a tiny
fragment of mud, he was floating in a world of cocaine or
morphine reveries, improvising wild gypsy melodies on his
violin. Garbo was an extraordinary combination in one figure
of the warm, earthy girl next door and the woman of ineffable
mystery. Chaplin's creation of the tramp was characterized by
an even more striking linkage of conflicts: the tramp was funny
and sad, gentle and sadistic, loving and hating, awkward and
graceful, hopelessly incompetent and brilliantly capable. Fleming was no Chaplin, nor even, I think, a Conan Doyle. His
invention lacks the universally human conflicts of qualities
that characterize Shakespearean characters or Chaplin's tramp.
But James Bond, like Sherlock Holmes, is a striking com-
pendium of conflicting cultural themes. Holmes unified in one
person the contending cultural forces of poetry and science,
the "two cultures," which since the mid-nineteenth century
have been so ambivalently hostile to each other. Bond's character and activities bring together a number of the conflicting

cultural values of the mid-twentieth century: he is an organization man who remains a determined individualist; he is
cool and detached, yet committed to his country; he is a man
of technology yet capable of exercising the brute physical force
of a primitive savage; he is a bureaucrat and a killer; he is
sexually liberated but capable of romantic love; he is an affluent
consumer, yet alienated from a corrupt and decadently mater-
ialistic society; he is something of a racist, yet he loves the
exotic and is always involved with men and women of other
races and cultures. While these may be superficial conflicts
which reflect the limited ideologies and attitudes of a specific
culture, they are nonetheless a source of frustration and anxiety
for mid-twentieth-century Americans and Europeans. Fleming's 007 saga enables us to participate vicariously in the
adventures of a character who contains and transcends these
conflicts. This yoking together of conflicting characteristics
and values is one major reason why James Bond has become
such an archetypal character for the contemporary public imagination.

There is another reason for Fleming's unique position in
the tradition of the secret agent thriller. No other writer so
simply and forcefully expresses the basic formulaic structure
of the heroic spy romance. If we assume that the various popular
genres develop and persist because they appeal to some complex
of interests and emotional needs in the culture which produces
and consumes them, then it seems likely that those writers
whose own imaginations work most directly in terms of the
formula are likely to have a unique kind of success. This is
surely the case with Mickey Spillane for the hard-boiled detective story and with Agatha Christie for the classical version
of the detective. Neither of these two writers has as much
literary distinction or variety of interest as others who have
written versions of these formulas, yet both have been uniquely
successful with the public. Spillane, for example, despite his
almost total lack of literary virtues, has been able to construct
his stories so that their structures and images dramatize the
attitudes of fear and hostility toward women and the city which
underlie the hard-boiled detective story. Despite their greater

subtlety—perhaps because of it—Hammett and Chandler dealt with these themes in a less open and forceful fashion. This makes for greater artistry and long-term interest, but not for immediate popularity of the sort Spillane has achieved. Fleming's fantasy has always centered around the basic structures of the secret agent story—its fundamental pattern of mission, entry of the enemy's lair, capture, torture, and escape—and he has presented this basic structure in striking images and symbols. More complex spy thriller writers, like Ambler, Greene, and le Carré, have used these structures as a basis for more complex and varied artistic constructions, but they have not, like Fleming, used their imaginative powers to make a narrative which continually reflects the essence of the formulaic pattern. Those other thriller writers who have commercial success as their primary and sole intention—like the authors of the contemporary Nick Carter series—have tried the same presentation of the bare bones of the secret agent formula, but they have mostly lacked Fleming's ability to create character, incident, and setting, which project the underlying meanings of the formula. These are writers who only understand the surface characteristics of the formula, and they achieve a moderate success in satisfying the emotional needs of those who have become addicted to spy stories. Fleming understood, or was at least able to project, the emotional and cultural concerns which give the spy story its peculiar power. Because of this, he became the king of the secret agent adventure. The unique integration between his imaginative powers and the patterns of the formula will probably make his work last, even after the general popularity of the secret agent thriller has given way to other formulas, just as Conan Doyle's Sherlock Holmes stories have far outlasted the age of their broad general popularity and even show signs of surviving the decline of the classical detective story. While Ian Fleming cannot be compared to the serious novelists of his era, there will probably always be a significant place for him in the history of literature and culture.

7   The Complex Vision of John le Carré

The spy story was largely a British invention. Hence it is appropriate that an English writer, John le Carré, more than any other practitioner, has transformed the secret agent adventure story created by earlier writers like Buchan, Rohmer, LeQueux, and Kipling into a distinctive genre of its own. Of course, le Carré's accomplishments were preceded by a long evolution. In the 1930s Eric Ambler and Graham Greene had already changed the original heroic spy story into an altogether different sort of adventure. After World War II, Ian Fleming's revival of the heroic spy story dominated the secret agent genre, but this new heroic spy was a very different figure from the gentleman amateurs of Buchan. The new spy was a professional working for a clandestine organization, and the postwar spy story showed an increasing preoccupation with the machinations of the espionage bureaucracy. The new heroic spy was molded less in the image of a gentleman adventurer and more in the synthetic mold of the playboy. One might say that the underlying message of the postwar heroic spy story was that one can be both

156

a bureaucrat and a hero and that the great reward of the world of corporate bureaucracies is the easy availability of sexy women and fancy products.

Against this background, and after several years in the foreign service, David Cornwell began his own clandestine career as writer John le Carré. His first novel, *Call for the Dead,* was published at the height of the Bond craze in 1961. Indeed, le Carré may have written his early books at least in part as a corrective to Fleming's extravagant fantasies. His third novel, *The Spy Who Came In from the Cold* (1963), was so successful that le Carré was able to leave the foreign service and devote his full time to writing. Since then, he has gained increasing critical acclaim and popular success. Graham Greene called *The Spy Who Came In from the Cold* "the best spy novel I have ever read." By the publication of *The Honourable Schoolboy* (1977) the appearance of a new le Carré book had become a major public event greeted by front page reviews in *The New York Times Book Review* and cover essays in *Time* magazine (3 Oct. 1977). Le Carré has not only achieved both popular success and critical acclaim, he has made the spy story into one of the most important literary genres of the mid-twentieth century.

As le Carré's conception of the spy story gradually evolved, he recapitulated the history of the thriller. His first two novels have more in common with the classical detective story than with his later works. In his next phase, le Carré drew more heavily on the tradition of the American hard-boiled detective story and the closely related Ambler-Greene secret agent adventure. Finally, in his mature phase, le Carré synthesized elements from all these earlier traditions, including the heroic spy story of John Buchan, into a remarkable artistic pattern of his own.

In spite of espionage elements in its plot, *Call for the Dead* (1961) is much like a classical detective story. It narrates the investigation of a suicide, which turns out to be a murder. The crime is solved by a detective figure who must puzzle out a number of riddlelike clues: a wake-up call left by a man who apparently intended to commit suicide the previous evening, a mysterious cup of cocoa, a license plate, a disappearing foreigner, and so forth. After many red herrings, the detective finally realizes the true solution to the murder in one of those moments of insight so characteristic of the classical detective story. Also typical is the way in which the solution dramatically reverses what was thought to be the state of affairs. The suicide turns out to have been murder, and the victim, thought to have killed himself because of an involvement in espionage, has been innocent. It is his wife who has been the real spy.

Other formulaic elements of the classical detective story shaped *Call for the Dead*. The detective is a man of thought rather than action. Though he is a deskman in the Secret Service at the beginning of the story, he resigns his position when his superior refuses to let him carry through his investigation. Thus, he concludes his work as an amateur. The detective even recruits an assistant to help him investigate the crime. This character, a police inspector near retirement, is more intelligent and independent than Sherlock Holmes's Dr. Watson, but, like Watson, he provides the detective with someone to talk over clues and tentative solutions.

Yet, in spite of this array of classical detective story devices, there is much in *Call for the Dead* which foreshadows the later le Carré. Most important, le Carré introduces the character George Smiley as his detective. Smiley returns as the detective in le Carré's second novel, as a minor figure in *The Spy Who Came In from the Cold* and *The Looking Glass War*, eventually becoming the major protagonist in the later Smiley-Karla trilogy. Unlike the classical detective, Smiley is given a life and a set of feelings outside of the particular crime he is investigating. He is an aging spy being pushed to the margins of his profession by younger bureaucrats. He has an unhappy marriage, and at the beginning of *Call for the Dead* his wife, Lady Ann Sercombe, has left him for a Cuban racing driver. Also, Smiley was involved in espionage during the war, a past which enables him to deduce the involvement of one of his former agents in the crime he is investigating by recognizing this agent's "tradecraft," or typical espionage practices. Though Smiley's character and background will be much more fully developed in later books, he is already a figure of considerable complexity and interest.

The espionage background of *Call for the Dead* is not untypical of classical detective stories. Several of Sherlock Holmes's adventures such as "The Bruce-Partington Plans" involve the recovery of stolen military secrets, and so do a number of the cases of Hercule Poirot. Holmes's brother Mycroft is an important official in some mysterious clandestine branch of the government and may even have been one of the literary figures who suggested to le Carré some of the characteristics of George Smiley. Le Carré's early treatment of the Secret Service already shows some of the characteristics of the fully developed "Circus." Maston, the new head of the Circus, is a typical government bureaucrat concerned mainly with keeping things quiet while he consolidates his power. When Smiley concludes that the apparent suicide was actually a murder, Maston is desperately afraid of the political implications of this revelation, and he refuses to let Smiley continue the investigation. Maston is the first in a long line of service bureaucrats who are more concerned with their own power and their agency's relationship to its minister and parliament than with the mounting of espionage operations.

A Murder of Quality (1962) is even more like a classical detective story than *Call for the Dead*. In this mystery, the least likely person turns out to be the killer after Smiley has investigated several false suspects. Smiley is now completely in retirement, and his espionage background is marginal to the plot. A former associate of Smiley's during the war asks him to investigate the murder, and a brother of the murderer is briefly mentioned as a wartime spy hero, presumably captured and executed by the Germans.

In this novel, le Carré doesn't whip up much excitement about clues, suspects, and red herrings. What truly engages his attention and brings forth his best stylistic efforts is the setting of the mystery, an English public school called Carne. His descriptions of the school, its students, and the vicious backbiting that goes on among the faculty is at times Dickensian in its satiric comedy and at times reminiscent of Joyce's description of an Irish public school in *Portrait of the Artist as a Young Man:*

> Gloom and the cold. The cold was crisp and sharp as flint. It cut the faces of the boys as they moved slowly from the deserted playing fields after the school match. It pierced their black topcoats and turned their stiff, pointed collars into icy rings around their necks. Frozen they plodded from the field to the long walled road which led to the main tuck shop and the town, the line gradually dwindling into groups and the groups into pairs. Two boys who looked even colder than the rest crossed the road and made their way along a narrow path which led towards a distant but less populated tuck shop. (*A Murder of Quality*, p. 2)

The English public school plays an increasingly important role in le Carré's work, both as an institution and as a symbol of some of the most basic patterns of traditional British life. Indeed, one might almost call the Smiley-Karla trilogy a sardonic and ironic commentary on the famous statement attributed to the Duke of Wellington: "The battle of Waterloo was won on the playing fields of Eton."

The other aspect of *A Murder of Quality* which presages le Carré's later work is his further development of the character of George Smiley. In doing so, le Carré emphasizes the difference between real spies and the heroes of secret agent fiction:

> Smiley himself was one of those solitaries who seem to have come into the world fully educated at the age of eighteen. Obscurity was his nature, as well as his profession. The byways of espionage are not populated by the brash and colorful adventurers of fiction. A man who, like Smiley, has lived and worked for years among his country's enemies learns only one prayer: that he may never, never be noticed. Assimilation is his highest aim, he learns to love the crowds who pass him in the street without a glance; he clings to them for his anonymity and his safety. His fear makes him servile—he could embrace the shoppers who jostle him in their impatience, and force him from the pavement. He could adore the officials, the police, the bus conductors, for the terse indifference of their attitudes. (P. 77)

Le Carré, in *A Murder of Quality,* also presents Smiley as a man of divided morality, a conflict of motive and action which will become central to the later trilogy:

> It was a peculiarity of Smiley's character that throughout the whole of his clandestine work he had never managed to reconcile the means to the end. A stringent critic of his own motives he had discovered after long observation that he tended to be less a creature of intellect than his tastes and habits might suggest; once in the war he had been described by his superiors as possessing the cunning of Satan and the conscience of a virgin which seemed to him not wholly unjust. (P. 73)

After *A Murder of Quality,* le Carré was not yet ready to go on with the story of George Smiley. Instead, in his next three books *The Spy Who Came In from the Cold* (1963), *The Looking Glass War* (1965), and *A Small Town in Germany* (1968), le Carré turned away from George Smiley and what he represented to explore the conflict between ends and means in a harsher, more sordid, and ultimately more tragic way. *The Spy Who Came In from the Cold* was a tremendous success and showed, for the first time, an aspect of le Carré's artistic gifts that differed from anything previously published within the genre of the spy story.

Though George Smiley hovers in the background of *The Spy Who Came In from the Cold,* the protagonist is a very different kind of figure. Alec Leamas is not a contemplative man; on the contrary he is extremely hostile to philosophy of any sort. When his lover asks him what he believes in, he replies, "I don't like Americans and public schools" (p. 35). His East German interrogator challenges him to state his philosophy and his answer is, "I just think the whole lot of you are bastards" (p. 124). This rejection of ideology is related to his spying. Leamas believes that philosophies are dangerous because they make people willing to destroy for their sake. His ultimate justification of secret service is that it helps keep the ideologists from destroying the world:

> I don't believe in anything, don't you see—not even destruction or anarchy. I'm sick, sick of killing but I don't see what else

[the Secret Service] can do. They don't proselytize; they don't stand in pulpits or on party platforms and tell us to fight for Peace or for God or whatever it is. They're the poor sods who try to keep the preachers from blowing each other sky high. (P. 215)

Like an American hard-boiled detective, Leamas is a man of action, suspicious of words. He is strong, tough, and resilient. Skillful in violence, Leamas is able at one point in the story to kill an enemy with one blow of his fist. Like Hammett's Sam Spade, he faces the world with hostile suspicion and cynicism. His capacity for love and trust has been almost totally blunted by his lifetime experience of corruption and betrayal. His fulfillment comes in action, and, when, at the beginning of the novel, circumstances conspire to transfer him to a desk job, he is ready to do anything to get back into the field.

Leamas is also, as are so many of the characters of Graham Greene, a "burnt-out case." Early in the story Control asks, "I wondered whether you were tired. Burned out." Leamas typically answers, "That's up to you," (p. 18) because being burned out in this instance has a double meaning. The operation he is enlisted in requires Leamas to pretend to go to seed in order to make the Communists think he might be willing to defect. Leamas carries out this act with skill and even enthusiasm:

> The process of going to seed is generally considered to be a protracted one, but in Leamas this was not the case. In the full view of his colleagues he was transformed from a man honorably put aside to a resentful, drunken, wreck—and all within a few months. (P. 24)

However, Leamas's very intensity in pretending to decline suggests the emptiness and lack of interest in life with which Leamas begins his last adventure. This hollowness, this inability to feel ordinary human emotions and feelings drives Leamas to seek fulfillment in the risks and heightened excitement of espionage operations. He has been out in the cold too long and it has burned out his capacity to find satisfaction in ordinary life.

Yet, behind his facade of toughness and moral exhaustion, Leamas remains a deeply feeling human being. His hard-boiled attitude is a mask which he wears to conceal from others and from himself his true sensitivity to people and events, a sensitivity he has not lost in spite of the horrors and betrayals he has experienced. When his best agent is killed, Leamas feels a good deal more than disappointment in the failure of his operation, for he has become fond of the man.

Even Control understands this and says rather facilely to Leamas:

> "We have to live without sympathy, don't we. That's impossible of course. We act it to one another, all this hardness; but we aren't like that really. I mean . . . one can't be out in the cold all the time; one has to come in from the cold." (P. 19)

Ironically, Control is quite capable of taking calculated advantage of Leamas's underlying humanity to further his devious plots. In his professional stance, Leamas is even willing to condone such deceit, but he is afflicted with what Control calls "recurrent fever," a sudden abhorrence at what he has committed himself to do. In Leamas's case his fever takes the form of two recurrent nightmarish memories, one from his experience during the war and one from the time of his involvement with East German double agent, Karl Riemeck:

> Leamas saw. He saw the long road outside Rotterdam, the long straight road beside the dunes, and the stream of refugees moving along it; saw the little airplane miles away, the procession stop and look toward it; and the plane coming in, neatly over the dunes: saw the chaos, the meaningless hell, as the bombs hit the road. (P. 19)

> As he passed the car he saw out of the corner of his eye four children in the back, waving and laughing, and the stupid, frightened face of their father at the wheel. He drove on, cursing, and suddenly it happened; suddenly his hands were shaking feverishly, his face was burning hot, his heart palpitating wildly. He managed to pull off the road into a lay-by, scrambled out of the car and stood, breathing heavily, staring at the hurtling

stream of giant lorries. He had a vision of the little car caught among them, pounded and smashed, until there was nothing left, nothing but the frenetic whine of klaxons and the blue lights flashing; and the bodies of the children, torn, like the murdered refugees on the road across the dunes. (P. 106)

Graham Greene's burnt-out cases are usually defined by their alienation from God, like the drunken priest in *The Power and the Glory*. Their redemption involves a renewal of their faith which, in turn, enables them to act morally in the world. Le Carré's burnt-out cases, are, like Alec Leamas, alienated from their fellow human beings by the dehumanizing forces of twentieth-century society. Their redemption is not religious, but humanistic and involves a new growth of trust in the ordinary pleasures of life and in friendship and love with others. As Leamas leaves England to enter into what he believes to be the final phase of his mission, he considers how his relationship with Liz Gold has made it possible for him to live again as a human being:

He knew then what it was that Liz had given him; the thing that he would have to go back and find if ever he got home to England; it was the caring about little things—the faith in ordinary life; that simplicity that made you break up a bit of bread into a paper bag, walk down to the beach and throw it to the gulls. It was bread for the sea gulls or love, whatever it was he would go back and find it; he would make Liz find it for him. (P. 93)

Unfortunately, in le Carré's middle-period spy novels the protagonist is so caught up in the corruption, deceit, and crosspurposes of espionage bureaucracies that the only way he can express his newfound sense of life is by refusing any further to be used, a decision which invariably implies his death.

In *The Spy Who Came In from the Cold,* as in its immediate successors, *The Looking Glass War* and *A Small Town in Germany,* le Carré typically deals with operations initiated by the protagonists' own espionage organization which not only betray the protagonist himself, but become so intricate in their webs of betrayal and reversal that the distinction between means and ends is completely lost. The operation that generates the action of *The Spy Who Came In from the Cold* is basically a complex cover-up of what le Carré would later call a "mole," a double agent planted in an enemy espionage bureaucracy. In this case, the mole is Hans-Dieter Mundt, the assassin responsible for several murders and an attempt on George Smiley's life in *Call for the Dead*. In exchange for help in escaping from England, Mundt has agreed to become an agent for the Circus. He returns to East Germany, where his ruthlessness and ability quickly help him rise to the top of the Abteilung or East German counterespionage bureaucracy. Mundt is an anti-Semite, and one of his assistants, an East German Jew named Fiedler, soon suspects Mundt's double agentry and begins to amass evidence of his betrayals. Control decides that he must mount an operation to protect Mundt not only by eliminating Fiedler, but by removing any grounds for suspicion against Mundt. The scheme he arrives at is to make the East Germans think that the Circus is mounting a plot against Mundt and that Fiedler is a knowing or unknowing participant in that plot. Thus, when the supposed plot is exposed to the East Germans, Fiedler will be accused either of gross negligence or complicity, and Mundt will be exonerated beyond the slightest doubt.

In order to execute his scheme, Control enlists Leamas in what he says is a plot to destroy Mundt. He persuades Leamas to pretend to go to seed and become a defector so that he can plant information with the East Germans that will incriminate Mundt as the recipient of large funds from the Circus. He does not tell Leamas that the real object of the operation is not the destruction but the protection of Mundt. Instead, he uses Leamas's hatred of Mundt, who murdered his own East German network, to insure Leamas's participation in the plot. Since Leamas is only partially in on the plot, Control must devise another way of exposing the supposed scheme.

With complete indifference about the fate or identity of his victim, Control assumes that, during the period of his pretended decline, Leamas will strike up at least one friendship or affair. As it happens, Leamas does enter into what becomes a serious love affair with a young woman named Liz Gold. Conveniently for the operation, Liz is a Communist party member who can be manipulated into going to East Germany. She is victimized into doing so and becomes an innocent witness at the trial of Mundt. Her testimony proves that in spite of his apparent separation from the service, Leamas is still involved in some sort of Circus business, thus establishing that he is not a confused defector, but an active agent and part of a plot to destroy Mundt. Liz Gold's innocently delivered evidence seals the fate of Fiedler and brings about her own death and that of Leamas.

Both the reader and Alec Leamas are misled about the true nature of the plot until the very end of the novel, though on re-reading, one notes that le Carré has skillfully planted clues along the way. Le Carré's narrative skill is remarkably well-developed in *Spy*. He is able to maintain the reader's interest while at the same time misleading him until the true solution of the mystery has the impact of a brilliantly crafted classical detective story: "And suddenly, with the terrible clarity of a man too long deceived, Leamas understood the whole ghastly trick" (p. 202).

Even more significant, le Carré is able to invest his brilliant command of the plotting and narrative techniques of the thriller with a richness of character and a complexity of imagery and symbolism, that makes his creations much more deeply engrossing than the entertaining stock figures of the heroic spy tradition. The relation between Alec Leamas and Liz Gold is much more human than the casual amours James Bond indulges in with such sterotypical sexpots as Pussy Galore, Honeychile Rider, and Domino Vitale. Alec and Liz exemplify that antithesis between innocence and experience which le Carré develops in many of his later novels. However, as is often the case with le Carré's exploration of this paradigm, Liz Gold has had a good deal of experience, but it has not touched her deeply because her commitment to the Communist ideology has prevented her from integrating experience into thought. Her political naïveté will ultimately destroy her. Liz Gold's innocence resembles that of Lizzie Worthington in le Carré's

later novel *The Honourable Schoolboy,* though Lizzie's innocence
is due to her indifference to politics rather than to ideological
commitment.

Alec Leamas is a man of too much experience. He has seen
so much suffering and betrayal that he has largely ceased to
believe in anything. Yet there remains a kind of innocence at
the core of his being; he still feels outrage at the bombing of
children in his "recurrent fevers." This residual humanity makes
him vulnerable to the innocence of Liz Gold, and his experience
with her almost brings him back to life. The growing relationship between the two promises a new kind of fulfillment
for them since Liz's naïveté is challenged by Leamas's cynicism
and Leamas's despair is mitigated by Liz's simple trust in
ordinary experience. Just as burned-out Jerry Westerby in *The
Honourable Schoolboy* is given a new concern for people through
his encounter with Lizzie Worthington, so Leamas becomes a
much fuller person through Liz Gold's reawakening of the inner
vulnerability he has so carefully concealed with his mask of
toughness. Ironically, it is too late for both Leamas and Westerby since both are trapped by plots and counterplots from
which they cannot escape. Their deaths, however, take on a
tragic magnitude because they have changed from clandestine
agents to caring people. The last paragraph of *The Spy Who
Came In from the Cold* brilliantly evokes this aspect of Alec
Leamas. Choosing to die at the Berlin Wall rather than continue to live as a pawn in Cold War machinations, Leamas
finally identifies himself with the vision of children being
destroyed which had so often haunted him:

> They seemed to hesitate before firing again; someone shouted
> an order, and still no one fired. Finally they shot him, two or
> three shots. He stood glaring around him like a blinded bull
> in the arena. As he fell, Leamas saw a small car smashed between
> great lorries, and the children waving cheerfully through the
> window. (P. 223)

George Smiley plays a strangely enigmatic role in *Spy,* as
if le Carré cannot quite decide just where he stands. At the

beginning of the novel, Control tells Leamas that Smiley "isn't with us any more" (p. 21). In *Call for the Dead* Smiley had resigned from the service in order to pursue his investigation into the death of Arthur Fennan, an investigation which implicated Hans-Dieter Mundt. Sometime later, however, Control explains to Leamas that Smiley "doesn't like the operation. . . . He finds it distasteful. He sees the necessity but he wants no part in it" (p. 52). When Leamas asks Control if Smiley finds something immoral in the operation, Control insists that this is not the case: "It isn't a question of moralities. He is like the surgeon who is tired of blood. He is content that others should operate" (p. 53). As the operation proceeds, however, Smiley seems to be fully involved in it behind the scenes. He contacts Liz Gold after Leamas has "defected," and it is apparently he who arranges to pay Liz the money which later becomes the damning evidence in Mundt's trial. Finally, it is Smiley who meets Leamas and Liz at the Berlin Wall and tries to help them across before Mundt's prearranged murder of Liz and Leamas's own death. It seems probable that at this point le Carré was beginning to think of Smiley in terms of still more complex exploration of the means-end dilemma in secret service, but that he had not yet found the appropriate type of story with which to develop this theme. He would, in fact, write two more espionage stories and one novel before returning to the career of George Smiley.

In addition to a richer treatment of character and plot, *The Spy Who Came In from the Cold* also shows more fully some of the devices of narration and language which mark le Carré's mature style. One of his most interesting innovations is a narrative point of view which might be best described as "rumor." The first part of chapter 3, "Decline," is an excellent illustration. This section is replete with such phrases as "It surprised no one very much. . . . Rather to people's surprise. . . . Some said. . . . Then there was the story about the money. It leaked out—no one, as usual, knew from where . . . a few people wondered. . ." (pp. 21–26). Such a point of view works well in the narration of a spy novel by casting a haze of mystery and obfuscation about what is taking place, but it also enables le Carré to contrast the opinions, legends, and rumors bandied about by those not "in the know," with the feelings and actions of the protagonist and his antagonists. Le Carré evidently found the narrative use of "rumor" helpful, for he developed it even more complexly in his later novels. In books like *Tinker, Tailor, Soldier, Spy* intricate tapestries of many different narrative voices comment on the action, but none possess the truth in its entirety. For example, *The Honourable Schoolboy* begins: "Afterwards, in the dusty little corners where London's secret servants drink together, there was argument about where the Dolphin case history should really begin" (p. 3).

The most important aspect of le Carré's style as it coalesced in *The Spy Who Came In from the Cold* was his development of a special espionage vocabulary, based in part on the actual lingo of the Secret Service. One example will indicate how le Carré could make richly symbolic use of special terminology, such as the phrase "the cold." As used by Control and other spies, "the cold" refers to the condition of an agent being in jeopardy because he is part of an operation against the enemy. Being "out in the cold" also means that the agent is in a clandestine role where he must act a part and consequently cannot establish meaningful human contact. As part of a clandestine scheme, he is separated from the ordinary human world, and by never being able to be his real self, because it would risk his life, he even risks alienation from himself. Leamas must experience all of these feelings as aspects of being out in the cold. The cold is also a condition of the weather. While le Carré restrains himself from actually mentioning it until the third page ("Pushing up the collar of his jacket, Leamas stepped outside into the icy October wind"), the weather plays a constant role in the novel from that point on. All the major turning points—the murder of Riemeck, Leamas's defection, the trial, and the tragic climax at the Berlin wall—take place in cold weather. Finally, cold is also a traditional symbol of death. At the beginning of what he hopes will be his last operation, Leamas is told by Control that he must "stay out in the cold a little longer" implying that he can then come in, that is, retire from spying and live a normal life. By the end of the novel the only way Leamas can come in from the human death of espionage is by entering the eternal cold of physical death.

The Spy Who Came In from the Cold is a concentrated work of fiction in which every tiny action and detail assumes symbolic importance. The looser structures of the remaining novels of le Carré's second phase can be seen as preliminary studies for the much broader canvas of the Smiley-Karla trilogy. *A Small Town in Germany* and *The Looking Glass War* are clearly related to *Spy* in that they are both stories about tough and bitter agents who become entrapped in the devious machinations of their own organizations. One of them utterly fails to accomplish the moral purpose he has defined for himself and the other is destroyed by his organization's total incompetence.

The Looking Glass War is the bleakest and most absurd of all le Carré's novels. Its story tells how Leclerc, the head of a nearly defunct military espionage department, decides to send an undercover agent into East Germany because he has heard rumors of a new military installation (which probably does not exist) and because one of his couriers has been killed in Finland (probably an accident). Leclerc persuades a former wartime agent who had become bored with his peacetime life to undertake the mission. Out of shape, badly retrained, and provided with a totally obsolete radio, Leiser makes his "run," but it turns into a tragic comedy of errors, and he is almost immediately detected and trapped by the East German police. The final irony emerges when it becomes clear that Control of the Circus has assisted Leclerc in setting up the operation and provided him with obsolete equipment because he is sure the rival agency will so thoroughly bungle the operation that the ministry will finally abolish it. In essence, a man's life is sacrificed in the cause of bureaucratic infighting.

War is, among other things, le Carré's valedictory to the heroic spy tradition. Beginning with Buchan's *Thirty-Nine Steps,* the image of a man on the run was one of the basic structures of the heroic spy story. Thus, the three sections of

War are entitled "Taylor's Run," "Avery's Run," and "Leiser's Run." The sections have epigraphs from Rudyard Kipling, John Buchan, and Rupert Brooke, two writers associated with the heroic spy tradition and a poet who glorified sacrificial death in war and was himself killed in World War I. Leiser is literally an "old school" hero in that he has not been involved in espionage since World War II. Leclerc, Haldane, and the other department officials are constantly reminiscing nostalgically about their great days during World War II—"we had a whole motor pool then"—and their operation design is not only based on wartime practices, but employs World War II equipment. Leiser's first action on his run is to kill a sentry with a knife, a classic image of World War II commando operations—and he is last seen as "a man once more intent upon appearances, conscious of tradition" (p. 274).

Yet, if Leiser's fate seems to illustrate Ambassador Bradfield's insistence, in *A Small Town in Germany,* that "there's no room for his kind anymore" (p. 292), le Carré is not simply saying that. Department head Leclerc's name has a double meaning. He is the cleric or keeper of the faith; in this role he tries, however ineffectively, to maintain the heroic tradition. But he is also the clerk, the professional bureaucrat whose main concerns are to maintain and expand the power of his own department. This divided role makes him neither a true guardian nor an effective powerbroker. He is, instead, a pathetic clown, and, at the end of the novel, he really has no idea of what has happened to him.

Le Carré, however, is hardly an exponent of the bureaucratic dehumanization he sees replacing the heroic tradition. In *War,* George Smiley must perform the extremely distasteful job of making Leclerc and his group abandon their operation, leaving their agent defenseless in the field, knowing as he does that Control's original willingness to support the operation was a corrupt one. More clearly than ever before, le Carré portrays George Smiley as a man of sensibility and conscience, who is also committed to the goals of the clandestine organization and willing to act to accomplish these goals. His character poses such questions as whether the right person might learn to use power responsibly, to balance the claims of ideal and reality, thought and action, means and ends. Based in part on le Carré's own experiences as a foreign service officer in Bonn, *A Small Town in Germany* has a much wider cast of characters and a broader canvas than the much tighter structures of investigation and detection which characterized his earlier novels. This time the object of the investigation is not murder, but an ongoing espionage operation. In addition, the detective undergoes an important transformation of character in the course of his inquiry. This double structure in which the protagonist investigates an antagonist who has his own operation going on foreshadows the major structure of the Smiley-Karla trilogy. In *A Small Town in Germany,* the detective protagonist is Alan Turner, a foreign office security officer. Like Alec Leamas, Turner is a physically powerful man: "He was a big, lumbering man, fair-haired, plain-faced and pale, with the high shoulders and square fingers of an alpinist, and he walked with the thrusting slowness of a barge; a broad, aggressive policeman's walk, wilfully without finesse" (p. 380). He shares with Leamas a deep bitterness, partly the result of his puritanical lower-middle class upbringing and his lack of a public school background: "The Official Foreign Office publications were reserved. While they shed a merciless light on the origin of all their other Turners, in the matter of Alan they remained tight-lipped, as if, having considered all the facts, they felt that silence was the kindest policy" (p. 38). Thus, Turner has always felt an outsider from the old boy network of the Foreign Service. He is tough, conscientious, and contemptuous of human weaknesses, dedicated to his job, but alienated and unhappy, a failed marriage in his background.

Leo Harting is the object of Turner's investigation. Harting is a minor embassy employee who has mysteriously disappeared along with a top security file. Turner discovers that Harting, a concentration camp survivor, has been secretly investigating the background of Dr. Klaus Karfeld, the leader of a new West German political force and almost certainly the winner in the next major election. Harting has recognized

Karfeld as a concentration camp doctor who conducted experiments on human beings with various poison gases. Trying to find evidence to indict Karfeld before the statute of limitations on war crimes runs out, Harting comes across the transcript of a secret conversation between Karfeld and the British ambassador Bradfield from which it is clear that the British have struck a deal with the formerly anti-British Karfeld. Deeply concerned that this secret agreement will, like the Munich pact of 1938, foster the rise of neo-Nazism in Germany, Harting decides to assassinate Karfeld. It is for this reason that he has gone into hiding.

The more Turner discovers about Harting's life, the more he comes to admire him. He understands that like himself, Harting has been embittered by his past suffering and has gone through a long period of alienation in which survival was his only goal. Apparently a passionate love affair with the ambassador's wife has reawakened his human sympathies and driven him to commit himself to risk and action again.

The climactic scene of *A Small Town in Germany* is an argument between Turner and the British ambassador. The ambassador defends the destruction of Harting because his actions threaten the fragile appearance of British power in Europe. When Turner remonstrates that he cannot be that obsessed with surfaces, the ambassador replies: " 'What else is there when the underneath is rotten? Break the surface and we sink. That's what Harting has done. I am a hypocrite,' he continued simply. 'I'm a great believer in hypocrisy. It's the nearest we ever get to virtue. . . . I serve the appearance of things. It is the worst of systems; it is better than the others. That is my profession, and that is my philosophy' " (p. 291). Outraged at the ambassador's bureaucratic cynicism, Turner makes his own judgment: " 'Of all of you [Harting's] the only one who's real, the only one who believed and acted! For you it's a sterile, rotten game, a family game, that's all—just play. But Leo's *involved*! He knows what he wants and he's gone to get it' " (p. 292). Just as Leamas was characterized by the new men in the service as hopelessly "old school," so the ambassador tells Turner that there is no room for people like Harting anymore. "We've learned that even *nothing* is a pretty tender flower" (p. 292).

Turner is drawn out of his alienation, but his sympathy for Harting does little to avert the tragedy. In a climactic scene of a mass political rally where Karfeld speaks, Harting is himself killed, possibly by British agents. *A Small Town in Germany* is a powerful novel which, though lacking the taut coherence of *The Spy Who Came In from the Cold*, even more explicitly explores the political and ethical issues at the heart of le Carré's novels: the decline of Western democratic power and the rise of sterile and manipulative bureaucracies; the increasing problem of alienation and lack of commitment; the tendency of means and appearances to become much more important than ends.

Le Carré's re-creation of the spy story culminated in a series of three novels narrating the conflict between George Smiley of the British Secret Service and Karla, head of the espionage division of the Russian secret service, known as Moscow Centre. The three novels, *Tinker, Tailor, Soldier, Spy* (1974), *The Honourable Schoolboy* (1977), and *Smiley's People* (1980), were published separately. Each novel is an autonomous unit in a larger structure and can be read, understood, and interpreted individually. In fact, as each novel appeared, it quickly became an international best-seller. Two of the novels, *Tinker, Tailor, Soldier, Spy* and *Smiley's People*, were made into television miniseries by the BBC, starring Alec Guinness as George Smiley; both were widely shown in Britain and America. *The Honourable Schoolboy* poses much larger problems of location and cast than either of the other two novels and has not yet appeared in cinematic form.

Independent treatment of each of the novels would show that they are very different in character. *Tinker, Tailor* resembles *The Spy Who Came In from the Cold* in that it is a very tightly constructed narrative of plots within plots, betrayals within betrayals. *The Honourable Schoolboy* is more like *A Small Town*, with its variety of settings, broader cast of characters, and less concentrated structure, while *Smiley's People* is more like *The*

Looking Glass War, with its bleaker tone, its single-minded pursuit of an objective, and its ruthless manipulation of relatively innocent individuals to accomplish its end. Despite the three novels' qualities, they were clearly conceived as a trilogy and have been recently republished as such under the title *The Quest for Karla.* We will therefore discuss le Carré's transformation of the traditional secret agent adventure into a contemporary form by analyzing the trilogy as a unit.

The basic action of *Karla* begins with the expulsion of George Smiley from the service after an operational disaster leads to the disgrace and death of Control. Smiley is brought back into the service when rumors of a "mole" at the highest levels of the Circus reach Oliver Lacon, the parliamentary secretary in charge of espionage. Smiley carries out an extraordinarily complex and subtle investigation, which finally reveals that Bill Haydon, a man in the mold of John Buchan's Richard Hannay and one of the most respected and best-liked men in the Circus has been a Russian spy at least since the 1950s, and possibly since his undergraduate days before the war.

Haydon, based on the real double agent and defector Kim Philby, has not only betrayed government secrets and been responsible for the death of many Circus agents, he has also used his sexual attractiveness to betray those who consider him their friend. Haydon has seduced Smiley's wife Ann and, with Karla's help, has invented a false source of Russian information to destroy Control and insure that his own puppet, Percy Alleline, will become head of the Circus. Finally, in order to prevent Control from confirming his suspicion that the Circus harbors a double agent, Haydon is willing to risk the life of his oldest friend and homosexual lover, Jim Ellis.

After successfully exposing the treachery of Bill Haydon, Smiley is asked to accept a temporary assignment as head of the Circus in order to rebuild the department's now shattered reputation as an effective espionage agency. In *The Honourable Schoolboy,* Smiley discovers signs of a camouflaged flow of laundered money from Moscow to Hong Kong. His investigations suggest that the money is payment from Karla to a long-time double agent in Communist China. This agent, Nelson Ko, had been planted by Karla many years ago and has now become very important in the Chinese government. Ko also has a brother in Hong Kong who is trying to help him escape from the mainland. Smiley decides to capture Nelson Ko as he comes out of China. The final section takes place against the chaotic background of war and revolution in Southeast Asia. A Circus agent, Jerry Westerby, the "honourable schoolboy" of the novel's title, has been looking into the background of various characters associated with the Ko brothers. Like Alec Leamas in *Spy* and Jim Ellis in *Tinker, Tailor,* Westerby has human feelings which finally make him reject the complex web of betrayals in which he has become involved. When he tries to warn Nelson Ko of the plot to kidnap him, he is shot by a Circus agent from an American helicopter. The novel's final betrayal involves Saul Enderby, a Foreign Office bureaucrat who wishes to become head of the Circus. Enderby has conspired with one of Smiley's subordinates to turn Nelson Ko over to the American CIA in exchange for its support in his bid for power. Smiley is once more forced into retirement.

Smiley's return and his final ambiguous triumph over Karla are the subject of *Smiley's People.* The murder of an aging anti-Soviet emigré, Vladimir, sets Smiley off on another investigation. Shortly before his death, Vladimir had telephoned a contact at the Circus to ask for a meeting with Max, Smiley's code name. Pursuing the meaning of this mysterious message, Smiley follows a complex trail from Paris to Hamburg to Switzerland. Acting as a private citizen, with the assistance of some of the people who had formerly worked with him at the Circus, Smiley discovers that Karla's one vulnerability is a beloved schizophrenic daughter. Karla has tried to forge an identity for this daughter in the West so that she may receive decent care for her illness in a Swiss clinic. Smiley uses his knowledge of Karla's daughter to force Karla to defect from the Soviet Union and become a Western informer. At the end, Smiley and his former assistant Peter Guillam meet Karla briefly at the Berlin Wall as he is picked up by British agents.

"George, you won," said Guillam, as they walked slowly toward
the car.
    "Did I?" said Smiley. "Yes. Yes, well I suppose I did."
(P. 374)

That nothing is as it seems has always been a basic principle
in the spy story, but in *The Quest for Karla,* it reaches the level
of a metaphysical axiom. The espionage device that dominates
the first two volumes of the trilogy is that of the mole, a
prominent member of the bureaucracy who is actually a long-
term espionage agent. In the world of the mole, friends are
actually enemies, lovers are betrayers, and plots turn out to
be counterplots. The most important way in which this principle is exemplified in the trilogy as a whole is that Smiley's
apparent victory at the end of *Smiley's People* is, in fact, a defeat
in terms of the real issues that le Carré understands to be at
stake. This ultimate defeat is brilliantly summed up in a
seemingly trivial action toward the end of the book. As Karla
comes through the checkpoint into the waiting arms of Smiley
and his people, Smiley

> heard Guillam telling someone to get that bloody car up here
> before they come over the bridge and get him back. He heard
> the ring of something metal falling onto the icy cobble, and
> knew it was Ann's cigarette-lighter, but nobody else seemed to
> notice it. They [Smiley and Karla] exchanged one more glance
> and perhaps each for that second did see in the other something
> of himself. (P. 373)

A few moments later

> Something in Smiley's stiffness made Toby pull away and Smiley
> himself stepped quickly out of the halo, passing very close to
> Ann's lighter on his way. It lay at the halo's very edge, tilted
> slightly, glinting like fool's gold on the cobble. He thought of
> picking it up, but somehow there seemed no point and no one
> else appeared to have seen it. Someone was shaking his hand,
> someone else was clapping him on the shoulder. (P. 373)

These scenes are rich in symbolic implication: the cold ex-
changed glance, Smiley's stiffness, stepping out of the halo,
Ann's lighter at the halo's edge, glinting like fool's gold, no
one else appearing to see it. The key to these implications lies
in the lighter Karla drops and what it has come to mean. The
lighter is inscribed "To George from Ann with all my love"
and was given to Smiley by his wife at an earlier time, before
Ann's manifold infidelities had eroded their marriage. The
lighter came into Karla's possession during his only previous
meeting with Smiley in the summer of 1955 in India. At this
time Karla had fallen from power and was in danger of being
killed. He had been arrested in New Delhi on immigration
charges, and while he was held in prison there, Smiley had
flown to India hoping to persuade Karla to defect. At the end
of their first interview, Karla picked up a pack of cigarettes
and Smiley's lighter and did not return them. Smiley later
recalled, "I would never have dreamed of letting him take it
in the ordinary way; but this was not the ordinary way. Indeed
I thought it thoroughly appropriate that he should take her
lighter; I thought it—Lord help me—expressive of the bond
between us" (*Tinker, Tailor,* p. 209). However, Smiley's sense
of kinship with Karla is not returned. His pleas make no impact
on the totally committed Karla:

> I behaved like a soft fool. The very archetype of a flabby Western
> liberal. But I would rather be my kind of fool than his, for all
> that. I am sure . . . that neither my arguments, nor his own
> predicament at Moscow Centre would ultimately have swayed
> him in the least. I expect he spent the night working out how
> he would outgun Rudnev when he got home. It's odd to reflect
> that all the time he was looking at me, he could have been
> thinking of Gerald [code name of Haydon, the Circus mole]. I
> expect they've had a good laugh about it since. (P. 213)

At this early stage of his pursuit of Karla, Smiley may
feel a momentary bond between himself and another person
caught up in the clandestine world, but he understands himself
to be fundamentally different from Karla. He rejects Karla's
total willingness to use any human being including himself

to gain his ends. In fact, in the course of *Tinker, Tailor* we learn that Karla is not only capable of murder, but of the most brutal manipulation of other human beings. He is quite willing to use people and situations outside the clandestine world to attain his ends. Thus, in order to protect Bill Haydon from suspicion, Karla instructs him to initiate an affair with Smiley's wife, knowing that Smiley will conscientiously avoid being professionally suspicious of any person he is jealous of. In this way, Karla ruthlessly exploits not only Smiley's conscience but Ann's desperately needful promiscuity. The final irony is that Bill Haydon is primarily a homosexual and has no real desire for Ann. Haydon later explains to Smiley: "But you had this one price: Ann. The last illusion of the illusionless man. [Karla] reckoned that if I were known to be Ann's lover around the place you wouldn't see me very straight when it came to other things" (p. 364).

Returning Smiley's lighter is Karla's contemptuous gesture indicating that Smiley has become another Karla since he has been willing to exploit a young girl's pathetic madness and her father's profound love—a love so deep that Karla has been willing to risk not only his career but his life and, in the end, to reject his life's work in order to protect his daughter. It is no wonder that Smiley has no wish to pick up the lighter. It is also significant that the others do not see it. Unlike Smiley, they see only his triumph and do not recognize his even greater defeat.

This is le Carré's major reshaping of the spy story genre. He has changed it from a story of heroic, or at least, accidental triumph into a much more complex and ambiguous narrative of ironic failure in which the protagonists succeed only at the cost of becoming as dehumanized, as distorted in their conception of ends and means as their adversaries. In the modern world of clandestine bureaucracies and Cold War, the only choice open to a decent individual seems to be complicity, like Smiley, or destruction, like Leamas, and Westerby. Le Carré does not, however, give us simply an easy condemnation of the excesses of clandestine agencies. The spy story is as le Carré sees it, a statement about the inescapable dilemma of the mid-twentieth century.

Appropriately enough, *The Quest for Karla* begins with a "new boy" entering a minor English public school. The symbol of the school returns time and again throughout the trilogy: Smiley is often mistaken for a schoolmaster and in his retirement he carries out scholarly research on German baroque literature; Karla is described by Smiley as a "little wiry chap, with silvery hair and bright brown eyes and plenty of wrinkles . . . he could have been a schoolmaster" (*Tinker, Tailor*, p. 204); Jerry Westerby is "the honourable schoolboy." The appropriateness of this recurrent symbol is manifold. Espionage has always been associated with schools because of the special intelligence and training needed for espionage work. Both the British and the American secret services have always recruited primarily through colleges and universities. In England, particularly, the Oxford-Cambridge colleges, largely drawn from public schools, were the center of Secret Service recruitment until well after World War II. In addition, the public schools are connected with many of the traditions of British imperial administration and military success, for they instilled a deep loyalty and a ruthless discipline as well as creating an informal network of "old boys" whose personal acquaintance with each other often transcended the limitations of governmental bureaucracies. In this way, the public school symbolizes for le Carré an earlier stage of British cultural history, which, whatever its virtues and faults has become as obsolete in the contemporary world as the heroic spy tradition with which it is associated. Finally, school represents the period of first learning, the beginning of experience, and the end of innocence which is so pervasive a theme in le Carré's work.

The other institution that plays a major role in *The Quest for Karla* is the Circus, le Carré's version of the British Secret Service. The Circus is a major espionage bureaucracy with worldwide branches and the power to play an important role in shaping history. It is also a perverted family with siblings constantly squabbling with each other for their father's attention. Many of the major departments are given code names taken from family life: there are "mothers" or comptrollers, "babysitters" or bodyguards, "housekeepers" or specialists in cover-ups, and the Saratt "nursery" or clandestine training program. Le Carré uses the heavy-handed humor in these attempts to give an espionage bureaucracy some human qualities to ironically call attention to the essentially dehumanizing nature of bureaucratic life.

Smiley's individual drama in the trilogy is a recapitulation of the postwar history of the British Secret Service and, in a broader, more general way, of Western democracy in the Cold War. Emerging from school with a training in the imperial tradition, Smiley is recruited from university into the Circus. During the war, he is a heroic spy, daily risking his life in occupied Europe to uncover the enemy's secrets and sabotage his war effort. After the war, however, things gradually change. The Cold War with Soviet Russia creates new and more complex problems which cannot effectively be dealt with by the traditional methods and attitudes. Adventure becomes bureaucratized as the espionage organization must respond not only to its traditional mission of finding out enemy secrets, but also to the frustrations and limitations inherent in its role as part of an increasingly complicated political and economic bureaucracy. Those who still imagine that they live in the heroic tradition are unable to adapt to the new structures and attitudes. With Alec Leamas and Jerry Westerby, they share a traditional sense of honor which makes them reject the complex moral ambiguities of the Cold War. Their sense of right destroys them. Others, like Bill Haydon, are lured into the excitement of betrayal as a substitute for the decay of the heroic tradition. One character, Connie Sachs, understands this well. "Poor loves," she says. "Trained to Empire. Trained to rule the waves. All gone. All taken away. Bye-bye world. You're the last, George, you and Bill" (*Tinker, Tailor*, p. 113).

Smiley does attempt to adapt to the new moral environment of the Cold War, while trying to retain his basic sense of humanity and decency. In many ways, Smiley understands the working of the new clandestinity. He is a master of plots and counterplots and is highly skilled in the intricacies of the "paper chase," the assembling of information through the comparison of files and records. He understands the necessity of teamwork and the use of specialists like Connie Sachs, the Circus' retired Moscow Centre expert. In fact, much of the suspense in *The Quest for Karla* arises not from overt action, but from the search for vital bits of data that will link one set of facts and inferences to another. So long as Smiley is investigating the betrayals of others, he retains his moral perspective. In spite of Haydon's seduction of Ann, his murderous plots, his many betrayals, Smiley still feels some sympathy for a defeated man and eschews vengeance. But when he is himself involved in planning and executing an operation against an adversary, his moral judgment is increasingly obscured and he becomes more like Karla in his willingness to use any means to entrap his foe. The George Smiley of *The Spy Who Came In from the Cold* found Control's manipulation of Leamas and his victimization of Fiedler and Liz Gold morally repugnant. Though he continued to participate in the operation, we sense that he is at least partly concerned with protecting Leamas and Liz as much as he can. In *The Looking Glass War* Smiley is able to justify the abandoning of Leiser to his destruction, but is obviously not very happy about it. In *The Honourable Schoolboy,* Smiley's obsession with Karla has grown to the point where he is willing to connive at almost anything to entrap him. That operation gets out of his control at the end because of betrayal within his own organization. Nonetheless, Smiley is perfectly willing to do things which the more idealistic Jerry Westerby finds unjustifiable. Smiley himself is deeply worried about what has happened to him. At the end of *The Honourable Schoolboy* he writes to Ann:

> I honestly do wonder, without wishing to be morbid, how I reached this present pass. So far as I can ever remember of my youth, I chose the secret road because it seemed to lead straightest and furthest toward my country's goal. The enemy in those days was someone we could point at and read about in the papers. Today, all I know is that I have learned to interpret the whole of life in terms of conspiracy. That is the sword I have lived by, and as I look round me now I see it is the sword I shall die by as well. These people terrify me, but I am one of them. (Pp. 532–33)

Smiley's People completes the process of corruption. So concerned is Smiley to entrap Karla that he is prepared to use the weakness of an innocent young woman to accomplish his end. Unlike *The Honourable Schoolboy*, *Smiley's People* gives us a Smiley who is totally in control as he moves implacably from the first hint of Karla's weakness to its full exploitation in the forcing of Karla's defection. In spite of occasional moments when he wonders about his course of action ("he read as far into his own past as into Karla's, and sometimes it seemed to him that the one life was merely the complement to the other; that they were causes of the same incurable malady" [p. 281]), he does not hesitate until his complex plotting brings him to that ambiguous moment at the Berlin checkpoint when Karla returns his lighter.

Smiley's ultimate willingness to use any means to achieve his goal is probably the end of the story of George Smiley since he has failed to resolve those modern dilemmas of means and ends, action and thought, reality and ideal which can be summed up in the basic question that haunts all of le Carré's mature work: Do the ends of human survival and peace require such means that humanity will be destroyed in its effort to save itself?

The underlying theme of le Carré's portrayal of the human dilemmas of the mid-twentieth century is stated most obviously in his one novel without espionage as an explicit theme, *The Naive and Sentimental Lover* (1972). The protagonist of this novel, Aldo Cassidy, is a highly successful designer and manufacturer of baby carriages.

Cassidy is less than happily married and is on the verge of purchasing a run-down country house in which he can live the life of a country gentleman. In the process of inspecting a decaying mansion he meets a wildly irresponsible writer Shamus and his wife, Helen. Cassidy is immediately drawn to the spontaneity, the excitement, the reality, and the passion that he feels emanating from the couple. He enters into a secret affair with them, but is ultimately unable to commit himself fully to Shamus and Helen. He gives them up and returns to his former way of life, aware that he has somehow failed to meet the challenge of life. He moves with his wife to a country mansion and prepares to finish out the rest of his life, knowing that he has become an empty and burned-out person. His wife kindly "accepted that Cassidy had suffered spiritual death, but she was prepared, for the children's sake, to overlook it" (p. 452).

The significance of Aldo Cassidy's experience, as le Carré interprets it, is suggested by the title of the novel, which is taken from a famous essay on aesthetics and modernism "Über naive und sentimentalische Dichtung" by the German dramatist and philosopher Friedrich von Schiller. Schiller's essential argument was that in the earlier stages of human culture men lived in harmony with nature and with themselves. There was no separation between thought and action, between imagination and reality. But the evolution of culture alienated man from this basic unity with life. In the modern age man experiences a condition of disharmony and alienation. He can only yearn for his original wholeness of being as an ideal. For Schiller, "naive" poetry is that which grows out of man's original wholeness of being. Modern poetry and experience can only be "sentimental," that is, it must reflect the disunity of experience, the inescapable gap between ideal and reality, and the terrible burden of self-consciousness. As Helen explains this theory to Aldo Cassidy:

> Schiller had split the world in two. "It's called being *naive*," she said. "Or being sentimental. They're sort of different kinds of *things,* and they interact.". . .
>
> "Which am I?" he asked.
>
> "Well Shamus is *naive*," she replied cautiously, as if remembering a hard-learned lesson. "Because he lives life and doesn't imitate it. Feeling is knowledge," she added rather tentatively.
>
> "So I'm the other thing."
>
> "Yes. You're sentimental. That means you long to be *like* Shamus. You've left the natural state behind and you've become . . . well part of civilization, sort of . . . corrupt . . .
>
> "And Shamus . . . being *naive,* part of nature in fact, longs to be like *you.* He's natural, you're corrupt. That's why he loves you." (Pp. 62–63)

Le Carré is too good an artist to state explicit philosophic principles without qualifying ironies. Yet it is surprising how much Schiller's distinction plays a part in his work and in his thought. [1] For example, we have already seen how the dialectic between innocence and experience, one way of expressing the antithesis between "naive and sentimental" as Schiller conceived it, plays a very important part in his work, as in the relationship between Alec Leamas and Liz Gold.

George Smiley is le Carré's most complex expression of a man caught up in the "sentimental" mode of experience. Smiley is a reflective and contemplative person who has, until his involvement with Karla, a healthy suspicion of action that risks ends in the pursuit of means. This is the "recurrent fever," which characterizes Smiley's doubts about some of Control's more unscrupulous plots. However, Smiley is fascinated by men in whom thought and action seems inseparably united. He recognizes this as the apparent quality that gives Bill Haydon his power over the other leaders of the Circus—"the same unattainable ideal of the rounded man, even if the ideal was itself misconceived, or misplaced" (*Smiley's People,* p. 156). It is also this quality which Smiley ascribes to Karla, the power of reflecting and acting without his resolution becoming "sicklied o'er with the pale cast of thought." Smiley is fascinated by what seems to be Karla's complete lack of the ambiguity, alienation, and indecision that plague him. Though he seeks to justify his "sentimentality" by making it out to be a more human quality than Karla's "naïveté," he is nonetheless compelled to prove himself as capable of real action as Karla is. By the second volume of the trilogy, Smiley is beginning to act without human reservations; his former role as a "sentimentalist" is taken over by the disappointed idealist Jerry Westerby. In *Smiley's People,* Smiley has achieved a balance between thought and action in which his imagination and his intellect have become totally devoted to the destruction of Karla. But, in the process he becomes as "spiritually dead" as Aldo Cassidy.

1. I would like to express my indebtedness to Professor David Monaghan for first pointing out the significance of Schiller's distinction in le Carré's thought.

The split between thought and action is one of the fundamental themes of modernism. Le Carré's ability to make this dialectic the central theme of his version of the secret agent genre suggests that it is a problem he has himself experienced deeply. Indeed, the way in which his career as a Foreign Service officer gave way to his life as a writer might be viewed as indicating his dissatisfaction with a life of action or of thought alone. Like his creation, Aldo Cassidy, he yearns to unite in himself the naive-sentimental division, yet as a product of modern experience he is keenly aware of the impossibility of establishing a lost harmony between man and nature. Perhaps what he recently wrote about another artist is as good a commentary on himself: "His work is the product of a restless and slightly puritanical nature, deeply ill at ease with the world's condition and his own" (le Carré, "Introduction" to Don McCullin, *Hearts of Darkness,* p. 10).

As le Carré presents it, the basic problem of modern society is our loss of touch with our full human nature and our consequent tendency to engage in meaningless but destructive action, or to wallow in contemplation and thought which leads only to more rationalization and justification of the process of dehumanization which engulfs us. Bureaucracy is, in his view, the reification of endless inaction while, on the other hand, a thoughtless commitment to action can lead only to destruction. The ultimate naive poem is nuclear war, while the final form of sentimentality is total bureaucratization. The spy is a figure of particular fascination to le Carré because he is forced to act out this basic modern dilemma in his own individual situation. As a professional secret agent, he is part of an increasingly ineffective bureaucracy, but, as an agent in the field, a man out in the cold, he is in a situation where every action is real, a matter of life or death to him. In this sense he is the modern Everyman and the appropriate protagonist of a literary genre especially expressive of the human condition in the latter half of the twentieth century.

8 Today's Spy: Recent Espionage Fiction

Eric Ambler thought that the Dreyfus affair was a great stimulus for the writing of spy stories; if it was, that was in another time and in another country, and only distantly related to the themes and plots of espionage fiction today. Many of the heroes of spy novels written during the first three decades of this century were amateurs (it is now a commonplace to note): they were usually gentlemen in the stereotyped clubland sense and their world was unmistakably good or cosmically evil. But after World War II our understanding of the many facets of the spy's occupation has been tremendously expanded, and the moral parameters of his job have clouded many previously unambiguous moral issues. We now know that the secret agents of all nations, whether members of the KGB, CIA, MI6, BND, or the Mossad, assassinate enemies, steal hardware of military and strategic importance from friendly nations and neutrals, manipulate political and public events, finance revolutions and nationalizations, make secret deals with the enemy, conduct counterinsurgency operations, as well as perform the more

187

traditional tasks of gathering and evaluating intelligence data and uncovering the enemy's agents. Likewise, the secret agents of espionage fiction have expanded their roles by so much that it is now nebulous to speak of "the spy novel" and to be sure that we can all agree on what it means to spy.

Many novels written during the past three decades have more than kept pace with our understanding of the profession of espionage. It is no longer as simple as it once was. Today's spy is not always certain which side is the "right" one and which side he ought to be unfailingly serving and protecting. And, of course, neither are we. In *Saving the Queen* an American agent infiltrates the British Establishment to seek out moles who have infested the Queen's household. *The Looking Glass War* uses the conventional formula of the spy going over into enemy territory on the old-fashioned mission of gathering information—in this case to verify questionable information about a reported Russian missile emplacement in East Germany, an emplacement which may not exist at all—and though the territory is not that of a wartime enemy, the danger and the thrill are just as great. The danger of death, if the spy is caught, remains: in *The Looking Glass War* the British agent is captured and presumably killed. In the more recent *Firefox,* by Craig Thomas, the agent's mission is to steal a new Russian supersonic fighter (NATO code-named Firefox) from a closely guarded airfield deep in Soviet territory. If he had been caught he would most certainly have gotten shot—either before a public trial or shortly after. Cold wars can be deadlier than hot ones for the spooks who are the unsung combatants in them.

Good guys and bad are no longer recognizable by the hats they wear, and the governments they represent are equally ambiguous and thus at least suspect. Geoffrey Household's *Rogue Male* narrates the hairbreadth escapes of a man who has attempted to shoot Hitler—no ambiguity there. But less clear-cut in its morality is Frederick Forsyth's update of that plot in *The Day of the Jackal,* whose anonymous assassin is a professional killer in the employ of the OAS, hired to take the life of Charles de Gaulle: Whose side should we be on? The reader has an inevitable problem of empathetic identification in this novel. In other tales the ambiguity resides elsewhere: Jack Higgins's *Eagle Has Landed* engages us entirely with the German airborne commandoes whose assignment is the assassination of Winston Churchill; though on the "wrong" side they are very brave and commendably honorable throughout. Even though they are German, English-speaking readers are on their side. No one would want to have seen Churchill killed, and yet many readers on some level want the Germans to succeed. Higgins makes that decision making easy for us, since we eventually learn that "Churchill" was merely a double anyway, planted to obscure the real prime minister's secret movements. In Thomas Harris's *Black Sunday* Palestinian agents make plans to kill eighty thousand American football fans at a Super Bowl game, an extravagant plot which does not cause readers any problems of identification regardless of how they feel about the Middle East situation. In *The Rhinemann Exchange* Americans deal clandestinely with roughly their German counterparts at the height of World War II hostilities, though Robert Ludlum makes it quite explicit who are the good guys and who are the worms. In Len Deighton's *Spy Story* several wealthy and politically influential Englishmen take their nation's foreign policy into their own hands by dealing privately with the Russians. They are the bad guys of course, even though they are thoroughly patriotic Englishmen. In another of Ludlum's best-sellers, *The Gemini Contenders,* a small group of disaffected American army officers, chiefly Vietnam veterans, plan to expose corruption, inefficiency, and various other failings for their own purposes. Forsyth's experience as a journalist in Africa gave him the background for *The Dogs of War,* which is chiefly concerned with the attempt of a particularly rapacious English capitalist to take over a platinum-rich nation in a covert operation employing mercenaries. Once into this novel there seems little problem about the right side, but the reader will most likely have to forget that he is involved (even fictionally) in a real continent (Africa), though the targeted country is given a fictional name—"Zangaro." We all have opinions about mercenaries in Africa, especially those who have been hired to overthrow governments there, but those feelings may not correspond with the judgments that Forsyth is trying to elicit. It is fiction, of course, but does that mean that we can immediately forget the realities of the everyday-life world, that we can so readily and willingly suspend disbelief?

When the spy novel operative finds that his agency is inept or its administrators unwilling to carry out what he knows to be justice, he has—especially in recent years—taken justice into his own hands. In the old West he would be a vigilante. Caruthers (*The Riddle of the Sands*) returns briefly to London in the middle of his adventure off German waters, but while there he decides that Whitehall either will not want to get involved in what he knows to be a serious matter, or else British officialdom will botch it. So, he becomes one of the first of the secret agents to do it himself. In more recent years the menaces have been more personal, and the hero-spies have become, when they respond personally, in effect, vigilantes settling private scores. Robert Littell's Charlie Heller, in *The Amateur*, is a prime example of these; when the CIA is loath to find the terrorists who have killed his fiancé, Charlie blackmails his bosses into training him and sending him into Eastern Europe to do the job himself. Vengeance is his; by the end of his adventure he has successfully killed each member of the terrorist gang, evading not only the Communist's counterespionage agents but the assassins that the CIA have sent to eliminate him. So, too, with the marathon man who, at the novel's climax, declares to his teacher at Columbia University that he no longer wants justice, he wants blood. The parallel with several (fictional) police officers (especially Dirty Harry) will come immediately to mind; he, and those of his like-minded friends, are too obvious to justify elaboration, but also too obvious not to be mentioned.

As fictive intelligence agents have many of the same missions as their real-life counterparts, so have they by and large become more credible as people. James Bond and to a lesser degree Matt Helm are exceptions, but nearly all of the spy novel's heroes after 1945 have quite human failings and weaknesses, a theme which dates back to Ambler's 1937 *Background to Danger* and especially to Graham Greene's *The Confidential Agent* (1939). One of the functions of the real spy while on duty is to merge into his background, to be socially camouflaged; in espionage fiction he is actually often on the verge of losing his individuality as well as his identity, not what the home office had in mind. The fictional agent is victimized not only by his role in society but by technology, which not even James Bond ever seemed to get mastery of.

Adam Hall's secret agent Quiller is several cuts above his fellow operatives, yet even he (or especially he) can complain that his status is often reduced to that of an automated lever within a massively intricate machine:

> The Bureau is a government department but officially it doesn't exist, and this nihilistic status has long ago cast a sort of creeping blight over the people who work here. Most of them don't even know each other by our code name because we're a shifting population of rootless souls and our business is our own business and we're not interested in anyone else's. (*The Quiller Memorandum*, p. 216)

One of the few public evaluations of a spy's life may occur at his death; but since his life is so evanescent and seemingly insubstantial, his death will present problems to his survivors. Le Carré captures such a painful moment in *The Looking Glass War* when the colleagues of a recently deceased agent try to tell the widow (she does not yet know that she is a widow) of the disaster. Sweating palms and scraping feet; Avery and Leclerc have barely known the agent, Taylor, and know his widow even less well. They are relieved when a small girl answers their knock to say that Mommy has "gone to work" and more comforted to be able to give the girl two half crowns (*Looking Glass War*, pp. 40–41). More explicitly, Adam Hall has Quiller soliloquize:

> Except for the fact that we worked for the same outfit, I had nothing to do with North and he had nothing to do with me, but some of his misery had rubbed off and I knew I wouldn't sleep if I went back to the flat, and anyway we all seem to

gravitate to that dreary bloody building whenever there's trouble. Comfort in numbers, I suppose, when the nerves start playing up. (*The Quiller Memorandum*, p. 12)

Not that we'd ever hear of him again. Outside the hermetically sealed circle of his immediate contacts—his briefing officer, mission controller, and director in the field—there wouldn't be any inquiry. After tonight, along those warrenlike corridors of that anonymous building in Whitehall where no one officially exists even when they're alive, there'd be no questions asked, and the name of North would never be mentioned again. In the Bureau, death is a disease with no complications. (*The Quiller Memorandum*, p. 15).

Or the agent may be able to establish his identity only through his possession of a plastic security card—the predicted nightmare of many of us who have long complained that we are (or will shortly be) merely numbers, or that we will be known only by our Social Security or dog tag numbers. Just such a situation has been dramatized in Len Deighton's *Spy Story* when the protagonist-agent makes one of his infrequent visits to an adjacent headquarters building, but finds on entering that the guard does not know him personally and so challenges his identity because his card is missing from its proper place in the file—indicating that "he" is already inside:

The policeman at the door took my security card.
"Armstrong, Patrick," he announced to the other man, and not too fast. The other man searched through the cards on the wall. "Did you just come out," said the first cop. . . . "No, of course not, I'm just going in."
. . . "your card is not in the rack," he explained. "What happens to the cards is strictly your job," I said. "Don't try and make me feel guilty about it." . . . "I'm only going to the library," I explained. "Ah," said the gateman, smiling as if he'd heard this explanation from any number of foreign spies. "It's all the same in'it? Ther library is on the third floor."
"You come with me, then," I said.
He shook his head to show that it was a good try for a foreigner. . . . He put glasses on and read my security card

again. Before we had the security cards, there had been no delays.
I was a victim of some Parkinson's law of proliferating security.
(Pp. 152–53)

Nearly every fictional agent of the past two decades feels
this isolation and identity loss. It was not that way in the old
days, we are led to believe; the agency—the conglomerate,
ponderous, dispassionately paternal agency—had only in recent
times enveloped its own agents. Neither Buchan's Hannay nor
Childers's Caruthers nor Maugham's Ashenden were company
men; hardly. Len Deighton's Charlie, of *Yesterday's Spy*, com-
plains about life under the newly imposed working conditions,
wistfully reminiscent about former times, with his old friend,
Steve Champion:

> "The days of the entrepreneur are over, Steve," I told him. "Now
> it's the organization man who gets the Christmas bonus and the
> mileage allowance. People like you are called heroes, and don't
> mistake it for a compliment. It just means has-beens who'd
> rather have a hunch than a computer output. You are yesterday's
> spy, Steve." (P. 48)

And somewhat later, Charlie reflects on the new breed of
intelligence expert, in this case the American on temporary
duty, Schlegel, at poolside:

> He swam underwater, turning his head only enough to bite air.
> I envied him. Not only the ability to swim like a basking shark,
> but also the jet-jockey readiness to press buttons, pull triggers,
> and dive into the deep end of life, while people like me drown
> in indecision, imagined loyalties and fear. If Champion was
> yesterday's spy, Schlegel was tomorrow's. I can't say I looked
> forward to it. (P. 148)

Not all heroism is passé in modern fiction, of course, but
it seems difficult for American, British, and Western European
writers to write about the heroic except ironically. In *Not the
Glory* Pierre Boulle's double agent in London, the Polish ref-
ugee William Conrad, is at first sincerely spying for his real

country, Germany. But during the course of his mission he experiences a conversion: having been instructed to "fuse your own life into the life of those decadents. . . . You will induce them to recognize in you a reflection of themselves" (p. 218). Conrad succeeds far too well. Enlisting in the British army, he is quickly commissioned and eventually dies a "hero's death . . . hand-to-hand fighting in the jungle. . . . One of the finest officers in the unit . . . deeply missed by all his comrades-in-arms" (pp. 219–20). There is heroism, but in our world it can hardly be depicted without irony. Conrad fulfills the instructions of his superiors when he successfully induces the British to see in his life a reflection of their own; it is at first a mask, but his Anglo friends eventually induce him to respond as they perceive him. His death, in Her Majesty's service, is somewhat less dramatic than is advertised to the folks back home, yet his original enemies (and latterly his friends) interpret it in the most favorable light. Boulle's hero is a spy for the wrong side, a spy who changes sides silently and invisibly during the course of his mission. His betrayal of his German superiors becomes his salvation. Appropriately, in his death, appearances are more significant than reality.

More conventional in his heroism is William F. Buckley's agent (in *Saving the Queen*) who is by no means conservative in his accomplishments: he successfully "infiltrates" Buckingham Palace, uncovers the traitor who is among Her Majesty's entourage (ironically and unintentionally anticipating the scandal about Sir Anthony Blunt) and forces his suicide during an aerial combat simulation, and sleeps with Her Majesty in the course of his mission. All in a day's work in the life of a secret agent. As Buckley's old-fashioned heroism is shared by relatively few in the West—Robert Ludlum is another extoller of traditional heroic virtues—writers from some militantly nationalistic nations, notably Israel, have found this formula viable (more about this later).

Barely credible is the bravery and noble-spiritedness of Jack Higgins's Lt. Col. Kurt Steiner, of *The Eagle Has Landed;* the mission which, in code, gives the book its title—the attempt to kidnap or kill Churchill—turns out to be more believable than Steiner's defense and protection of Jewish victims of the Warsaw ghetto in defiance of SS troops stationed there. This act of unlikely humanity and bravado gets him and his men assigned to a suicidal post in the Atlantic, from which he is "rescued" when he and his men agree unanimously to the Eagle operation. His behavior, once he has landed, so impresses his English "victims" that after the Germans have all been killed they arrange to have their enemies buried with dignity and honor. But since neither Steiner nor most of the other characters are believable as people, the novel suffers from the reader's lack of faith, an incredulity exacerbated by the pretense that Steiner's biography had been uncovered during the course of a journalist's vacation in eastern England.

Fleming's hero's skill and poised courage we never take quite seriously; Boulle has the craftsmanship to invest his adventure stories with irony, as we have just seen. Higgins and Buckley do not make moral demands on the reader; both have enjoyed tremendous commercial success (though in Buckley's case his celebrity status has had a lot to do with it), suggesting that though in a minor key prewar heroism still has its admirers. Of all these writers, Robert Ludlum is the epitome of the novelist whose heroes, motivated by the purest of intentions, always succeed. Critics of this enormously popular writer complain that though Ludlum creates a nearly universal conspiracy for his heroes to combat, they are nevertheless uninterruptedly successful. The evil conspiracies are well-planned and huge in scope, and the enemy's agents are well-trained and ruthless and seem to have unlimited resources. Nevertheless, they are in the end always defeated. Obviously, Ludlum is not appealing to his readers' sense of what is realistic; just as obviously, he has been able to engage his reader's sympathy because the covert message of his fiction is that despite the seemingly overwhelming scope of the enemy the individual can survive, even overcome. For Ludlum that enemy is a wide range of powerful institutions: the FBI, Nazi Germany, the Catholic Church, secret cabals of highly placed and powerful army officers, neo-Nazi groups with extraordinary wealth. Yet his heroes have the ability, the cleverness, the skills, and the plain dumb luck to win out when the final gun sounds. We believe in Ludlum's heroes because we want to see such projections of ourselves get the bigger score.

In those olden days when good was instantly recognizable and evil was as cosmic as it was lethal, their side had its outstanding champions to challenge ours. Now, commonly enough, the other side's agents are individually no more able than the protagonist (or pivotal character) and are, despite the international scope of their conspiracy, quite ordinary. They too put on their pants one leg at a time. When Richard Hannay confronted the enemy, he was taking on evil; when George Smiley begins an operation, it is to combat his opposite number Karla in Moscow Centre. After Graham Greene allowed us to see that no side was distinctly better than any other, the confrontation in spy novels was necessarily between individuals and their agencies. No hero gains in stature by defeating weak or inept opponents. Great victories require opponents of great stature. In this respect the heroes of the 1920s and 1930s had an advantage because their amateur status by comparison enlarged still further the size of the Goliaths they faced. Hannay is all the more impressive for having outwitted the Black Stone professionals. If Caruthers's discovery of the riddle of the sands is going to be easy and simple to accomplish, we will not think so much of him. And we may think even less of Erskine Childers. Hence, the formula of the amateur whose commitment to the right cause enables him to win persists. In the 1980s, the enemy in the novels of Helen MacInnes are usually Russians (or other Communists) whose agents can be dealt with capably by her American private citizens. Graduate student Thomas Babington McCauley ("Babe") Levy, the marathon man, becomes hunter and executioner only after a very long spell as victim of the *bund* of *der Weisse Engel* and other former Nazis. But we remember Babe far more vividly as the victim of the Angel's dental drill than as his executioner, a humanizing touch, making Levy's final triumph over Szell all the more impressive and satisfying.

In these cases, as in many others, we may not feel that the "good guy" is really anything special, aside from being "good."

He persists, he survives, he is cleverer than many, but as much as anything he has only luck and (usually) our good wishes on his side. When the spy is thus humanized, he may not have, like us, much more than luck on his side. This is certainly true of *The Wind Chill Factor*'s John Cooper who, it is clear, could not survive, let alone effectively fight the enemy, were it not for his brutal and eminently able friend, Olaf Peterson. Yet the Cooper-Peterson "triumph" is one of survival only: they uncover a global neo-Nazi plot but are allowed to live only because they swear to maintain absolute secrecy about it. Cooper is under a psychiatrist's care and the Nazis consequently find him harmless enough anyway. (In the old days they would have gassed him.) *Firefox*'s Gant is a salad of nearly incapaciting neuroses. The same apparent handicap, however, does not incapacitate Piet Maas (*A Kind of Anger*) from coping effectively. Dogged determination as well as luck drive *The Odessa File*'s Peter Miller to ferret out former SS men, one of whom has killed his father; nearly all the while he hunts he is also hunted, and while on the run his inconspicuousness helps keep him safe. But of all of those opposed to Nazi conspiracies, the most capable is Quiller; in *The Quiller Memorandum* the West's premier agent joins the company of an illustrious few, including John Drake, though several notches below James Bond.

True to Cold War realities the enemy agency is often the KGB, as in *Moscow Letter*, the Smiley series, *Agent in Place*, *The Sixth Directorate*, or *Gentleman Traitor*, and many others; in each of these books the hero has moral stature. His opposite numbers are usually unextraordinary, though they often have great resources at their command. The hero's mission (or his flight) will still be fraught with peril, but luck and/or the agent's invisibility will help bring him through. The KGB, in nearly all books written this side of the curtain, cannot be permitted to struggle for a good cause. For the most part— James Bond and his ilk excepted—the days of the superagent or supcramateur are numbered. We soon will not have any Richard Hannays to kick around. The KGB will have to be defeated by the hero-as-victim, particularly so now that le Carré has put Smiley on a back shelf.

Graham Greene's *The Confidential Agent* (1939) is the first important spy novel to give its leading actor-agent a flawed personality along with a private life and so weaken him as a secret agent that he fails in his mission. Agent D is a tired, middle-aged university professor and patriot traveling to England to purchase essentially needed coal for his side. Memories of his deceased wife so encumber him that he cannot break loose to begin life anew, at the moment of the novel, with an inexplicably appealing, yet spoiled and stylish blonde whom he meets on the boat to England. Once ashore he is beaten up by a hostile agent and is continually shadowed and harrassed by agents of the other side as well as by his own. Self-doubts plague him. He becomes paternally fond of a waifish chambermaid at his boardinghouse, but that relationship only gets her murdered. Finally, the mission fails: the mine owners will not sell their coal to him. During his last days in England he is on the run, making a narrow escape with the help of the blonde, who we are led to feel will direct him toward a new life, wherever that is going to be. A compelling and important novel, *The Confidential Agent* explores the lives and personalities of its main characters more than it does the profession of espionage, more than exploiting the thrills of the thriller. In that way it anticipates that greatest of all spy novels, *The Human Factor*.

Greene chose irony, satire, and a sardonic weltanschauung to confront the private life of a spy in *Our Man in Havana* (1958). In this comic gem the hero agrees to spy for the British in order to earn enough money for his daughter's private school education. He sends London headquarters the enlarged schematics of the vacuum cleaner innards which he sells, passing them off as secret installations. Meanwhile, other writers who have seen in the spy novel a potential for a commentary on much in modern society that is not directly related to formal espionage, that goes beyond the mere thrills of the thriller, developed the notion of the spy with a private life. These are the writers who have brought the spy thriller back into the mainstream of modern fiction.

Helen MacInnes's characters—the positive ones at least—
are embarrassingly domestic in and around their middle-class
Manhattan apartments or Long Island summer houses. Mac-
Innes's stories are so consistently naive, in tone as well as in
the thrust of the plot, that invoking the sinister as a serious
force is often a problem. But it has been le Carré who (aside
from Greene) has most thoroughly explored his character's
human qualities, while at the same time revealing the agency
as merely another kind of bureaucracy, and its operatives often
as shallow, unthinking, inept, occasionally traitorous but always very human people (Smiley excluded from this scurrilous
description), and yet telling a convincing and riveting tale.
George Smiley, the most memorable hero of le Carré's fiction,
is overweight, middle-aged, and unsuccessful in his married
life. Ambler and Greene knew that spies were primarily people,
but le Carré's Smiley is the first spy novel character to survive
several books and to become something of a cult figure.

In still other narratives, this now humanized spy is seen
as being little better—either morally superior or technically
adept—than the enemy. To counter amateur Charlie Heller
there are the Company men who want him liquidated, as well
as the avuncular Czech chief of the secret police; for every
Maurice Castle there is the agency physician, Dr. Percival, who
poisons the wrong man, Davis; for every Avery who has un-
reflective faith in his agency there are his superiors who callously send agents to a pitiless destiny. A few spies succeed
because they are cleverer than their opponents; a few others
because they can match the enemy in cunning and brutality.
We have already mentioned Olaf Peterson, of *The Wind Chill
Factor*, whose rugged assertiveness balances John Cooper's fragility and neurotic persistence. In *The Moscow Letter* the section
chief of American espionage has ruthlessly sold out the agents
on a mission he is himself coordinating as part of a secret deal
with the Russians. Hungarian intelligence agent Paul Rappaport, in *The Winter Spy*, is not the unfeeling brute he once
was, though at the beginning of his narrative he is assigned
to murder an American diplomat—double agent. But being a

hatchet man for the secret police is not the way to arouse sympathy, and for the novel to succeed we must feel along with Rappaport all the dangers and threats that beset him and have compassion for his role as victim on the run. Paul Henissart succeeds by backgrounding Rappaport's unsavory past and by allowing us the human feelings of caring for another human being. Hunted by the KGB, cynically exploited by the CIA, he is finally shot by the daughter of one of his earlier victims.

Unameliorated brutality is now de rigueur. Gavin Lyall's hero in *Midnight Plus One* is hired to convey his patron across Europe and just short of his destination kills off the team sent to block him with explosives and a machine pistol in a mutually brutal duel. Matt Helm, recurrent hero of Donald Hamilton's many novels, is usually a match for the opposition in physical encounters, but for a genuine relish in inflicting physical pain, for joy in the smashing of noses and bones, the squirting of blood, and sadistic deaths inflicted on bad guys, Trevanian's Jonathan Hemlock is probably unparalleled. The narrative situation is unlikely from the character's premise: "a world renowned" art critic and connoisseur, Hemlock works as a paid assassin for the CII, SS Division (Search and Sanction). "Jonathan had made a moral bargain with himself to work for CII only when it was fiscally necessary" (*The Eiger Sanction,* pp. 19–20). Trevanian's whimsicality and irony are too heavy-handed to describe them by those names, but this only further foregrounds his hero's brutality. Hemlock is as murderously brutal as recent publics demand, and while we might not expect an art critic to be a widely popular folk hero, the popularity of *The Eiger Sanction*—the movie version of which stars Clint Eastwood, who plays the hero "straight," without Trevanian's ironies and academic posturing—suggests that in whatever context, brutality toward one's enemies is la mode. The Eiger expedition ends when all three of Hemlock's companions fall hundreds of feet to their icy deaths (one having died earlier), all this beyond his control as he struggles desperately to survive. At the operation's debriefing, the department chief, Eurasis Dragan (no one has yet denounced Trevanian for subtlety) congratulates his man on what he considers the surest way of eliminating the guilty spy from among the group of suspects.

The spy novel has kept abreast of recent world politics as well. We have already seen that the Ambler novels begin in the Balkans, Turkey, and certain parts of central Europe, but that the later works are sited in Malaysia, Africa, and, recently, the Middle East. The latter region has gained popularity as a spy fiction setting, in, for example, Barak's *Secret List of Heinrich Roehm,* even Geoffrey Household's *Arabesque,* and in part *Black Sunday,* and Berlin has become even more a center for international intrigue, in *The Quiller Memorandum, Funeral in Berlin, Berlin Game,* and *The Spy Who Came In from the Cold.* Berlin has symbolic value as well as its political importance, since it has become a transition area between East and West, and such anomalous no-man's-lands have been the secret agent's spiritual and topographical home ground since Cooper's *The Spy.*

But for the most part these settings are superficial. One feels that the Berlin novels could as well have taken place in Lisbon, Frankfurt, or Baltimore, and little save a modicum of atmosphere would be lost. Spy novelists have seldom been interested in imparting a sense of place. Deighton's *Funeral in Berlin* might well take place elsewhere—most of the action actually does—and Berlin seems to have been named because it is a crossing point between two political worlds. *The Spy Who Came In from the Cold* ends in Berlin with Leamas and his lover shot at "the Wall," but the scene is only slightly more localized than the other novels which are set in Berlin, or the Middle East, or wherever. *A Coffin for Dimitrios* takes us to Istanbul, Sophia, Bucharest, and Belgrade and does not waste a word on description. Locale imparts atmosphere simply by its being named; spy writers have done very little to enhance their topographical settings with descriptive writing. The Asia of *The Honourable Schoolboy* is a rare exception.

Closer attention is being paid to technological and scientific advances as employed by spies, counterspies, and torturers. James Bond is said to be fascinated by the technical properties of machines and particularly weapons; when M. orders him to turn in his old .25 Baretta for a more powerful weapon, "Bond felt unreasonably sad. How could one have such ties with an inanimate object, an ugly one at that, and, he had to admit it, with a weapon that was not in the same class as the ones chosen by the Armorer? But he had the ties and M. was going to cut them" (*Doctor No*, p. 23). Compared with Quiller, Bond is a maudlin sentimentalist. When Quiller buys a rifle in *The Ninth Directive,* it is quite another kind of love affair:

> All the Husqvarnas are beautiful but the finest they make is the 561. It is a .358 Magnum center-fire, with a three-shot magazine, 25½ inch barrel, hand-checkered walnut stock, corrugated butt-plate and sling swivels. The fore-end and pistol grip are tipped with rosewood. The total weight is 7¾ pounds and the breech pressure is in the region of 20 tons p.s.i., giving a high muzzle velocity and an almost flat trajectory with a 150-grain bullet. . . . I had chosen an exemplary Balvar 6 by Bausch and Lomb with an optical variable from $\times 2\frac{1}{2}$ to $\times 5$. Its feature is that as the magnification power is increased the crosshair reticle remains constant in size and does not therefore tend to obscure the target. (P. 74)

But attention to technology becomes more ominous when the ends are torture. Bond is placed on a moving conveyer to be sliced in half by a rotary saw; the steel blade is upgraded in the movie version to a laser, though in both versions Bond, of course, escapes. Yet this is high-school stuff compared with the technological deaths conceived by the anonymous protagonist-agent of Jerzy Kosinski's *Cockpit:* arranging with the pilot of a radar-equipped plane that is to be exhibited at an air show to fatally irradiate the victim as she stands in front of the nose cone, he laconically comments that "invisible missiles were assaulting her body and brain" (p. 164). At another moment, Kosinski's protagonist lures a pursuer into a room equipped with powerful quartz lights; when the gunman enters the room, the agent, wearing safety goggles, switches on the power and blinds his enemy with light that "tore through the room like an explosion" (p. 259).

But even this is kindergarten stuff. Induced psychological stress, which gives us the acronym "Ipcress," causes kidnapped British scientists to forget their most useful theories and experiments, a new and sinister version of the brain drain. (The novel does not make very much of this altered psychic state; the movie version enlarges this aspect greatly.) Drugs are used for the usual information-extracting purposes in *An Expensive Place to Die,* and they are threatened in *Tremor of Intent* and *The Quiller Memorandum.* But once we can speak of the "usual purposes," we have come a long way toward accepting these chemical intrusions into our innermost lives, particularly when used by the hostiles. Nearly all fictional agents at one time or another succumb to being forcibly injected, one of the rare exceptions being Quiller, who identifies the injected drug by its effects and then through the force of will alone overcomes its influence.

But if we want to see how the spy novel has developed in its brutality, the most telling exemplum is not drug-related, but has to do with a dentist's drill. Before World War II, in Ambler's *Background to Danger,* Col. Saridza threatens to force the reluctant Kenton to reveal certain secrets by referring to that painful instrument of torture, the dental drill. Nearly forty years later, Goldman's Dr. Szell actually uses that device on Babe, the marathon man, in an episode intensified by the movie version, made so real that it is the most painfully memorable scene in that movie. Mere threat has now become excruciating reality. During the time of the first great war, plus or minus a decade or so, the spy of fiction was a heroic patriot, motivated by a desire to serve his country. Ambler changed that formula slightly by focusing on an innocent amateur who may never become patriotic, but who sees a commitment to a cause in those around him, as Kenton comes to see and admire this trait in the Russian agent Zaleshoff. After 1945, however, the hero—the principal actor, by whatever term—is usually the agent on the mission and not just a bystander. Like James Bond, he may be impelled to adventure by his reaction to boredom, but he is never uncommitted, though that commitment varies among secret agents.

The British agent in Len Deighton's *Yesterday's Spy* discovers an old friend's schemes while on assignment. Motive? "Champion did it for money?" he asks incredulously, not wanting to believe *that* of an old friend. "My dear fellow," is his informant's reply, "what else?" "Trouble is," the agent hears in dismay, "a chap's got to have a little bread, while he's figuring out what the better way is"—the better way to earn a living (p. 66). But spying merely for money is not what heroes do, nor is it a motive we are often asked to identify with; we expect to be shown some transcendent loyalty, to one's country or even merely to the agency, as behavior to be emulated.

Helen MacInnes is probably the most widely read of that dwindling group of spy novelists for whom the old-fashioned patriotism of the twenties and thirties is still valid. Her positive characters are usually amateurs, occasionally in the midst of a professional spook war, as in *Agent in Place,* but as often as not are forced to work against the enemy on their own. Such is the case with Rona Metford and Paul Hayden in *Neither Five nor Three,* denizens of Madison Avenue. Rich and wellborn Scott Ettley, Rona's fiancé, has been recruited by the local Communist party to infiltrate the editorship of *Trend* magazine, for which the principal characters in this novel work. The FBI works behind the scenes somewhat, but to the civilians goes most of the credit for the eventual smashing of the commies' plans, and though Scott is one of their fatal casualties, we share the triumph of those who have labored and suffered for the American way.

The political crisis in Scott's life explodes upon him when Comrade Nicholas Orpen tells him that a recent party visitor to their meetings, code-named "Jack," has been denounced back in Czechoslovakia as a spy: "now they say he was in Nazi pay. Now they say he's an American spy. That's Jack—a man who devoted thirty-four years of his life to the Party, five of them in prison, eighteen months of them in a German concentration camp—a man who helped make Czechoslovakia a Communist State" (p. 220). Orpen's humane instincts will not permit him to believe that his lifelong friend is a traitor, regardless of party denunciations. In contrast, Scott has been thoroughly programmed to accept what his superiors tell him; however, he has just enough human doubts to bring on a crisis of disbelief.

He goes at once to Rona's apartment and is no sooner inside the door when he begins an abstract discussion of loyalty and treason. When does disillusion become treason? he asks her:

> "Well. . . . I suppose you can shift from some loyalties without betraying them. I mean if you—if someone finds that he has been loyal to a delusion, then I wouldn't call it treachery when he sees his mistake and admits it. If he stayed loyal to something that was false, knowing it was false, then he would only start betraying himself." (P. 224)

Scott blurts out a few nearly incoherent words about Jack. Rona is confused: "but I don't know what this man has betrayed . . . friendship or—love? Or his country?" Scott's reply is contemptuous: "is that all you see in life, is that all?" But for the readers of *Neither Five nor Three* that is the crux. Friendship, love, and country—these are the enduring values. The Communists' rejection of them, articulated by Scott Ettley, condemns the movement with its own false beliefs.

Loyalty to one's country is still a viable commitment in many of those novels having to do with the Middle East, where nationalism is not a decadent ideal. This is particularly true of books by and about Israelis. The Israeli major of intelligence in Harris's *Black Sunday* has come to the United States to prevent an attack on the Super Bowl crowd (though the target of Arab terrorists is unknown to him when he first arrives); he is fully aware of the consequences to his nation of a dramatic "incident" perpetrated by extremists upon Americans and their reaction toward Israel as a result. Despite FBI and CIA casualness toward the possibility of Arab terrorism in America, the Israeli agents first expose the plot but are finally killed in preventing its execution. *The Secret List of Heinrich Roehm,* by Israeli Michael Barak, has its patriot-hero, Lt. Col. Joe Gonen of Air Force Intelligence, endure intense physical torture but also risk losing the woman he loves to discover the Arab plot that results in the outbreak of the Yom Kippur war. Thanks to Col. Gonen's dedication to his duty and his country, Israel is able to avert irretrievable disaster. Most recently, not even Israel is safe from the novelist's acidic observations; le Carré's *Little Drummer Girl* recoils from the exploitation of the girl's deepest emotions by cynical Mossad agents. The English are more cynical, probably with reason. Avery's great loyalty, in *The Looking Glass War,* is primarily to his own agency, and his great passion is to return it to its former, wartime status when it had power, influence, and a huge budget. Quiller, on the other hand, is moved to undertake a dangerous mission in *The Quiller Memorandum* to avenge the death of a friend, and in *The Mandarin Cypher* it is "out of sheer stinking pride" (p. 192). Different agents are motivated by various commitments; as Quiller tells us,

> [Egerton] works for the good of the cause. They all have their different motivations, the London controls. Loman's working for a knighthood and he doesn't give a damn for his ferrets. . . . Parkis is working for some grand and distant checkmate when the board is cleared of the pawns. . . . But Egerton works for Queen and Country and his morality is First World War, with tattered banners and muted bugles and the Greatest Game of them all to win. (*The Mandarin Cypher,* p. 162)

Steve Champion, in spite of his friend's dismay, is now in business for himself: as he explains it to Charlie Bonnard, "I'm cold and hungry, at least I was until a few years ago. I've done my bit of villainy for God, King and country. And now I'm doing a bit for my own benefit" (Deighton, *Yesterday's Spy,* p. 105).

Steve Champion, yesterday's spy, has no transcendent commitments. And Charlie hunts him down because he is doing wrong. The situation, as in all of Deighton's novels, is fairly clear-cut: our agent against theirs. But one recent development with ominous implications—if we are to take these fictions at all seriously as reflective of our lives—is the foregrounding of betrayal, one of the most common formulas in the contemporary spy novel. The agent must always be on his guard against it, and consequently he cannot allow himself to trust anyone. Hartley Howard's agent Philip Scott, in *Assignment K,* expresses it succinctly: "even if I were imagining things I could still trust no one. The world was my enemy" (p. 20). Yet the particularly insidious form Scott's betrayal takes is not without analogues in contemporary espionage fiction. One day an anonymous caller informs Scott that his fiancé has been abducted and that if Scott does not cooperate, "pity if another man were to usurp your nuptial rights . . . don't suppose she'd enjoy being taken against her will" (p. 9). The caller does not want money, but Scott's treasonous complicity against his own agency. In the end Scott is able to track down Mr. Smith and his accomplices, but the end has led him to discover that the enemy includes Woden, his own field officer, and that his beloved Jane has been a willing part of the conspiracy all along.

Ominously, betrayal by one's own agency is not rare in recent spy story plots. In Grady's *Six Days of the Condor* the victim-agent is working quietly in his office—officially reading spy novels to see whether or not they come too close to actual operations—when the entire office staff is attacked by several assassins with automatic weapons, from another CIA bureau. The Condor not only escapes the initial raid, but remains elusively on the run for the next six days while his own people hunt him down. In Robert Duncan's *Dragons at the Gate* a CIA agent stationed in Japan discovers that he is to be the victim of his own agency; as the man betrayed, he cannot turn either to his own people or even to other agents of his government since his own agency is his country's representative. Harry is thus cut loose from most of the usual anchors of the secret agent and is left, finally, to rely upon the loyalty of a few close friends, including a former lover, and his own cunning. The CIA has forced Harry not to rely on any transcendent entity and to trust only those who truly love him, and they are very few in number. Abstract loyalties are neutralized; personal attachments are the only ones Harry can trust.

Treason or murderous incompetence in high places is, after all, no more than we read about in our newspapers. Kim Philby actually appears as himself in *Gentleman Traitor* and *The Sixth Directorate*, and is a model for le Carré's most famous traitor, Bill Haydon. Like Philby, Haydon had betrayed everything that was important:

> Haydon had betrayed. As a lover, a colleague, a friend; as a patriot; as a member of that inestimable body that Ann loosely called the Set; in every capacity, Haydon had overtly nursed one aim and secretly achieved its opposite. Smiley knew very well that even now he did not grasp the scope of that appalling duplicity. (*Tinker, Tailor*, p. 332)

In *The Honourable Schoolboy*, he will find out.

Earlier, in *The Looking Glass War*, the agency uses a really fragile pretext to gear back up to a wartime footing. They scantily train one of their old agents, by now middle-aged, underequip him for his job, and drop him over the East German border. We slowly come to realize that the very shaky evidence they have used to convince themselves and their superiors that they should rearm is dangerously suspect and that they have interpreted it for their own purposes. It is a classic case of overreading the text. When the extent of their network of errors is made clear to them, the agency executives coldly abandon their agent to the encircling enemy, dispassionately cutting his electronic umbilical cord with "home." In *The Ipcress File* the traitor is Harry Palmer's superior within the apparatus, Dalby, who has all along been working for the other side, tipping them off about Palmer's inroads into their secrets and his whereabouts. And in le Carré's first important novel, *The Spy Who Came In from the Cold*, treachery in high places brings about the hero's death—when he thinks (and we hope) that he is about to make good his escape.

Cynicism about patriotism, and loyalties of any kind to people or to institutions, is currently the prevailing mood. Americans, particularly, feel that they have seen their patriotism exploited for specious reasons benefitting others in Viet

Nam. Many feel that they have been lied to by a variety of official government spokesmen, including the president, on a variety of issues for many years. This complex of feelings is best summarized by Jimmy Carter's phrase, "crisis of faith." And we have seen a number of officials in high places exposed as agents for a foreign power. In a lesser, and more domestic vein, many have felt that influential components of government owe their chief allegiance to private corporations or other interest groups. This civic cynicism about issues and leaders finds an outlet in reading about traitors in high places in the spy novel. Times of stress foster paranoia. In our times the secret agent, caught in his own crisis of belief, becomes a projection of our own doubts. The highly placed traitor, while not yet commonplace in the news, is heard of with sufficient frequency to be believable in fiction.

Yet the contemporary spy novelist does not stop there. Betrayals are often as personal as they are political. In *Marathon Man,* grad student Babe Levy is victimized because his revered brother, unknown to him, has for years been a secret agent— assassin; the CIA is not named by Goldman as the employer. Babe knows very little about his brother's other life, either as a professional killer or as the gay lover of another apparatus employee, Janey: "he and Janey had been an item for five years now" (p. 48). Janey, we eventually discover, on occasion cooperates with the other side (as expedience demands), plans Scylla Levy's death, and helps track down the escaped Babe. The bait originally tendered the younger, innocent brother is an attractive young woman placed strategically in the Columbia University library. Babe is smitten with Else on sight, is lured into making the first advances, then the first date. But when he introduces her to his secret agent—brother, Scylla sees through her cover right away. There is no firmer innocence than being in love; Babe refuses to believe that she is anything but lovingly devoted to him until, at the end, the truth is forced upon him. In a paroxysm of retribution, he guns down Szell's men, Janey, and his beloved.

We have seen how, in *Assignment K,* agent Philip Scott is led to believe that his fiancé has been abducted and threatened with a degrading debauch if he does not cooperate. When he resolves the mystery of his blackmailer's identity, he also learns that his fiancé has been part of the conspiracy all along. No one is immune; Harry Palmer's lover loyally reports his whereabouts and intentions to her boss, Harry's superior, who is in fact a double agent in the movie version of *The Ipcress File*. This may be more or less a betrayal (depending upon one's moral values) than the plight of the agent in Deighton's *Catch a Falling Spy* who has become deeply infatuated with a woman he has met at a party. Later he is delighted to learn that the attractive and seductive Red Bancroft is also an agent; they have something in common. But somewhat later he is devastated to discover that their blossoming affair is doomed because the enthralling Ms. Bancroft is a lesbian; she is caught in flagrante delicto with a Russian woman prisoner whom she has been assigned to guard.

But at least Red is on the right side: the marathon man's Else has been in the enemy's pay all along; Jonathan Hemlock is seduced by the charms of Jemima Brown, but that is part of E. Dragan's plan to keep track of his paid killer; John Cooper has for a lifetime trusted and befriended his family attorney (in *The Wind Chill Factor*) who is in his other life the führer of a worldwide neo-Nazi conspiracy; all are betrayals of friendship, of love, of a commitment that the individual makes in reaching out beyond the bounds of his own ego space to touch another person. We should not wonder that Dante placed such betrayers so deep in his circles of Hell. Loyalty, one of the few cherished universal constants in our civilization, is turned inside out and upside down in the modern spy novel. While on the run for his life in *The Winter Spy*, turned AVH agent Paul Rappaport appeals to a former aide for help, but to himself has to wonder, "was Sandor loyal? And, in this case, to whom? To Ana? [AVH department chief who has ordered his execution] Or his arrangement with the CIA? Or loyal to no one but himself?" (pp. 100–101).

That is the world in which the secret agent in contemporary espionage fiction finds himself; we, as empathetic readers of spy novels, find in our own lives some psychic analogue.

Our political leaders, our immediate superiors, our putative friends, even our lovers do not seem to have lasting commitment to us; ours to them must then be, out of self-protection, expedient. Agencies, even one's country, can be unreliable bases of security and certitude. In such a situation, the agent, or we, must, like Sandor, be loyal to no one but ourselves. And again like Sandor, we must pretend loyalty to those individuals, agencies, and countries whose favors are required. Thus the individual perpetuates the circle of clandestinity, deceit, and betrayal.

The spy, in short, is as humanly vulnerable as we.

The data in this analysis have been drawn from several important novels—important in their influence on the direction of the genre—several popular books, and several others chosen more or less at random. And while we cannot speak of a monolithic vision of the world, certain themes and moods are foregrounded. The spy, compositely, in modern fiction signifies a man in an impalpable world of shadows, one who fears to express his genuine feelings, whose work cannot be discussed with others, and the precise nature of which he may himself be unaware. In *The Ninth Directive* Quiller is assigned to prevent the assassination of an English VIP in Bangkok. At about the same time that he learns the whereabouts of the suspected killer, he discovers that he is himself being tailed. But the plot is not to murder the VIP at all—Quiller learns after he thwarts the murder attempt—but rather to kidnap him. Quiller's tail is from another British secret agency whose mission is to protect him from kidnapping, not from the ostensible "enemy" but from a local potentate who had been helping the British all along. Thanks to Quiller's good luck, a bit of sharp reasoning, and a few deus ex machinas, Adam Hall is able to resolve all satisfactorily in the end.

The spy's organization is narrowly and tightly compartmentalized, fostering clandestinity, and the agent may not be aware of his co-worker's real purposes or intentions. Adam Hall's *Ninth Directive* illustrates this as well; so does *Spy Story*, in which the protagonist-spy has to identify himself through the ownership of a security card: one day the records of the

security card disposition show that the agent must be somewhere else or that he is an imposter. The spy's relation to his
world is remote and ephemeral; like the protagonist of Kosinski's *Cockpit,* he may lament that

> As a result of the circumstances under which I left that service,
> I cannot join any professional, social or political group. Yet, to
> live alone, depending on no one, and to keep up no lasting
> associations, is like living in a cell; and I have never lost my
> desire to be as free as I was as a child, almost flying, drawn on
> by my wheel. (P. 163)

Given the milieu in which many are hostile and so everyone
must be suspect, the spy's world must grow continually nar-
rower, so that finally he himself becomes the only reliable
element in his life. But that way paranoia lies.

The threat of the loss of his freedom of action unsettles
the fictional spy, yet it also presents him with the potential
for heroism. Gifford's John Cooper, in *The Wind Chill Factor,*
is victimized by an incomprehensible and bewildering hostile
conspiracy that has engulfed his life: "Everything I believed
in has been proven a lie, everything I had ever looked to as
an anchor in my life. Nothing is what it seemed" (p. 367).
His foil—his friendly and crudely protective foil Olaf Peterson—survives because he is as ruthless and as cruel as the other
side, as is Maj. Mann in *Catch a Falling Spy* or Schlegel in
Yesterday's Spy.

In this environment of deceit and betrayal the spy's moral
commitment must transcend the values in which he is im-
mersed and which, in large measure, he must himself live by.
Many, as we have just noted, are forced to abandon loyalties
to country or agency in their flight to protect themselves from
their own people. And the spy who can only rely on his own
values in a world that provides only negative standards—and
those often evanescent—is "heroic" simply in reaffirming his
personal commitments. Without them, survival is the only
goal. This is the new heroism. Succumbing to the values of
the other side may be an unfortunate fall—if they are nor-

matively evil or even hostile—and the agent's heroism lies in his ability to perceive the correct course of action, as much as it resides in his ability to carry out his assignment.

When everyone threatens, either overtly or potentially, the secret agent must remain detached, unemotional, distanced from all those he encounters so that he may evaluate the people and the situations around him all of the time. A detached, analytical, and impersonal stance toward everyone is the mental mode of his existence. Emotional involvements are exploitable, so his ideal behavior is not to get involved with anyone. This will be shown by glibness to his enemies, even while he is on the brink of death at their hands, and by a witty insolence to his superiors. The legacy of the hard-boiled detective is obvious here. The agent thus emotionally forearms himself for his mission, which is inevitably fraught with danger. He threads his way along a twisting path where danger is concealed and unknown, where no one is to be trusted, where no solace proves lasting. It is like a blindfolded man groping through an unmarked minefield. His world is one in which the

> creak of a stair that had not creaked before; the rustle of a shutter when no wind was blowing; the car with a different number plate but the same scratch on the offside wing; the face on the Metro that you know you have seen somewhere before. . . . Any one of these was reason enough to move, change towns, identities. (Le Carré *Tinker, Tailor, Soldier, Spy,* p. 328)

The spy's heroism derives, ultimately, from his physical and psychic self-reliance, his self-possession and containment, the moral and psychological strength to maintain his individuality in a world of ciphers and to confront a society of deceit with poise and confidence, usually manifested as a cynical sophistication. As his environment presses him continually in upon himself, he must find the resources within himself if he is to survive.

Isolated as he is, the spy's position is both his strength and his vulnerability. Though he lives in close physical proximity with those around him, and must constantly guard against being "touched" by them, he moves freely, almost invisibly, through his host society. His identity, a contrived cover, enables him to live among others without being known by them. He need not comply, therefore, with society's rules or laws because his real purposes are not those of his neighbors; he is not really a member of an open society. He may feel like Kosinski's protagonist, caught in an elevator out of control in its roof-to-basement cycle:

> Although I have always thought of myself as moving horizontally through space, invading other people's spheres, my life has always been arranged vertically: all my apartments have been at least midway up in tall buildings, making elevators absolutely essential. Now, one of those necessary devices had suddenly become a windowless cell. (*Cockpit*, p. 272)

Often the spy's moral and ethical commitments are not those of his habitat society. This occurs most dramatically in the instance of those agents who, like 007, have a license to kill (or who are members of some such search-and-sanction unit as is Jonathan Hemlock). In enemy territory, of course, capture may well mean death, preceded by some torture "worse than death," but evasion is enhanced by the agent's invisibility. At home his own agency may assist him, and usually that organization is itself invisible. The spy violates the laws and codes of his heritage and his society on behalf of his clandestine agency; if he loses faith in that agency, he loses that moral and ideological center of his life which justifies his existence. And then he has nothing.

Nearly everyone feels oppressed by the rules and stipulations and laws of society; some more than others, at certain times more than at others. But the feeling, centuries old, is as strong today as ever, and apparently widespread. And these wary responses intensify as society becomes more bureaucratic and more rule-governed. We yearn to be free of societal restraints, like the romantic in his flight from the city to untrammeled regions or the pioneer with his canvas-topped wagon trudging across the prairie. Unlike the rest of us, the spy is able to move freely and invisibly through society, and this ability makes him ideal as the reader's vicarious projection; we can envy him his freedom from restraint. If we were invisible, we too could move unhindered through the walls and partitions that now separate and isolate the corporations, bureaucracies, and organizations that constitute contemporary industrialized society. Normal life today limits free movement of this kind; we are compartmentalized, in the dark about much that goes on around us, much that is about us. In this respect there is an element of voyeurism in the idea of the spy, and that is one of its attractions. The spy has access, so we think, to the other side of the wall, the fence, the office partition; he can find out what is happening there, what "they" are thinking about. But our envy stops at that point; we do not want to share the spy's isolation, his enforced distance from personal contacts, his professional separation from the values and traditions—the anchors—of his culture.

The world evoked by the spy novel is paranoia dramatized. The spy moves continually through these signifiers, and the reader—who understands these impulses and to varying degrees shares them—is brought imaginatively into this realm. Psychologist David Shapiro described one type of paranoiac as suspicious, people who were constantly apprehensive but also continually alert and sensitive. Paranoiacs are often intellectually keen and exhibit "acuteness and intensity of attention" (Shapiro, *Neurotic Styles*, p. 60); their mistakes in judging the world are often brilliantly perceptive ones. We may think of the spy as "normal," as making correct calculations and balanced evaluations, and so he must to survive; but the psychic mode of his minute-by-minute life is suspicion. His environment has made suspicion mandatory, but an author has created it all—spy, situation, the enemy, neutrals, all the paraphernalia of clandestinity, physical and psychic—so that not only the characters but to some extent the author and sympathetic reader participate in this world.

The clever agent is suspicious where we would be oblivious—to the creak on the stair, the rustle of the shutter, and the like. As Shapiro says of the paranoid,

Suspicious people are also conspicuously hypersensitive and hyperalert. These people are exceedingly, nervously sensitive to anything out of the ordinary or unexpected; any such time, however trivial or slight it might seem from the standpoint of the normal person, will trigger their attention in its full, searching intensity. (P. 61)

We have seen with repeated examples how the secret agent copes with his hostile medium either by anticipating dangerous situations or by adjusting very rapidly to them. So too does the paranoiac respond:

> he avoids surprise by virtually anticipating it. The paranoid quality that we describe as "hyperalertness" consists of exactly this, and it is this activeness that distinguishes hyperalertness from a merely frightened or startled response. The suspicious person is ready for anything unexpected and immediately becomes aware of it. And he does not merely become aware of the unexpected, but must then bring his full attention to bear on it. He must scrutinize it, cover it, or, as it were, get on top of it. He must, in other words, bring it into the orbit of his scheme of things and, in effect, satisfy himself that it is not or at least is no longer surprising. (P. 62)

Pierre Boulle expressed the paranoidal style eloquently when he made the hero of *A Noble Profession* a certifiable paranoid whose case officer is a psychiatrist. On a dangerous mission in Nazi-occupied France, agent Arvers feels that

> Suddenly the forest seemed extraordinarily hostile, concealing in the shadow of every bush someone bent on his destruction. His enemies—by whom he meant anyone who discussed him behind his back—he imagined those enemies gathered together this evening in this secluded corner of Brittany, temporarily united in their common feeling of ill-will toward him. (P. 211)

When Robert Duncan's hero Harry Calder, in *Dragons at the Gate,* is imprisoned by his own people in an interrogation room, he soon suspects that the looking glass on the wall is an observation mirror, and the thought that he is under constant surveillance induces a breakdown. It is only a conventional mirror; yet in this homily very real problems are identified. The spy is threatened with exposure, and dangers to his identity may be constantly felt, whether real or imagined. He is always tottering on an abyss in which his identity may be lost: "Secret Agent man / Secret Agent man / They've given you a number / And taken 'way your name." He may regret establishing personal contact with others even if he is able to do so: like Leamas, in *The Spy Who Came In from the Cold*, not until he loves someone does he have something of great value to lose. And that vulnerability is what is exploited. Or like the agent in Howard's *Assignment K*, emotional attachments are merely other kinds of vulnerabilities which the marathon man and the agent in Deighton's *Catch a Falling Spy* found to their anguish are not always what they seem. So, as Harry Palmer and Alec Leamas learn, as many of us may learn, the message derived from spies' lives and their adventures is to stay clear of emotional entanglements.

The secret agent man, with a number instead of a name— how unlike Richard Hannay or Caruthers or even Zaleshoff!— is continually tested, by implication more than by his author-creator, for his commitments. Le Carré's Leiser probably discovers that MI 6 is no better ethically than the KGB, though his betrayal by his English masters may not even leave him time to reflect on that discovery; Avery, whose burgeoning faith in the agency is shattered in the end of *The Looking Glass War* will live with the revelation. To which belief, which society, which moral dictate should we commit ourselves? If we ask that question of ourselves seriously, we are in a sense in the position of the double agent, for whom loyalty and betrayal, national interest and conscience are elusive and evanescent concepts which he may avoid confronting entirely. The spy in such dilemmas projects these problems; "the soul of the spy," Jacques Barzun has written for the most willfully wrong-headed reasons, "is somehow the model of our own; his actions and his trappings fulfill our unsatisfied desires" ("Meditations on the Literature of Spying," p. 168). The spy novel is a wish-fear medium of our projection, a sign of our society as many now perceive it. These popular fictions both reflect our society and evoke our psychic directions, what we are and what we fear we are becoming. The spy is a man for our times.

Appendix: Motif and Type Index of the Spy Story

Plot Types

> The spy goes over
> The big job
> The hero as victim
> Journey into fear
> To catch a spy

Characteristic Episodes (motifs)

> Initial ennui
> Assassination (attempted assassination)
> Abduction
> Close call
> Confrontation
> Disguise
> Disguised encounter/confrontation
> Narrow escape
> Chase
> Evasion
> On the run

Capture
Interrogation
Torture
The drop
Exchange
The plant
Planted misinformation
Doubling/turning (an agent)
Turnabout (the hunted becomes hunter)
Betrayal
Counterspying
The tag

Dramatis Personae of the Spy Novel

The Hero's Company
    The hero agent
    Control (the agency director)
    Control's immediate subordinate
    Control's satellites
    Heroine (often a lure, and thus a false heroine, sometimes
        for the other side, when the male protagonist is the
        hero)
The Adversary's Company
    Enemy agent
    Enemy control
    Enemy control's henchman
    Enemy agency entourage or natives of country hostile to
        hero
    False heroine
Ambiguous Personae
    Defectors (can defect to either side)
    Double agents
    Plants (whose ultimate loyalties may not be apparent)
Neutrals
    Neutrals may initially have innocent intentions but are
    usually exploited by one side or the other and eventually
    become unwilling helpers or dupes.

A Guide to the Spy Story

Books and Articles on the Spy Story

I. Bibliography

Smith, Myron, Jr. *Cloak and Dagger Fiction: An Annotated Guide to Spy Thrillers.* 2d ed. Santa Barbara: ABC-Clio, 1982.

An outstanding work of bibliography, useful both to scholars and to fans. Individual works of special importance and major authors are annotated. Indexed by title and author. Also contains guides to pseudonyms, main characters in series, and intelligence and terrorist organizations.

II. Spy Stories in Literature and Film

Barzun, Jacques. "Meditations on the Literature of Spying." *American Scholar* 34 (1965): 167–78.

Clark, I. F. *Voices Prophesying War, 1763–1984.* London: Oxford, 1966.

An important scholarly study of the future wars genre which flourished in the late nineteenth century and had an important influence on both the spy story and science fiction.

221

Davis, Brian. *The Thriller: The Suspense Film from 1946.* London: Studio Vista/Dutton, 1973.
Studies several different kinds of film thriller, but includes a brief chapter on the spy film.

Gow, Gordon. *Suspense in the Cinema.* New York: A. S. Barnes, 1968.
Suggestive analysis organized around such psychological themes as "isolation," "irony," "phobia," etc. Treats spy films in relationship to other examples of suspense.

Harper, Ralph. *The World of the Thriller.* Cleveland: Case Western Reserve University Press, 1969.
An existential study of the central psychological appeals of the thriller. One of the first full-length books on the spy story and still useful. See introduction.

Hay, Eloise Knapp. *The Political Novels of Joseph Conrad.* Chicago: University of Chicago Press, 1963.
Particularly useful for its discussion of the sources of Conrad's novels of espionage. Establishes that in spite of many similarities, Conrad's Verloc could not have been based on the character of Aseff.

McCormick, Donald. *Who's Who in Spy Fiction.* New York: Taplinger, 1975.
A delightful dictionary of the major spy writers. See introduction.

Merry, Bruce. *Anatomy of the Spy Thriller.* Montreal: Queen's University Press, 1977.
A good analysis of the major narrative structures characteristic of the spy story, though limited in usefulness by a rambling structure and an overly reductive treatment of the spy story as an epic archetype. See introduction.

Neuse, Steven M. "Intrepidity and Ideology in Eastern Bloc Chillers and Thrillers: A Case Study in System Legitimation." Paper prepared for the annual meeting of the American Political Science Association, August 1984.
Interesting study of Russian, Bulgarian, Czech, and Polish spy stories. The author concludes that the Russian stories are primarily concerned with reaffirming the Soviet ideology, while Czech and Polish thrillers tend to be at least subtly critical.

Monaghan, David. *The Novels of John le Carré: The Art of Survival.* Oxford: Blackwell, 1985.

The first major study of the spy stories of John le Carré. Excellent literary and cultural analysis.

Palmer, Jerry. *Thrillers: Genesis and Structure of a Popular Genre.* New York: St. Martin's Press, 1979.

Concerned with the spy story only as a type of thriller. Best account of general cultural significance of the thriller, though Palmer's argument raises some basic questions. See introduction.

Panek, Leroy L. *The Special Branch: The British Spy Novel, 1890–1980.* Bowling Green, Ohio: Bowling Green University Popular Press, 1981.

A good collection of essays on most of the major spy writers. Particularly good on the earlier period and on writers like LeQueux and Oppenheim. See introduction.

Perry, George. *The Films of Alfred Hitchcock.* London: Studio Vista/Dutton, 1965.

Standard study of the master of the movie spy story.

Rubenstein, Leonard. *The Great Spy Films: A Pictorial History.* Secaucus, N.J.: Citadel Press, 1979.

The best study of spy films. Rubenstein does not attempt a complete history. Rather he analyzes a small selection of films categorized by narrative themes, "A Sense of Adventure," "The Problem of Loyalty," "The Possibility of War," and "The Edge of Paranoia."

Sauerberg, Lars Ole. *Secret Agents in Fiction: Ian Fleming, John le Carré, and Len Deighton.* New York: St. Martin's Press, 1984.

Recent study of structural patterns and themes in Fleming, le Carré, and Deighton.

Symons, Julian. *Mortal Consequences: A History, from the Detective Story to the Crime Novel.* New York: Harper, 1972.

Chapter 16 presents a brief history of the spy story.

Truffaut, Francois, with Helen G. Scott. *Hitchcock.* New York: Simon & Schuster, 1967.

Based on a series of interviews with the filmmaker, this book offers many insights into Hitchcock's use of espionage as a subject for film.

Usborne, Richard. *Clubland Heroes: A Nostalgic Study of Some Recurrent Characters in the Romantic Fiction of Dornford Yates, John Buchan, and "Sapper."* London: Constable, 1953.

The earliest book on spy stories. Usborne studies the heroic spy story of World War I and the 1920s.

A Selected Bibliography of the
History and Practice of Espionage

I. Bibliography

Blackstock, Paul W., and Frank L. Schaf, Jr. *Intelligence, Espionage, Counterespionage, and Covert Operations: A Guide to Information Sources.* Detroit: Gale Research Co., 1978.
An excellent annotated bibliography, divided into four major categories (General Bibliographic Resources; Strategic Intelligence; Espionage and Counterespionage; Covert Operations) and 21 subdivisions. Indexed by author and title separately. Also includes a very useful list of fifty most important titles covering the area.

Smith, Myron, Jr. *The Secret Wars: A Guide to Research in English.* 3 vols. New York: ABC-Clio, 1980–81.
Concentrates on espionage and covert activities since 1939.

II. History of Espionage

Bakeless, John. *Turncoats, Traitors, and Heroes.* New York: Lippincott, 1958.
Detailed history of espionage on both sides during the American Revolution.

Blackstone, Paul W. *Agents of Deceit: Fraud, Forgeries and Political Intrigue Among Nations.* Chicago: Quadrangle, 1966.
Analysis of forgeries like the Protocols of Zion and the Zinoviev letters used for purposes of political agitation. Includes discussion of disinformation as political warfare in the 1920s and during the Cold War.

Bum, Michael. *The Debatable Land: A Study of the Motives of Spies in Two Ages.* London: Hamish Hamilton, 1970.
Blackstone and Schaf describe this as "a scholarly, brilliantly written survey of espionage during the Elizabethan age in England, followed by an analysis and comparison of the motives of spies then and in the post–World War II period."

Deacon, Richard (pseud.). *A History of the British Secret Service.* London: Taplinger, 1970.
————. *History of the Russian Secret Service.* New York: Taplinger, 1972.

Farrago, Ladislas. *The Game of the Foxes: The Untold Story of German Espionage in the United States and Great Britain during World War II.* New York: Bantam, 1973.

Fitzgibbon, Constantine. *Secret Intelligence in the Twentieth Century.* New York: Stein & Day, 1977.
The best recent short history of its subject.

Ind, Allison. *A History of Modern Espionage.* London: Hodder & Stoughton, 1965.

Kahn, David. *The Codebreakers: The Story of Secret Writing.* New York: Macmillan, 1967.
At 1,164 pp. a backbreaker as well as a magnum opus. Fascinating history of cryptography.

Kane, Harnett Thomas. *Spies for the Blue and Gray.* Garden City, N.Y.: Doubleday, 1954.
Espionage during the Civil War.

Rowan, Richard Wilmer, with Robert G. Deindorfer. *Secret Service: Thirty-Three Centuries of Espionage.* New York: Hawthorn, 1967.
The nearest thing to a definitive history of espionage that is likely to be written.

Seth, Ronald. *Encyclopedia of Espionage.* Garden City, N.Y.: Doubleday, 1974.

Taylor, A. J. P. "Through the Keyhole." *New York Review,* 10, February 1972, pp. 14–18.
An argument that most espionage activity is useless by a controversial British historian.

III. Modern Espionage Organizations and Practices

Agee, Philip. *Inside the Company: CIA Diary.* New York: Stone Hill, 1975.
Highly critical and disturbing exposé of the CIA's role in covert operations. Every effort was made to suppress this book.

Blackstock, Paul W. *The Strategy of Subversion: Manipulating the Politics of Other Nations.* Chicago: Quadrangle, 1964.
Scholarly study of the methods and effects of covert operations.

Dulles, Allen. *The Craft of Intelligence*. New York: Harper & Row, 1963.
Essays on espionage techniques by the first director of the CIA.

Eells, Richard, and Peter Nehemkis. *Corporate Intelligence and Espionage: A Blueprint for Executive Decision Making*. New York: Macmillan, 1984.
A handbook for business espionage, indicating how intelligence, espionage, and counterespionage have become vitally important for the modern corporation.

Greene, Richard M., Jr., ed. *Business Intelligence and Espionage*. Homewood, Ill.: Dow Jones–Irwin, 1966.
Textbook on industrial espionage edited by an experienced management consultant.

Johnson, Lock K. *A Season of Inquiry: The Senate Intelligence Investigation*. Lexington: University of Kentucky Press, 1985.
Recent study of the Senate's attempt to bring the CIA under some form of congressional control.

Marchetti, Victor, and John Marks. *The CIA and the Cult of Intelligence*. New York: Dell, 1975.
Critical but balanced analysis of the CIA by a disillusioned former intelligence bureaucrat. Highly readable.

Oseth, John M. *Regulating United States Intelligence Operations: A Study in Definition of the National Interest*. Lexington: University of Kentucky Press, 1985.
An attempt to define the best method for regulating espionage activity.

Ransom, Harry Howe. *The Intelligence Establishment*. Cambridge: Harvard University Press, 1970.
Excellent analysis by the dean of espionage scholars. Blackstone and Schaf call it "the best single scholarly work on the subject."

Rositzke, Harry. *The KGB: The Eyes of Russia*. Garden City, N.Y.: Doubleday, 1981.
Semipopular account by a CIA Soviet specialist, which seeks to justify CIA activity. Ends by warning against "the decay of allegiance" in Western democracies which will make Soviet subversion easier.

Powers, Thomas. *The Man Who Kept the Secrets: Richard Helms
  and the CIA.* New York: Pocket Books, 1981 (1979).
  Excellent study of a CIA careerist.
Shils, Edward. *The Torment of Secrecy.* Glencoe: Free Press,
  1956.
  Classic study of the national hysteria that surrounded the fear
  of Communist espionage during the McCarthy era. Stresses
  the dangers of secrecy for democracy.
Ungar, Sanford J. *FBI: An Uncensored Look behind the Walls.*
  Boston: Atlantic, Little, Brown, 1976.
  A balanced history of the FBI containing much information
  on intelligence and counterintelligence activities.
Wise, David, and Thomas B. Ross. *The Espionage Establishment.*
  New York: Random House, 1967.
  Useful analysis of the espionage systems of the U.S., Great
  Britain, Russia, and Communist China.
Wise, David. *The Politics of Lying: Government Deception, Secrecy,
  and Power.* New York: Random House, 1973.

IV. Major Spies and Espionage Episodes

Brown, Anthony Cave. *Bodyguard of Lies.* New York: Harper &
  Row, 1975.
  Detailed and thoroughly researched account of deception and
  intelligence operations in World War II.
Dulles, Allen. *Great True Spy Stories.* Secaucus, N.J.: Castle,
  1983 (1968).
Fitzgerald, Frances. *Fire in the Lake.* Boston: Little, Brown,
  1972.
  Includes account of covert operations and other special forces
  activities in Vietnam.
Halberstam, David. *The Best and the Brightest.* New York: Random
  House, 1972.
  Points up the failures of intelligence and covert operations in
  the Vietnam War.
Hoehling, Adolph A. *Women Who Spied.* New York: Dodd,
  Mead, 1967.
Maclean, Fitzroy. *Take Nine Spies: The Great Espionage Agents of the
  Twentieth Century—From Mata Hari to Oleg Penkovski.* New
  York: Atheneum, 1978.

Masterman, John C. *The Double Cross System in the War of 1939 to 1945.* New Haven: Yale University Press, 1972.
Fascinating account of the British use of German spies as double agents during World War II.

Moorehead, Alan. *The Traitors.* New York: Harper & Row, 1963.
Discusses Soviet atomic espionage and its use of British scientists.

Page, Bruce, David Leitch, and Philip Knightley. *The Philby Conspiracy.* Garden City, N.Y.: Doubleday, 1968.
The best book on the Kim Philby case in which an important British secret agent was finally exposed as a longtime Russian double agent.

Singer, Kurt, ed. *Three Thousand Years of Espionage: An Anthology of the World's Greatest Spy Stories.* New York: Prentice-Hall, 1948.

Weinstein, Allen. *Perjury: The Hiss-Chambers Case.* New York: Knopf, 1978.
A study of the Alger Hiss case based on documents released under the Freedom of Information Act. Weinstein argues rather conclusively that Hiss was guilty of passing information to the Russians.

Landmarks in the History of the Spy Story

1821   James Fenimore Cooper, *The Spy*

1871   Col. George Chesney, "The Battle of Dorking" launched the future wars genre, immediate precursor of the spy story.

1885   H. Rider Haggard, *King Solomon's Mines,* a highpoint of the colonial adventure genre, another precursor of the spy story.

1894   A. Conan Doyle, "The Naval Treaty." For the first time Sherlock Holmes confronts an espionage problem.
William LeQueux, *The Great War in England in 1897.* An early work by the man who would help develop the spy story.

1898   E. Phillips Oppenheim, *The Mysterious Mrs. Savin.* Another future war story.

1901   Rudyard Kipling, *Kim.* Colonial adventure and espionage meet in this classic, as in many of Kipling's stories.

1903   Erskine Childers, *Riddle of the Sands*. Two British gentle-
       men sailors expose a German invasion plot and launch
       the modern spy story.
1907   Joseph Conrad, *The Secret Agent*. Probably the first realistic
       and tragic spy novel.
1913   John Buchan, *The Thirty-Nine Steps*. First spy story classic.
       Arthur S. Ward (Sax Rohmer), *The Insidious Dr. Fu Man-
       chu*. First spy story series to gain mass popularity.
1920   H. C. McNeile (Sapper), *Bulldog Drummond*. First in a
       typical heroic spy story series.
1927   *Spies* (*Spione*). First major spy movie, directed by Fritz
       Lang and produced by German UFA.
1928   W. Somerset Maugham, *Ashenden*. Sketches based on the
       author's own experience as an agent in World War I.
       Generally considered the first realistic spy story.
1932   Graham Greene, *Orient Express*. The first of many
       espionage-centered thrillers by this modern master.
1935   Alfred Hitchcock, *The Thirty-Nine Steps*. Much changed
       adaptation to film of Buchan's original. Still one of
       the greatest spy films.
1937   Eric Ambler, *Background to Danger*. First spy novel by an-
       other major figure in the genre.
1938   Geoffrey Household, *Rogue Male*. Story of a man who al-
       most assassinated Hitler. First major thriller based on
       assassination.
1942   Michael Curtiz, *Casablanca*, with Humphrey Bogart and
       Ingrid Bergman, *the* espionage romance of World War II.
1945   Louis de Rochemont, *The House on 92nd St*. Documentary
       style of this film, based on a German espionage epi-
       sode, was very influential on the Cold War films of
       the 1950s.
1952   *Biff Baker, U.S.A.* The first spy series on American televi-
       sion, an American version of the heroic spy with
       Communist subversives as his antagonists.
1953   Ian Fleming, *Casino Royale*. The first in what would be-
       come the most successful series of spy stories and
       films in history.
1959   Alfred Hitchcock, *North by Northwest*. Another Hitchcock
       gem adapting his magical combination to the Ameri-
       can scene and the Cold War. Stars Cary Grant and
       Eva Marie Saint.

1961   British television produces *Danger Man* (later *Secret Agent*)
and the first version of *The Avengers* beginning the adaptation to television of a Bond-like formula.

John le Carré, *Call for the Dead*. First novel by the major
spy writer of the 1960s through the 1980s.

1962   John Frankenheimer, *The Manchurian Candidate*. Film
based on Richard Condon's novel begins a series of
assassination films which will culminate in *The Day of
the Jackal*.

Len Deighton, *The Ipcress File*. First novel by another major contemporary spy writer.

1963   John le Carré, *The Spy Who Came In from the Cold* begins
le Carré's great popular success. Made into a very successful film in 1965 by Martin Ritt with Richard
Burton as Alec Leamas.

Terence Young, *Doctor No*. The first James Bond film starring Sean Connery and produced by Broccoli and
Saltznan.

1964   *The Man from U.N.C.L.E.* debuts on television.

1965   Deighton's *Ipcress File* becomes a successful film and the
beginning of a series starring Michael Caine as
"Harry Palmer."

Amazing year for spies on television. Shows which debut
include *Secret Agent; I Spy; The Wild, Wild West; Honey
West; Get Smart;* and *The F.B.I.*

1966   *Mission: Impossible* begins the fad for clandestine group
operations.

1973   Success of *The Six Million Dollar Man* indicates a possible
confluence between the spy story and science fiction;
the delight in fancy technology especially marks the
later Bond films.

1974   John le Carré begins *The Quest for Karla* with *Tinker,
Tailor, Soldier, Spy*.

Two American films—Sidney Pollack, *Three Days of the
Condor* (Robert Redford and Faye Dunaway), and Alan
Pakula's *Parallax View* (Warren Beatty)—indicate that
le Carré's theme of internal corruption is becoming
increasingly influential.

1978   Graham Greene publishes *The Human Factor*.

The Greatest Spy Stories

Our own list of the twenty-five greatest spy stories in rank order.

1. Graham Greene, *The Human Factor* (1978)
2. John le Carré, *The Quest for Karla* (3 vols.), including *Tinker, Tailor, Soldier, Spy* (1974); *The Honourable Schoolboy* (1977); and *Smiley's People* (1980)
3. John le Carré, *The Little Drummer Girl* (1983)
4. Graham Greene, *Our Man in Havana* (1958)
5. John le Carré, *The Spy Who Came In from the Cold* (1963)
6. Graham Greene, *The Honorary Consul* (1973)
7. Rudyard Kipling, *Kim* (1901)
8. Graham Greene, *The Ministry of Fear* (1943); *The Confidential Agent* (1939); and *This Gun for Hire (A Gun for Sale)* (1936)
9. John le Carré, *A Small Town in Germany* (1968) and *The Looking Glass War* (1965)
10. Eric Ambler, *The Mask of Dimitrios* (1939)
11. W. Somerset Maugham, *Ashenden* (1928)
12. Jerzy Kosinski, *Cockpit* (1978)
13. Eric Ambler, *The Intercom Conspiracy* (1969)
14. Robert Littell, *The Amateur* (1981)
15. William Goldman, *Marathon Man* (1974)
16. Elleston Trevor (Adam Hall), *The Quiller Memorandum* (1965)
17. Len Deighton, *The Ipcress File* (1964)
18. James Grady, *Six Days of the Condor* (1974)
19. Ira Levin, *The Boys from Brazil* (1976)
20. Gavin Lyall, *Midnight Plus One* (1965)
21. John Buchan, *The Thirty-Nine Steps* (1913)
22. Frederick Forsyth, *The Day of the Jackal* (1971)
23. Noel Behn, *The Kremlin Letter* (1966)
24. Thomas Gifford, *The Wind Chill Factor* (1975)
25. Eric Ambler, *The Levanter* (1972)

The Major Spy Films

Leonard Rubenstein in *The Great Spy Films* (1979) offers the following list of major spy films:

A Sense of Adventure
Spies (Fritz Lang), 1927–28
The Scarlet Pimpernel (Alexander Korda and Harold Young), 1935

The Thirty-Nine Steps (Alfred Hitchcock), 1935
State Secret (*The Great Manhunt;* Sidney Gilliat and Frank
   Launder), 1950
Doctor No (Terence Young), 1963
The Ipcress File (Sidney Furie), 1965

A Feel for Politics

Watch on the Rhine (Herman Shumlin), 1943
The Iron Curtain (William Wellman), 1948
Walk East on Beacon (Alfred Werker), 1952
My Son John (Leo McCarey),
North by Northwest (Alfred Hitchcock), 1959
The Spy Who Came In from the Cold (Martin Ritt), 1965
La Guerre Est Finie (Alain Resnais), 1967
Executive Action (David Miller), 1974

The Problem of Loyalty

The Adventuress (Frank Launder), 1947
Decision before Dawn (Anatole Litvak), 1952
The Deadly Affair (Sidney Lumet), 1966
Scorpion (Michael Winner), 1973
Three Days of the Condor (Sidney Pollack), 1974

The Possibility of War

The Lady Vanishes (Alfred Hitchcock), 1938
Confessions of a Nazi Spy (Anatole Litvak), 1939
Foreign Correspondent (Alfred Hitchcock), 1940
Across the Pacific (John Huston), 1942
The Invaders (Michael Powell), 1942
The House on 92nd Street (Henry Hathaway), 1945

The Intricacies of War

The Spy in Black (Michael Powell), 1939
Five Graves to Cairo (Billy Wilder), 1943
Cloak and Dagger (Fritz Lang), 1946
13 Rue Madeleine (Henry Hathaway), 1946

The Man Who Never Was (Ronald Neame), 1965
The Counterfeit Traitor (George Seaton), 1961

A Touch of Romance

Dishonored (Josef von Sternberg), 1931
Mata Hari (George Fitzmaurice), 1932
Secret Agent (Alfred Hitchcock), 1936
Night Train (Carol Reed), 1940
Casablanca (Michael Curtiz), 1942
Notorious (Alfred Hitchcock), 1945
Golden Earrings (Mitchell Leisen), 1947

The Edge of Paranoia

The Ministry of Fear (Fritz Lang), 1944
The Manchurian Candidate (John Frankenheimer), 1962
The Quiller Memorandum (Michael Anderson), 1966
The Parallax View (Alan Pakula), 1974
Escape to Nowhere (Claude Pinotheau), 1974
Le Secret (Robert Enrico), 1974

The Urge for Humor

All through the Night (Vincent Sherman), 1942
To Be or Not to Be (Ernst Lubitsch), 1942
My Favorite Blonde (Sidney Lanfield), 1942
Our Man in Havana (Carol Reed), 1960
The Tall Blond Man with One Black Shoe (Yves Robert), 1973
A Pain in the A* (Edouard Molinaro), 1975

Rubenstein points out that more than 450 spy films have been produced. The following, in alphabetical order, gives a sampling of the multitude not on Rubenstein's basic list:

Above Suspicion (Richard Thorp), 1943. Based on a novel by Helen MacInnes.

The Amateur (Charles Jarrott), 1982. Terrorism and revenge are the background of this thriller. Hero is a computer expert turned violent by the murder of his wife. Some resemblance to the much superior *Three Days of the Condor*.

Background to Danger (Raoul Walsh), 1943. Good adaption of early Ambler novel.

Beyond the Limit (John Mackenzie), 1983. Film version of Greene's *The Honorary Consul*.

The Billion Dollar Brain (Ken Russell), 1967, and *Funeral in Berlin* (Guy Hamilton), 1966. Two additional Len Deighton adaptations starring Michael Caine.

Blow Out (Brian De Palma), 1981. Interesting use of similar plot gambit to Antonioni's *Blowup* using sound recording instead of photography as the recording mechanism.

Charade and *Arabesque* (Stanley Donen), 1963 and 1966. Two elegantly stylish thrillers, one starring Sophia Loren and Gregory Peck and the other Cary Grant and Audrey Hepburn.

Cloak and Dagger (Richard Franklin), 1984. Delightful spy fantasy with fine performance by Dabney Coleman. Young boy fantasizes about spy game hero until things turn "real."

The Day of the Jackal (Fred Zinneman), 1973. Highly successful adaptation of Forsyth's superb assassination novel.

The Eiger Sanction (Clint Eastwood), 1975. Adaptation of Trevanian's first novel.

Eye of the Needle (Richard Marquand), 1981. Excellent treatment of the Ken Follett novel with Donald Sutherland and Kate Nelligan.

Hopscotch (Ronald Neame), 1980. Brian Garfield's novel turned into a delightful vehicle for Walter Matthau and Glenda Jackson. About a rebellious CIA agent who does in his chief.

The Informer (John Ford), 1935. Great film classic based on the Irish revolution. Victor McLaglen plays the title role.

I Was a Communist for the FBI (Gordon Douglas), 1952. Influential early Cold War movie redolent of the paranoia of the McCarthy years.

The Kremlin Letter (John Huston), 1970. Flawed but interesting adaptation of Noel Behn's novel.

The Little Drummer Girl (George Roy Hill), 1984. Problematic adaptation of le Carré's most recent novel. Stars Diane Keaton in the title role.

The Looking Glass War (Frank Pierson), 1970. The worst of the various le Carré adaptions.

Man on a String (André de Toth), 1960. Ernest Borgnine and Colleen Dewhurst make this an outstanding Cold War film.

The Man Who Knew Too Much (Alfred Hitchcock), 1934 and 1956. Two versions of this same tale with a well-known cymbalic climax. The later version stars James Stewart and Doris Day.

The Mask of Dimitrios (Jean Negulesco), 1944. Superb Ambler adaptation with memorable performances by Peter Lorre and Sidney Greenstreet.

The Mask of Fu Manchu (Charles Brabin), 1932. One of the best of numerous Fu films. Stars Boris Karloff as the maestro of mystery.

Missing (Costa-Gavras), 1982. Powerful drama about CIA collusion in a South American coup. Unusually serious performance by Jack Lemmon.

Modesty Blaise (Joseph Losey), 1966. Somewhat in the manner of *Charade* and *Arabesque,* an attempt at a stylish spy spoof based on the long-running comic strip.

The Odessa File (Ronald Neame), 1974. Another Forsyth adaptation, not as good as *The Day of the Jackal.*

The Osterman Weekend (Sam Peckinpah), 1983. Like many directors and writers, Peckinpah turned from the Western to the spy story. Something was lost in the change in his version of Robert Ludlum's novel.

Our Man Flint (Daniel Mann), 1965, and *In Like Flint* (Gordon Douglas), 1976. These wacky Bond imitations starred James Coburn and were far better than the Dean Martin "Matt Helm" series, another ersatz Bond series.

The Passenger (Michelangelo Antonioni), 1975. Though as usual in Antonioni it's hard to tell what's going on, this Jack Nicholson film is nonetheless fascinating.

Rambo (Sylvester Stallone), 1984. The great hit of 84–85, this sequel to Stallone's *First Blood* is in the secret operation genre,

Vietnam prisoner of war subdivision. A flourishing story type
in the mid-1980s as America tried vicariously to refight the
Vietnam war and win. The hero's character and actions derive
from the "Enforcer" version of the crime thriller described in
Adventure, Mystery, and Romance, chapter 3.

The Riddle of the Sands (Tony Maylam), 1979. Faithful but slow
adaptation of the Erskine Childers classic.

The Silencers, 1966, *Murderer's Row,* 1966, *The Ambushers,* 1967,
and *The Wrecking Crew,* 1978. Dean Martin's poor Bond imitations based on Donald Hamilton's much better novels,
achieved considerable popularity in their day. For a more
faithful adaptation of Hamilton see *Matt Helm* (Buzz Kulik),
1975, the pilot for a short-lived TV series.

The Thirty-Nine Steps (Ralph Thomas), 1959 and (Don Sharp)
1978. Two remakes of Buchan-Hitchcock, the former more
like Hitchcock and the latter like the original novel. Neither,
however, are as good as the 1935 film.

This Gun for Hire (Frank Tuttle), 1942. Excellent adaptation of
Greene's *A Gun for Sale.* The film made Alan Ladd and Ve-
ronica Lake into major stars.

To Have and Have Not (Howard Hawks), 1943. Classic Bogart film
in the same league with *Casablanca.* Among other things, the
film introduced Lauren Bacall. Based *very* loosely on the
Hemingway novel, which is, in some ways, an improvement.

To Trap a Spy (Don Medford), 1965. Pilot film for the successful
TV series "The Man from U.N.C.L.E."

Torn Curtain, 1966, and *Topaz,* 1969. Two later Hitchcock spy
thrillers which lack the dazzling finesse of some of his earlier
work, but are nonetheless worth seeing for individual scenes.

Z (Costa-Gavras), 1969. Brilliant study of a political assassination
and its investigation.

The James Bond Movies

The Bond films were largely produced by the team of Albert R.
Broccoli and Harry Saltzman, who had purchased the option to
film Ian Fleming's novels even before their great popularity. The
films have been directed by a number of directors including Ter-

ence Young, Guy Hamilton, Lewis Gilbert, and John Glen.
Screenplays have been largely the work of Richard Maibaum.

With Sean Connery:
  Doctor No (1962)
  From Russia, with Love (1963)
  Goldfinger (1963)
  Thunderball (1965)
  You Only Live Twice (1967)
  Diamonds Are Forever (1971)
  Never Say Never Again (1983)

With Roger Moore:
  Live and Let Die (1973)
  The Man with the Golden Gun (1974)
  The Spy Who Loved Me (1977)
  Moonraker (1979)
  For Your Eyes Only (1981)
  Octopussy (1983)
  A View to a Kill (1985)

Major Series Writers and Characters

Writer	*Character*
Aarons, Edward S.	Sam Durell
Avallon, Michael	Ed Noon
(Several other writers have written volumes in the U.N.C.L.E. series based on the TV programs.)	The Man from U.N.C.L.E. The Girl from U.N.C.L.E.
Baker, W. Howard	Richard Quintain John Drake, "Secret Agent" (basis for the TV series)
Ballinger, Bill S.	Joaquin Hawke
Brust, Harold (pseud. Peter Cheney)	Lemmy Caution Peter Quayl et al.
Buchan, John	Richard Hannay
Buckley, William F., Jr.	Blackford Oakes

Writer	*Character*
Caidin, Martin	Steve Austin, "The Six Million Dollar Man" (basis for TV series)
Canning, Victor	Various characters
Various writers using the name Nick Carter (Over 100 volumes in this largest of all spy story series)	Nick Carter
Christie, Agatha (Though Christie is mainly a detective story writer, some of her Poirot stories and all of her Tuppence and Tommy series have espionage themes.)	Tuppence and Tommy Beresford Hercule Poirot
Clayton, Richard (pseud. William Haggard)	Col. Charles Russell
Cornwell, David (pseud. John le Carré)	George Smiley
Creasey, John (various pseuds.)	Gordon Craigie Dr. Palfrey The Baron Patrick Dawlish
Cussler, Clive (Specialist in nautical thrillers, including *Raise the Titanic*)	Dirk Pitt
Daniels, Norman, and various writers	The Avengers (based on TV series)
Dark, James	Mark Hood
Deighton, Len	Deighton's British Secret Service agent is anonymous, though he was given the name Harry Palmer in the film based on *The Ipcress File*.
Devilliers, Gerald	Malko
Duncan, Robert L. (pseud. James H. Roberts)	Various characters

Writer	Character
Egleton, Clive	Various characters
Fairlie, Gerald (pseud. Sapper) (Continued the Drummond series after McNeile's death)	Bulldog Drummond
Fleming, Ian	James Bond
Gainham, Sarah	Various characters
Gardner, John (appointed successor to Ian Fleming)	Boysie Oakes James Bond
Garfield, Brian	Various characters
Garner, William	Mike Jagger
Gibbs, Henry (pseud. Simon Harvester)	Dorian Silk
Gilman, Dorothy	Mrs. Polifax
Grady, James	Ronald Malcom, "Condor"
Gray, Rod	Eve Drum, "The Lady from L.U.S.T." (semi-pornographic)
Gribben, William L. (pseud. Talbot Mundy)	Various characters
Hamilton, Donald	Matt Helm
Herron, Shaun	Miro
Horler, Sydney	Various characters
Hunt, E. Howard (pseud. David St. John)	Peter Ward
Johnston, William	Maxwell Smart (based on the TV series *Get Smart* created by Mel Brooks, Buck Henry, and others)
Kenyon, Paul	The Baronness
Leasor, James	Dr. Jason Love
Lesser, Milton A. (pseud. Stephen Marlowe)	Chester Drum
LeQueux, William	Various characters
Loewengard, Heidi H. (pseud. Martha Albrand)	Various characters

Writer	*Character*
Luard, Nicholas	Various characters
Ludlum, Robert	Various characters
Lyle-Smyth, Alan (pseud. Alan Caillou)	Cabot Cain
MacCarthy, John L. (pseud. Desmond Cory)	Johnny Fedora
Maclean, Alistair	Various characters
McCutchan, Philip	Simon Shard
	Commander Shaw
Mack, Ted	The Man from O.R.G.Y. (semiporno-graphic spoof)
McNeile, H. C. (pseud. Sapper)	Bulldog Drummond
Mair, George B.	David Grant
Manning, Adelaide F. O., and C. Henry Coles (pseud. Manning Coles)	Tommy Hambledon
Marlowe, Dan J.	Earl Drake
Marquand, John P.	Mr. Moto
Mason, F. Van Wyck	Hugh North
Messman, Jon	Jefferson Boone, "The Handyman"
Mitchell, James (pseud. James Munro)	Callan
	Craig
Moore, Robert L. (pseud. Robin Moore)	Various characters
Nicole, Christopher (pseud. Andrew York)	Jonas Wilde
O'Donnell, Peter	Modesty Blaise (based on highly popular comic strip)
O'Malley, Patrick	Harrison and Hoeffler
Oppenheim, E. Phillips	Various characters
Palmer, John L., and Hilary St. G. Saunders (pseud. Francis Beeding)	Various characters

Writer	Character
Patterson, Harry (pseud. Jack Higgins)	Various characters
Perry, Ritchie	Philis
Phillips, James A. (pseud. Philip Atlee)	Joe Gall
Pollard, Alfred O.	Various characters
Price, Anthony	Dr. David Audley
Rosenberger, Joseph	"Death Merchant"
Ross, Angus,	Mike Farrow
Sapir, Richard, and Warren Murphy	"The Destroyer"
Sayer, Walter M., and various writers	Sexton Blake
Sawkins, Raymond H. (pseud. Colin Forbes)	Various characters
Sela, Owen	Various characters
Simmel, Johannes (German thriller writer)	Various characters
Sinclair, Upton	Lanny Budd
Smith, Don	Phil Serman "Secret Mission"
Spillane, Mickey (Like many detective story writers, Spillane dabbled in espionage themes and briefly developed the spy character Tiger Mann.)	Mike Hammer Tiger Mann
Stanton, Ken	The Aquanauts
Thomas, Craig (Author of *Firefox*, which became Clint Eastwood movie successful enough to inspire a sequel)	Various characters
Thomas, Ross	Padille and McCorkle
Thompson, Arthur L. B. (pseud. Frances Clifford)	Various characters
Thorne, F. P.	Major "Brains" Cunningham (series set in India)
Trevanian (pseud.; real name unknown)	Dr. Jonathan Hemlock
Trevor, Elleston (pseud. Adam Hall)	Quiller
Wade, Arthur Sarfield (pseud. Sax Rohmer)	Nayland Smith Dr. Fu Manchu

Writer	*Character*
Wager, Walter (pseud. John Tiger)	Various characters, *Telefon* (basis of Charles Bronson movie); *I Spy* (based on TV series)
Wallace, Edgar	Various characters
Ward-Thomas, Evelyn B. P. (pseud. Evelyn Anthony)	Various characters
Wheatley, Dennis	Gregory Sallus
Williams, Valentine (pseud. Douglas Valentine)	Desmond Okewood
Winterton, Paul (pseud. Andrew Garve)	Various characters
Woodhouse, Martin	Giles Yeoman
Wynd, Oswald (pseud. Gavin Black)	Paul Harris
Yin, Leslie C. B. (pseud. Leslie Charteris)	The Saint

The Best Spy Writers

A selected list of those writers who, while concentrating on the spy story, have achieved consistent excellence.

Allebury, Ted
Ambler, Eric
Behn, Noel
Boulle, Pierre
Buckley, William F., Jr.
Cornwell, David (John le Carré)
Deighton, Len
Follett, Ken
Forsyth, Frederick
Freemantle, Brian
Greene, Graham,
Household, Geoffrey
Littell, Robert
Ludlum, Robert
Lyall, Gavin
MacInnes, Helen
Maclean, Alistair
Sela, Owen
Trevanian
Trevor, Elleston (Adam Hall)

Novels Making Important Use of Espionage Themes

Espionage is such a central theme of twentieth-century life that a complete list of novels making use of spy themes would be very long. The following is a highly selective sample, which should give some indication of the variety of writers and types of novels in which spying and other clandestine activities have been important.

Joseph Conrad, *The Secret Agent* (1907) and *Under Western Eyes* (1911). One of the first major twentieth century novelists to center on spying as a major symbol of modern life.

Roman Gul, *Provocateur* (1930). Novelistic account of the life of Ievno Aseff.

Ernest Hemingway, *For Whom the Bell Tolls* (1938). One of Hemingway's best novels dealing with guerrilla activity during the Spanish Civil War. Hemingway's unsuccessful play *The Fifth Column* deals with attempted subversion during that conflict.

George Orwell, *1984* (1949). Orwell's classic dystopia shows secret police as a major feature of totalitarianism.

Ignazio Silone, *The Fox and the Camellias* (1961). Deals with the guerrilla activities of the Italian resistance.

Vladimir Nabokov, *Pale Fire* (1962). Though many of Nabokov's novels feature secret conspiracies of one sort and another, *Pale Fire*, which (possibly) depicts a coup d'état and an assassination, is perhaps the most striking.

Thomas Pynchon, *V.* (1963), *The Crying of Lot 49* (1966) and *Gravity's Rainbow* (1973). Pynchon remarks in the introduction to *Slow Learner:* "I had grown up reading a lot of spy fiction, novels of intrigue, notably those of John Buchan . . . The net effect was eventually to build up in my uncritical brain a peculiar shadowy vision of the history preceding the two world wars. Political decision-making and official documents did not figure in this nearly as much as lurking, spying, false identities, psychological games" (pp. xxviii–xxix).

Muriel Spark, *The Mandelbaum Gate* (1965). Set against the background of the Arab-Israeli conflict.

Alain Robbe-Grillet, *Le Maison de Rendezvous* (1965) and *Project for a Revolution in New York* (1972).

Anthony Burgess, *Tremor of Intent* (1966). An ironic spy story by a major contemporary British novelist.

Kinsley Amis, *The Anti-Death League* (1966). Satiric spy story by the author of *Lucky Jim.* Amis was also a great fan of Ian Fleming (see *The James Bond Dossier*) and wrote the first posthumous Bond adventure, *Colonel Sun* (1968).

Morris West, *The Tower of Babel* (1968).

E. L. Doctorow, *The Book of Daniel* (1971). Based on the Rosenberg atomic espionage case.

Irwin Shaw, *An Evening in Byzantium* (1973). Terrorism.

Robert Coover, *The Public Burning* (1977). A black comedy and satire based on the Rosenberg execution.

Mary McCarthy, *Cannibals and Missionaries* (1979). Hijacking and terrorism.

Many writers of contemporary best-sellers have drawn extensively on themes of espionage and clandestinity. See especially Irving Wallace, *The Plot* (1967) and *The R Document* (1976), and Leon Uris, *Topaz* (1967), *Exodus* (1958), *Trinity* (1976), and *The Haj* (1984).

Public Figures Who Have Published Spy Stories

William F. Buckley, Jr., conservative journalist and television personality, and author of the Blackford Oakes series.

William S. Cohen and Gary Hart, Democratic senators and authors of *The Double Man* (1985).

John Ehrlichman, leading figure in the Nixon White House and author of *The Company* (1976).

Jim Garrison, former New Orleans district attorney, a leading exponent of the conspiracy theory of the Kennedy assassination, and author of *The Star-Spangled Contract* (1976).

E. Howard Hunt, former CIA agent, Watergate figure, and author of the Peter Ward series under the name David St. John.

G. Gordon Liddy, major Watergate figure and author of *Out of Control* (1979).

Pierre Salinger, Kennedy's press secretary and author of *The Lollipop Republic* (1971) and *On Instructions of My Government* (1971).

Harrison Salisbury, Russian correspondent of *The New York Times* and author of *The Gates of Hell* (1975).

Tad Szulc, major foreign correspondent and author of *Diplomatic Immunity* (1981).

Television Spy Series

Biff Baker, U.S.A. (1952)	*O.S.S.* (1957)
I Led Three Lives (1953)	*Danger Man* (BBC, 1961)

The Avengers (BBC, 1961)
The Saint (BBC, 1962)
The Fugitive (1963)
The Man from U.N.C.L.E.
   (1964)
Amos Burke, Secret Agent (1965)
Secret Agent (1965)
Honey West (1965)
The Wild, Wild West (1965)
I Spy (1965)
Get Smart (1965)
The F.B.I. (1965)
The Girl from U.N.C.L.E.
   (1966)
The Man Who Never Was (1966)

T. H. E. Cat (1966)
Mission: Impossible (1966)
The Name of the Game (1968)
O'Hara, U.S. Treasury (1971)
The Men (1972)
Six Million Dollar Man (1973)
Bionic Woman (1975)
Return of the Saint (1979)
The New Avengers (1985)
John le Carré's *Tinker, Tailor,
   Soldier, Spy* and *Smiley's
   People* were produced as
   miniseries by the BBC
   (1980) starring Alec Guin-
   ness as George Smiley.

References

Ambler, Eric. *A Kind of Anger.* London: Bodley Head, 1964.
_____. *Background to Danger.* New York: Bantam, 1973.
_____. *Cause for Alarm.* London: Penguin, 1942.
_____. *Dirty Story.* London: Bodley Head, 1967.
_____. *Doctor Frigo.* New York: Atheneum, 1974.
_____. *Epitaph for a Spy.* London; Hodder, 1938.
_____. *Journey into Fear.* New York: Fontana, 1966.
_____. *Judgment on Delchev.* New York: Bantam, 1977.
_____. *Passage of Arms.* New York: Bantam, 1965.
_____. *State of Siege.* New York: Knopf, 1956.
_____. *The Intercom Affair.* London: Weidenfeld & Nicholson, 1970.
_____. *The Levanter.* New York: Bantam, 1973.
_____. *The Mask of Dimitrios.* London: Hodder, 1939. American title, *A Coffin for Dimitrios.*
_____. *The Schirmer Inheritance.* New York: Knopf, 1953.
_____. *Topkapi.* New York: Bantam, 1964. British title, *The Light of Day.*
Amis, Kingsley. *The James Bond Dossier.* New York: New American Library, 1965.
Barak, Michael. *The Secret List of Heinrich Roehm.* New York: Signet, 1977.

Barzun, Jacques. "Meditations on the Literature of Spying." *American Scholar* 34 (1965): 167–78.

Benson, Raymond. *The James Bond Bedside Companion.* New York: Dodd, Mead, 1984.

Boulle, Pierre. *A Noble Profession.* Trans. Xam Fielding. New York: Vanguard, 1960.

————. *Not the Glory.* New York: Manor Books, 1977.

Brosnan, John. *James Bond in the Cinema.* New York: A. S. Barnes, 1972.

Buchan, John. *Greenmantle.* London: Doran, 1915.

————. *Memory Hold the Door.* London: Hodder & Stoughton, 1940.

————. *Mr. Standfast.* Boston: Houghton Mifflin, 1919.

————. *The Thirty-Nine Steps.* New York: Popular Library, 1974. First published in 1915.

————. *The Three Hostages.* Boston: Houghton Mifflin, 1921.

Buckley, William F. *Saving the Queen.* New York: Avon, 1981.

Burgess, Anthony. *Tremor of Intent.* New York: Ballantine, 1967.

Cawelti, John G. *Adventure, Mystery, and Romance.* Chicago: University of Chicago Press, 1975.

Childers, Erskine. *The Riddle of the Sands.* New York: Dover, 1976. First published in 1903.

Condon, Richard. *The Manchurian Candidate.* New York: McGraw-Hill, 1959.

Conrad, Joseph. *The Secret Agent.* New York: Harper, 1907.

————. *Under Western Eyes.* New York: Harper, 1911.

Cooper, James Fenimore. *The Spy: A Tale of the Neutral Ground.* Philadelphia: Lea & Carey, 1821.

Deighton, Len. *Mexico Set.* New York: Knopf, 1985.

————. *Spy Story.* New York: Pocket Books, 1975.

————. *Yesterday's Spy.* New York: Warner, 1976.

Duncan, Robert. *Dragons at the Gate.* New York: New American Library, 1976.

Eco, Umberto, and Oreste del Buone. *The Bond Affair.* London: Macdonald, 1966.

Eells, Richard, and Peter Nehemkis. *Corporate Intelligence and Espionage: A Blueprint for Executive Decision Making.* New York: Macmillan, 1984.

Fleming, Ian. *Casino Royale.* New York: Signet, 1960. First published in 1953.

————. *Diamonds Are Forever.* New York: Signet, 1961. First published in 1956.

————. *Doctor No.* New York: Signet, 1958.

————. *From Russia, with Love.* New York: Signet, 1957.

————. *Goldfinger.* New York: Signet, 1960.

————. *Live and Let Die.* New York: Signet, 1959.

————. *Moonraker.* New York: Signet, 1955.

————. *On Her Majesty's Secret Service.* New York: Signet, 1964.

————. *The Man with the Golden Gun.* New York: Signet, 1965.

————. *The Spy Who Loved Me.* New York: Signet, 1962.

————. *Thunderball.* New York: Signet, 1961.

————. *You Only Live Twice.* New York: Signet, 1965.

Forsyth, Frederick. *The Day of the Jackal.* New York: Viking, 1971.

————. *The Dogs of War.* New York: Bantam, 1975.

————. *The Odessa File.* New York: Bantam, 1974.

Gifford, Thomas. *The Wind Chill Factor.* New York: Ballantine, 1975.

Goldman, William. *Marathon Man.* New York: Dell, 1974.

Grady, James. *Six Days of the Condor.* New York: Norton, 1974.

Greene, Graham. *A Gun for Sale.* New York: Penguin, 1973. First published in 1936 as *This Gun for Hire.*

————. *Orient Express.* New York: Bantam, 1955. First published in 1932 as *Stamboul Train.*

————. *The Human Factor.* New York: Simon & Schuster, 1978.

————. *The Ministry of Fear.* New York: Penguin, 1973.

————. *Ways of Escape.* New York: Penguin, 1981.

Halasz, Nicholas. *Captain Dreyfuss: The Story of a Mass Hysteria.* New York: Simon & Schuster, 1955.

Hall, Adam. *The Mandarin Cypher.* New York: Dell, 1975.

————. *The Ninth Directive.* New York: Pyramid, 1966.

————. *The Quiller Memorandum.* New York: Dell, 1975.

Harper, Ralph. *The World of the Thriller.* Cleveland: Case Western Reserve University Press, 1969.

Harris, Thomas. *Black Sunday.* New York: G. P. Putnam, 1975.

Henissart, Paul. *The Winter Spy.* New York: Pocket Books, 1976.

Higgins, Jack. *The Eagle Has Landed.* New York: Bantam, 1976

Hone, Joseph. *The Sixth Directorate.* New York: Dutton, 1975

Household, Geoffrey. *Arabesque.* London: Kaye & Ward, 1969.

————. *Rogue Male.* New York: Penguin, 1977.

Howard, Hartley. *Assignment K.* New York: Pyramid, 1968.

Kahn, David. *The Codebreakers: The Story of Secret Writing.* New York: Macmillan, 1967.

Kosinski, Jerzy. *Cockpit.* New York: Bantam, 1976.

Le Carré, John. [David Cornwell]. *A Murder of Quality*. New York: Pocket Books, 1970. First published in 1962.

————. *A Small Town in Germany*. New York: Dell, 1969.

————. *Call for the Dead*. New York: Pocket Books, 1970. First published in 1961.

————. *Smiley's People*. New York: Knopf, 1980.

————. *The Honourable Schoolboy*. New York: Knopf, 1977.

————. *The Little Drummer Girl*. New York: Knopf, 1983.

————. *The Looking Glass War*. New York: Bantam, 1975. First published in 1965.

————. *The Naive and Sentimental Lover*. New York: Knopf, 1972.

————. *The Spy Who Came In from the Cold*. New York: Dell, 1965.

————. *Tinker, Tailor, Soldier, Spy*. New York: Bantam, 1975.

LeQueuex, William. *Great War in England in 1897*. London: Tower, 1894.

Lesser, Simon. *Fiction and the Unconscious*. Chicago: University of Chicago Press, 1957.

Littell, Robert. *The Amateur*. New York: Dell, 1981.

————. *The Defection of A. J. Lewinter*. New York: Bantam, 1986.

Ludlum, Robert. *The Gemini Contenders*. New York: Dell, 1979.

————. *The Osterman Weekend*. Cleveland: World, 1972.

————. *The Rhinemann Exchange*. New York: Dell, 1979.

Lyall, Gavin. *Midnight Plus One*. New York: Scribner, 1965.

McCormick, Donald. *Who's Who in Spy Fiction*. New York: Taplinger, 1977.

McCutchan, Philip. *Gibraltar Road*. New York: Berkeley, 1965.

McCullin, Don. *Hearts of Darkness*. New York: Knopf, 1981.

MacInnes, Helen. *Agent in Place*. New York: Fawcett, 1976.

————. *Neither Five nor Three*. New York: Fawcett, 1951.

————. *Share of the Hunter*. New York: Fawcett, 1975.

Magruder, Jeb. *An American Life*. New York: Pocket Books, 1975.

Marchetti, Victor, and John Marks. *The CIA and the Cult of Intelligence*. New York: Dell, 1975.

Maugham, W. Somerset. *Ashenden; or, The British Agent*. New York: Doubleday, Doran, 1941. First published in 1928.

Merry, Bruce. *Anatomy of a Spy Thriller*. Montreal: McGill Queen's University Press, 1977.

Monoghan, David. *The Novels of John le Carré: The Art of Survival*. Oxford: Blackwell, 1985.

Nikolajewsky, Boris. *Aseff the Spy*. Trans. George Reavey. New York: Doubleday, Doran, 1934.

Palmer, Jerry. *Thrillers: Genesis and Structure of a Popular Genre*. New York: St. Martin's Press, 1979.

Panek, LeRoy L. *The Special Branch: The British Spy Novel, 1890–1980.* Bowling Green, Ohio: Bowling Green University Popular Press, 1981.

Parsons, Aarand. Chicago Symphony program notes, 26 October 1972.

Pearson, John. *Alias James Bond: The Life of Ian Fleming.* New York: Bantam, 1967.

Richler, Mordecai. "James Bond Unmasked." In Bernard Rosenberg and David Manning White, eds., *Mass Culture Revisited,* pp. 341–55. New York: Van Nostrand Reinhold, 1971.

Rockwell, Joan. "Normative Attitudes of Spies in Fiction." In Bernard Rosenberg and David Manning White, eds., *Mass Culture Revisited,* pp. 325–40. New York: Van Nostrand Reinhold, 1971.

Rohmer, Sax. [Arthur S. Ward]. *President Fu Manchu.* New York: Doubleday, Doran, 1936.

Rosenberg, Bernard, and David Manning White, eds. *Mass Culture Revisited.* New York: Van Nostrand Reinhold, 1971.

Rosenberg, Bruce A. *Custer and the Epic of Defeat.* State College, Pa.: Pennsylvania State University Press, 1974.

Rowan, Richard Wilmer, with Robert G. Deindorfer. *Secret Service: Thirty-Three Centuries of Espionage.* New York: Hawthorn, 1967.

Schlesinger, Arthur M., Jr. *A Thousand Days.* Boston: Houghton Mifflin, 1965.

Shapiro, David. *Neurotic Styles.* New York: Basic Books, 1965.

Shils, Edward. *The Torment of Secrecy.* Glencoe: Free Press, 1956.

Snelling, O. F. *007 James Bond: A Report.* New York: Signet, 1964.

Starkey, Lycurgus M., Jr. *James Bond's World of Values.* Nashville: Abingdon Press, 1966.

Stevenson, William. *A Man Called Intrepid.* New York: Ballantine, 1976.

Tanner, William. [Kingsley Amis]. *The Book of Bond.* New York: Viking, 1965.

Thomas, Craig. *Firefox.* New York: Holt Rinehart Winston, 1977.

Trevanian. *The Eiger Sanction.* New York: Avon, 1972.

Truffant, François, with Helen G. Scott. *Hitchcock.* New York: Simon & Schuster, 1967.

Uris, Leon. *Topaz.* New York: Bantam, 1968.

Usborne, Richard. *Clubland Heroes: A Nostalgic Study of Some Recurrent Characters in the Romantic Fiction of Dornford Yates, John Buchan, and "Sapper."* London: Constable, 1953.

Williams, Alan. *Gentleman Traitor.* New York: Pyramid, 1977.

Index